Statistical Methods
and
the Improvement of Data Quality

Academic Press Rapid Manuscript Reproduction

The Proceedings of The Small Conference on the Improvement of the Quality of Data Collected by Data Collection Systems, November 11–12, 1982, Oak Ridge, Tennessee

Statistical Methods
and
the Improvement of Data Quality

Edited by

Tommy Wright

Mathematics and Statistics Research, Computer Sciences
Oak Ridge National Laboratory
Operated by Union Carbide Corporation, Nuclear Division
Oak Ridge, Tennessee

1983

 ACADEMIC PRESS, INC.

(Harcourt Brace Jovanovich, Publishers)

Orlando   San Diego   New York   London
Toronto   Montreal   Sydney   Tokyo

ACADEMIC PRESS, INC.
Orlando, Florida 32887

United Kingdom Edition published by
ACADEMIC PRESS, INC. (LONDON) LTD.
24/28 Oval Road, London NW1 7DX

Library of Congress Cataloging in Publication Data

Small Conference on the Improvement of the Quality of
    Data Collected by Data Collection Systems (1982 : Oak
    Ridge, Tenn.)
    Statistical methods and the improvement of data
quality.

    Sponsored by the Oak Ridge National Laboratory.
    Includes bibliographical references and index.
    I. Sampling (Statistics)--Congresses. 2. Surveys--
Congresses. 3. Census--Congresses. 4. Errors, Theory of
--Congresses. I. Wright, Tommy. II. Oak Ridge
National Laboratory. III. Title.
QA276.6.S63 1982   001.4'222   83-22326
ISBN 0-12-765480-1 (alk. paper)

PRINTED IN THE UNITED STATES OF AMERICA

85 86 87 88   9 8 7 6 5 4 3 2

Contents

Response Effects to Behavior and Attitude Questions

Seymour Sudman

Error Profiles: Uses and Abuses

Barbara A. Bailar

Principles and Methods for Handling Outliers in Data Sets

Vic Barnett

Influence Functions, Outlier Detection, and Data Editing

Michael R. Chernick

Using Exploratory Data Analysis to Monitor Socio-Economic Data Quality in Developing Countries

Paul F. Velleman and David F. Williamson

Application of Pattern Recognition Techniques to Data Analysis

R. C. Gonzalez

Can Automatic Data Editing be Justified? One Person's Opinion

Gunar Liepins

Missing Data in Large Data Sets

Roderick J. A. Little and Donald B. Rubin

Reducing the Cost of Studying Survey Measurement Error: Is a Laboratory Approach the Answer?

Judith T. Lessler and Richard A. Kulka

The Implication of Sample Design on Survey Data Analysis

Rick L. Williams, Ralph E. Folsom, and Lisa Morrissey LaVange

An Approach to an Evaluation of the Quality of Motor Gasoline Prices

Arthur R. Silverberg

Health and Mortality Study Error Detection, Reporting, and Resolution System

Katherine C. Gissel, Martha L. Wray, and Martha S. Hansard

On Using Exploratory Data Analysis as an Aid in Modeling and Statistical Forecasting

Thomas A. Curran III and Robert D. Small

Contributors

Numbers in parentheses indicate the pages on which the authors' contributions begin.

Barbara A. Bailar (117), U.S. Bureau of the Census, Washington, D.C. 20233

Vic Barnett (131), Department of Probability and Statistics, University of Sheffield, Sheffield S3 7RH, England

Michael R. Chernick (167), The Aerospace Corporation, Los Angeles, California 90009

Thomas A. Curran III (333), International Institute for Comparative Social Research, Wissenschaftszentrum Berlin, Federal Republic of Germany

Tore Dalenius (1), Division of Applied Mathematics, Brown University, Providence, Rhode Island 02912

Ralph E. Folsom (267), Statistical Sciences Group, Research Triangle Institute, Research Triangle Park, North Carolina 27709

Katherine C. Gissel (321), Medical and Health Sciences Division, Oak Ridge Associated Universities, Oak Ridge, Tennessee 37830

R. C. Gonzalez (193), Electrical Engineering Department, The University of Tennessee, Knoxville, Tennessee 37916

Martha S. Hansard (321), Nuclear Data Power, Inc., Smyrna, Georgia 30080

Leslie Kish (73), Survey Research Center, Institute for Social Research, The University of Michigan, Ann Arbor, Michigan 48106

Richard A. Kulka (245), Statistical Sciences Group, Research Triangle Institute, Research Triangle Park, North Carolina 27709

Lisa Morrissey LaVange (267), Statistical Sciences Group, Research Triangle Institute, Research Triangle Park, North Carolina 27709

Judith T. Lessler (245), Statistical Sciences Group, Research Triangle Institute, Research Triangle Park, North Carolina 27709

Gunar Liepins (205), Energy Division, Oak Ridge National Laboratory, Oak Ridge, Tennessee 37830

Roderick J. A. Little* (215), Datametrics Research, Inc., Chevy Chase, Maryland 20015

Donald B. Rubin** (215), Datametrics Research, Inc., Chevy Chase, Maryland 20015

Arthur Silverberg (297), Rockville, Maryland 20857

Robert D. Small (333), The Wharton School, University of Pennsylvania, Philadelphia, Pennsylvania 19104

Seymour Sudman (85), Department of Business Administration and The Survey Research Laboratory, University of Illinois at Urbana–Champaign, Urbana, Illinois 61801

How J. Tsao (25), Energy Division, Oak Ridge National Laboratory, Oak Ridge, Tennessee 37830

Paul F. Velleman (177), Department of Economics and Social Statistics, Cornell University, Ithaca, New York 14853

Rick L. Williams (267), Statistical Sciences Group, Research Triangle Institute, Research Triangle Park, North Carolina 27709

David F. Williamson (177), Division of Nutritional Sciences, Cornell University, Ithaca, New York 14853

Martha L. Wray (321), Medical and Health Sciences Division, Oak Ridge Associated Universities, Oak Ridge, Tennessee 37830

Tommy Wright (25), Mathematics and Statistics Research, Computer Sciences, Oak Ridge National Laboratory, Oak Ridge, Tennessee 37830, and Department of Mathematics and Physics, Knoxville College, Knoxville, Tennessee 37921

*Present address: Biomathematics Department, University of California, Los Angeles, Los Angeles, California 90024.
**Present address: Department of Statistics, The University of Chicago, Chicago, Illinois 60637.

Preface

In recent years, the number of active large data systems has increased sharply with the demands for more information from decision makers. While recent observations suggest that this number may not be increasing for the moment, the need to improve the quality of collected data still exists. This need cuts across many fields, including agriculture, defense, economics, education, energy, environment, finance, health, labor, natural resources, population, and transportation. Practical experience in dealing with different types of data shows that they can contain gross errors. These errors, if left unchanged, directly affect analyses and decisions based on the data by leading to faulty decisions, inappropriate actions, and a loss of confidence in the data collection system.

In the late 1970s and early 1980s, Oak Ridge National Laboratory assisted the Energy Information Administration of the U.S. Department of Energy in evaluating the quality of the data produced by many of its data collection systems. Each completed study of a system revealed that the question of data quality assessment is indeed a complex one without any apparently complete answers. Figure 1 is a revision of a scheme included in a publication by the American Statistical Association entitled "What Is A Survey?" This figure gives a rough sketch of the phases of a typical data collection effort. It was felt that any effort to assess data quality should include the impact of each of these phases on the published data. It is clear from the sketch that there is a need for concern about the quality of data in the phases before and during the actual collection as well as after.

Realizing that there was much to be learned from others, we approached the Office of Naval Research with a proposal to sponsor a small conference that would be titled The Improvement of the Quality of Data Collected by Data Collection Systems. The purpose was to bring together experts who had demonstrated an understanding of the problems of data collection systems so that state-of-the-art techniques could be discussed for handling these problems

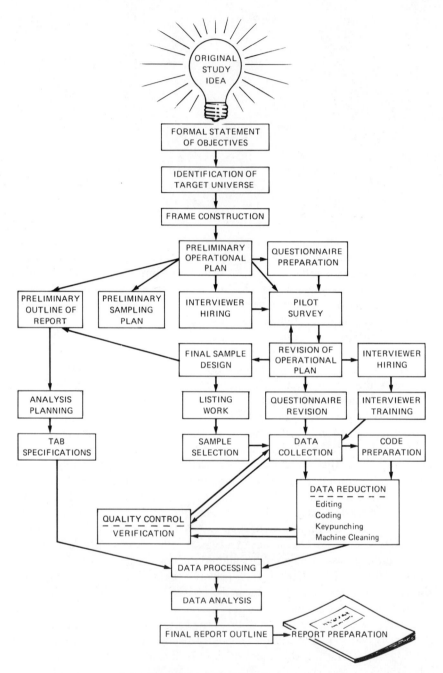

FIGURE 1. The phases of a survey.

and so that determinations could be made of the potential for developing a comprehensive research program aimed at improving the quality of data collected by data collection systems. Our request was granted and speakers were invited to prepare presentations for a program on improving the quality of data based on at least one of the following considerations:

1. A statement of the purpose(s) for the collection of the data
2. A clear statement as to what data are to be reported and who shall report them
3. A statement of the accuracy and precision requirements for the estimates of the primary parameters
4. A clear statement of the problems of the data collection system(s) and an understanding of the subject matter
5. A classification of errors and an error profile
6. Studies to determine the usefulness of error models
7. Statements that identify users' understanding of the data collection systems phenomena, evolution purpose, origin of requirements, who potential users are, and potential uses
8. Statements supporting the design of the data collection system(s) with special attention to the need to have a census, a sample survey, or a combination
9. Statements on the adequacy of the frame (including plans for updating)
10. A thorough review of the survey form design (questionnaire design)
11. An application of exploratory data analysis and pattern recognition techniques (including computer graphics)
12. An application of outlier detection methods and data editing techniques
13. A plan for dealing with incomplete data
14. A plan for internal and external consistency checks
15. Documentation

This volume contains most of the papers presented at The Small Conference on the Improvement of the Quality of Data Collected by Data Collection Systems, held on November 11–12, 1982, at Oak Ridge, Tennessee. They are ordered approximately as they were presented during the conference. The first 11 papers are by invited speakers; the remaining 5 were contributed. Each paper was read by at least one reviewer, and authors were given the opportunity to make appropriate revisions after the reviews. The papers in this volume are likely to be of primary benefit to individuals and groups throughout the world who deal with large data collection systems and who are constantly seeking ways to improve the overall quality of their data. The papers can also be used to complement the material presented in a general course in survey sampling techniques.

Acknowledgments

The success of this conference and the preparation of this volume are due to the efforts of many; therefore, a general expression of gratitude goes to all the conference participants and to those involved in preparing this volume.

The small conference was sponsored by the Oak Ridge National Laboratory* with major funding from the Office of Naval Research. Additional support was provided by the Energy Division of the Oak Ridge National Laboratory, the Quality Division of the Oak Ridge Y-12 Plant, and the Statistics Department of The University of Tennessee at Knoxville.

The planning committee consisted of D. A. Gardiner, Union Carbide Corporation, Nuclear Division; A. S. Loebl, Oak Ridge National Laboratory; and T. Wright (chairman). We are very grateful to the authors for their carefully prepared papers. Thanks are also due those who served as session chairmen: G. Dailey, D. Downing, D. Flanagan, D. Horvitz, W. Lever, V. Lowe, D. Pack, and V. R. R. Uppuluri. Special thanks go to the following persons, who assisted in reviewing the papers in this volume: B. Bailar, C. A. Brooks, T. Dalenius, D. Downing, E. Frome, R. S. Garfinkel, L. Gordon, B. Greenberg, D. Horvitz, D. Pack, and M. S. Rosenzweig.

I am grateful to Herman Postma, Director of the Oak Ridge National Laboratory, who welcomed the participants, and to the following individuals, who gave remarks during the opening session: D. DePriest, Office of Naval Research; A. S. Loebl; and Robin Textor, Oak Ridge Y-12 Plant. I also thank L. Kish, who delivered the after-dinner talk, which was enjoyed by all.

Finally, I greatly appreciate and thank for their assistance Donna Poole, Tammy Reed, and Karen Shultz, who expertly typed the papers; D. Barnes, who read a draft and found many errors; and the members of the staff of Academic Press.

*Operated by Union Carbide Corporation, Nuclear Division, for the U.S. Department of Energy under Contract W-7405-eng-26.

Statistical Methods
and
the Improvement of Data Quality

ERRORS AND OTHER LIMITATIONS OF SURVEYS

Tore Dalenius

Brown University
Providence, Rhode Island

I. INTRODUCTION

When statisticians are asked to assess the usefulness of
a data collection system, we tend to follow a classical tradition of oblique narration: we focus on the *limitations* of
the system and especially on the errors, which may impair the
results. To be sure, such an indirect assessment typically
provides a powerful guide to the development of efficient designs and their faithful implementation. It must, however, be
supplemented by a more comprehensive analysis which takes into
account that the usefulness of a data collection system is
determined by a great many other circumstances than those
discussed in terms of limitations.

In my paper, I will consider some of the limitations of a
special kind of data collection system, viz., the survey. Ad-
hering to the theme of this conference, I will take a broad
view, allowing a discussion of both negative and positive
aspects. The scope of the paper is indicated by the following
list of its six sections:

    II.   The Data Collection System Considered: A Survey.
    III. An Inherent Limitation.
    IV.   Errors in Surveys.
    V.   The Formal Basis for Comprehensive Quality Control.
    VI.   Quality Control of the Specifications.
    VII. Quality Control of the Survey Operations.

The objective of the paper is to provide a *holistic* picture of the ends and means of quality control in the realm of
surveys. References given should not be interpreted as
assignment of priority; several of them have been chosen for
their easy access.

STATISTICAL METHODS
AND THE IMPROVEMENT OF DATA QUALITY

1

II. THE DATA COLLECTION SYSTEM CONSIDERED: A SURVEY

A. *The Purpose of Section II*

     The purpose of this section is to provide a conceptual
framework for the discussion in sections III-IV, and sections
V-VII, respectively.

     Thus subsection B will present the special kind of 'data
collection system' which I will consider in this paper, viz. a
survey. Most of the discussion will concern a *sample* survey,
but many points are applicable to a total survey (= 'census')
as well. Subsection C will present three technical perspectives which underlie the discussion in sections V and VI.

B. *The Notion of a Survey*

     An examination of the specialist literature suggests that
there is no generally agreed upon definition of 'survey'.
Indeed, there is an abundance of different definitions.

     The term 'survey' will be used in this paper in a way
illustrated well by the following examples:

     Definition No. 1. In Kendall and Buckland (1960), the
following definition is given:

     An examination of an aggregate of units, usually
     human beings or economic or social institutions.
     Strictly speaking perhaps, 'survey' should relate
     to the whole population under consideration but it
     is often used to denote a sample survey, i.e., an
     examination of a sample in order to draw conclusions
     about the whole.

     Definition No. 2. In Campbell and Katona (1953), survey
is defined as follows:

     Many research problems require the systematic
     collection of data from populations or samples
     of populations through the use of personal inter-
     views or other data-gathering devices. These
     studies are usually called surveys, especially
     when they are concerned with large or widely
     dispersed groups of people.

Typically, as part of a survey, *observational* data – in contrast to experimental data – are collected from all or a sample of elements in a given population. The data are referred to as 'observational,' as they are as generated by Nature. With each element in the survey, we associate a vector of measurements (observations), which may exist independently of the survey, for example, in a population registration system. Alternatively, all or some of the measurements may be generated in the course of a measurement operation, which is part of the overall survey operations.

The description of a survey just given applies to a wide range of formats, such as interview and mail surveys ('surveys proper'), statistical investigations of administrative records, and data collection by means of satellites, to give but three examples.

C. *Three Technical Perspectives*

Following Hansen et al. (1961), I will view a survey from three perspectives: requirements, specifications, and operations.

First, there are the requirements imposed by some problem. Corresponding to these requirements, there is a design defined by reference to a relevant population, a relevant property, a method of measurement, and a method of summarizing the measurements. If this design is properly carried out, the survey will yield a set of statistics, the *ideal* goals (Z) of the survey.

Second, there are the specifications – the design – of the actual survey to be carried out. These specifications are arrived at by the choice of the population to be studied, the property to measure, the method of measurement to use, and the method of summarizing the measurements. Thus, the specifications identify the *defined* goals of the survey.

Third, there are the actual operations of the survey. These operations yield the actual set of statistics, *the results* of the survey.

FIRST PART - THE LIMITATIONS

III. AN INHERENT LIMITATION

A. *Two Inference Situations*

The usefulness of a survey will, of course, depend on our possibility of drawing valid inferences of the kind called for by the problem, to the solution of which the survey is expected to contribute. It is in that context of vital importance that we make a clear distinction between two fundamentally different inference situations.

Inference Situation No. 1. This is the situation wherein the survey is carried out to provide estimates of characteristics which describe the population from which a set of data has been collected. Thus the objective may be to estimate some means, sums or ratios for the entire population, or for specified parts ("domains") of that population. This is, by and large, the prevailing situation with respect to most surveys carried out by government statistical agencies.

Inference Situation No. 2. In this situation, the objective is to make inferences about the cause system which generated the finite population at hand. This is sometimes referred to as calling for "causal analysis" or "critical analysis".

B. *The Limitation*

The limitation to be discussed in this subsection concerns the use of a survey to make inferences about a cause system. I will use two real-life examples to illustrate the point to be made. Only the major design features of the surveys involved will be presented.

Example 1. A statistical study is expected to provide an answer to the following question: Is it economic to import fertilizer to a country in order to increase the use of fertilizer and hence increase the yield of a certain crop? This question was in fact asked during the Second World War in some countries, which had to import fertilizers.

In order to provide an answer, a sample survey of n farms may be carried out; in the subsequent discussion, I will put

n = 3, in the interest of perspicuity. The sample farms are
observed with reference to two variables:

    Y: the yield per acre of the crop; and
    X: the amount of fertilizer per acre.

The data may realistically look as in Figure 1:

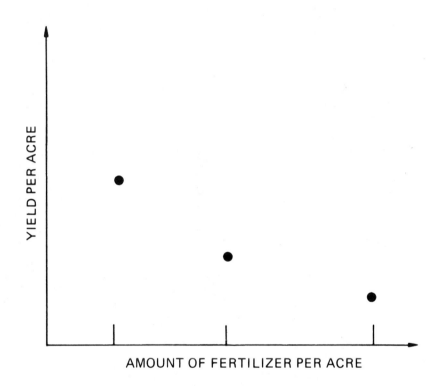

FIGURE 1

    The survey provides the following inference about the
finite population of farms: there is a negative correlation
between the yield and the amount of fertilizer used.   Granted
that the sample is a probability sample (of sufficiently large
size), this inference is perfectly valid.   It reflects, of
course, the impact of a third variable, viz., the soil
quality; the correlation is spurious.

But the survey does not provide a valid inference about
the cause system generating the yields. Realizing this fact,
it may be natural to extend the design as follows. Thus, the
sample of n farms already observed, as discussed above, may be
observed again next year. This may be expected to provide
different X-values and different Y-values. Denoting the
yields per acre with Y_{1j} for the first year and
Y_{2j} (j = 1, 2, 3) for the second year, and likewise the
amounts of fertilizer by X_{1j} and X_{2j}, the outcome may look as
follows:

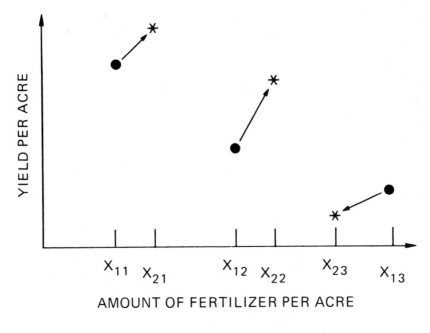

As in Figure 1, the dots denote observations from the first
year; the corresponding observations from the second year are
denoted by asterisks. For each farm, an arrow indicates the
direction of change from the first year to the second year.

This design has - at least superficially - some similar-
ity with experimental designs known as 'before-and-after

designs'. The outcome suggests that the cause system generating the yields is such as to make the association between
the two variables positive.

  Example No. 2. This example has been chosen to illustrate - among other things - that the use of a design of the
'before-and-after' type may not be sufficient to provide a
valid inference about the cause system. The problem to be
addressed by a survey is as follows. It has been proposed to
give young farmers extensive training in agronomy as a means
of making them better farmers. This proposal raises the question: Is the training program effective? The design of the
survey, which is expected to provide the answer to this question, is as follows.

  A sample of n farmers 20 years of age is selected for
participation in a training program, scheduled to last for 5
years. Before the training starts, they are observed with
respect to their performance as farmers; the outcome is given
by the average $\overline{y}_b$ (b for 'before'). At the end of the training period, they are observed once more; the outcome is given
by the average $\overline{y}_a$ (a for 'after'). The analysis of the survey
calls for a comparison of the two averages, say by means of
$\overline{y}_a - \overline{y}_b$.

  For the sake of the discussion, I will assume that $\overline{y}_a$ is
'significantly' larger than $\overline{y}_b$. It may then appear natural to
make the inference that the training program has a beneficial
effect and consequently consider it for use. Such an inference appears reasonable against the background of the use of a
'before-and-after design'.

  Upon closer examination, it is obvious that such an
inference may be erroneous. The outcome is - as in example
No. 1 - influenced by a third variable: the aging of the participants in the training program. More specifically, young
people who are working as farmers for some 5 years may by
themselves (i.e., in the course of their work) improve their
performance. It cannot be excluded that the training program
has no effect at all; that is, that $\overline{y}_a$ is larger than $\overline{y}_b$ solely
as a result of the farmers getting 5 years older in the course
of the training program. In fact, if the training program has
a negative effect, it may nonetheless happen that $\overline{y}_a$ proves to

be significantly larger than $\overline{y}_b$ as a consequence of a strong positive effect from the aging of the farmers!

In this second example, a better design would involve the use of a 'control sample', i.e., a sample of farmers who are not given the training program.

The discussion above must *not* be interpreted to mean that observational data cannot be used to provide valid inferences about cause systems.

For such inferences to be possible, a realistic model of the cause system concerned must be available; the term 'model' is used here in the sense of an 'explanation' of the phenomena generated by some mechanism. Given a realistic model, the role of a survey is to provide estimates of the parameters of that model.

This possibility has long been taken advantage of in the natural sciences; astronomy is but an example. In the social sciences – where experiments (in the sense of Fisher) seldom are feasible – we often do not have the information needed to build the model. If, nonetheless, inferences are drawn to a cause system, there is no statistical theory for assessing their uncertainty.

IV. ERRORS IN SURVEYS

A. *Two Kinds of Errors*

In section II-C, we introduced three terms: the *ideal* goals, the *defined* goals, and the *results* of a survey. If we denote these entities by Z, X, and y, respectively, we may define the following two kinds of errors:

i. the error y – X, i.e., the error relative to the defined goal; and

ii. the error y – Z, i.e., the error relative to the ideal goal.

Clearly, the following relation holds:

$$y - Z = (y - X) + (X - Z).$$

The subsequent discussion in this section will refer to the error relative to the defined goal, i.e., to y - X.

B. *Some History*

In the 1930s and 1940s, two lines of methodological developments concerning errors in surveys emerged. I will discuss them in turn.

   1. The First Line of Development. This line focused on the *sampling* error, the error introduced by the use of a sample survey rather than a total survey. In the infancy of survey practice, the control of the sampling error was typically carried out in terms of the 'representativity' of the sample at hand: the sampling design had as its aim to generate a sample, which in controllable respects was similar to the population. This idea was, for example, basic to 'quota sampling', sometimes referred to as 'the Gallup method' after one of its spokesmen, and also to various schemes for 'purposive selection'.

With Neyman (1934), a significant change was brought about. In this paper, Neyman gave a fundamentally new meaning to 'representativity'; he defined what he termed a representative method of sampling, viz., probability sampling, yielding what nowadays is referred to as 'measurable designs'. As observed in Sukhatme (1966), Neyman's paper "can be said to mark a beginning of a new era altogether"; the paper represented a "turning point in the history of sampling methods."

In Kruskal and Mosteller (1979 and 1980), a stimulating review is given of the use of the term 'representative'.

   2. The Second Line of Development.

The Government are very keen on amassing statistics.
They collect them, add them, raise them to the nth
power, take the cube root and prepare wonderful diagrams. But you must never forget that every one of
these figures comes in the first instance from the
village watchman, who just puts down what he damn
pleases.
                              Sir Josiah Stamp
         Inland Revenue Department (England) 1896-1919

Soon after the First World War, survey practitioners became concerned about *non-sampling* errors. In the 1930s and 1940s, important advances were made.

In many instances it was found that various sources of non-sampling errors (such as measurement errors, non-response, etc.) contributed significantly more to the total error than did the use of sampling. This observation served to stimulate important research and development. In the United States, much of this work was carried out in the context of surveys of human population by various government agencies and notably the Bureau of the Census. Mention should also be made here of the concerns that some 'opinion pollsters' felt; an example in kind is Connelly (1945), where it was stated:

> While perfection of sampling for all surveys must remain one objective, it alone will probably mean no more than an improvement of two or three percentage points, at the most. Errors of question interpretation, on the other hand, run the gamut.

In India, the focus was on non-sampling errors in crop estimation. For references to the literature, see Dalenius (1977).

C. *Survey Models*

The term 'survey model' has been coined to denote theory for measuring the impact of sampling and non-sampling errors in an integrated way. Endeavors to that end may be traced to the late 1940s; and in the 1950s these endeavors proved to be successful. In Hansen et al.(1961), the first complete survey model was presented.

In section VII, I will discuss the role of a survey model in an effort to control the survey operations.

D. *Error-Related Criteria for Survey Design*

A natural adjunct to the development of methods and theory for probability sampling (measurable designs) and survey models is the use of a design criterion which calls for striking a balance between the error of a survey result and the cost of the survey.

It is indeed desirable to go one step further. The public's concern about invasion of privacy – while not

necessarily reflecting objective considerations – may have to
be brought into the picture. Hence, an appropriate criterion
would have three ingredients: accuracy, cost, and privacy
protection. A beginning has been made in the development of
such a new criterion, but more work is needed.

SECOND PART – COMPREHENSIVE QUALITY CONTROL

V. THE FORMAL BASIS FOR COMPREHENSIVE QUALITY CONTROL

A. Measuring the Usefulness of a Survey

As suggested in the beginning of this paper, measures of
the limitations of a survey are not sufficient to assess the
usefulness of a survey: they must be supplemented by an
analysis which takes into account other pertinent circumstances. The circumstances which are applicable in a specific
instance will, of course, reflect e.g. the requirements in
response to which the survey is carried out. Examples of such
circumstances are

     i.   the relevance of the expected results
    ii.   the timeliness of the survey
   iii.   the wealth of details provided,

to give but three examples.

Accordingly, we may conceive of a 'quality measure
vector' $Q(.)$ such as

$Q(.)$ = (accuracy, cost, privacy protection, relevance,
        timeliness, wealth of detail,...),

which is to serve as the measure of the usefulness of a
survey.

B. Comprehensive Quality Control - An Overview

On the basis of such a quality measure vector, it is
natural to conceive of a program P for 'comprehensive quality
control', composed by two sub-programs P_1 and P_2:

$$P = (P_1, P_2)$$

where

    i. P_1 accounts for the control of the survey design

    ii. P_2 accounts for the control of the survey
        operations.

Selected aspects of these subprograms will be discussed in sections VI and VII, respectively.

VI. QUALITY CONTROL OF THE SURVEY DESIGN

A. *Three Quotations*

I will introduce my discussion in this section by three pertinent quotations.

Quotation 1: "Statistics must have purpose." Prashandra C. Mahalanobis.

Quotation 2: "Until the purpose is stated, there is no right or wrong way of going about the survey." W. Edwards Deming.

Quotation 3: "... it is often better to have reasonably good solutions of the proper problems than optimum solutions of the wrong problems." Herbert Robbins.

These quotations reflect a circumstance which cannot be compromised. The usefulness of a survey depends, in a decisive way, on how well the survey statistician is able to translate a user's substantive problem into a statistical problem (= the survey design), the solution of which will contribute to the solution of the substantive problem.

What the statistician needs is a scheme for a critical evaluation of the survey design. Such a scheme may consist of an extensive 'check list' addressing the major design problems. In subsection B, I will present an embryo of such a check list.

B. *Embryo of a Check List*

In order to elucidate the basic idea of a check list for a critical evaluation of a (preliminary) survey design, I will present a *selected* set of questions to ask concerning various design aspects.

1. *The Problem Situation.* The importance of having a good understanding of the problem situation is well stated in the following:

Quotation 4: "As the correct solution of any problem depends primarily on a true understanding of what the problem really is, and wherein lies its difficulty, we may profitably pause upon the threshold of our subject to consider first, in a more general way, its real nature; the causes which impede sound practice; the conditions on which success or failure depends; the directions in which error is most to be feared." Wellington.

I will give some examples of questions, answers to which may help the statistician to grasp the subject-matter problem:

    i.   How does the problem manifest itself?
    ii.   What action should be taken in order to reduce/eliminate the problem?
   iii. How important (in dollars) is it that the problem be reduced/eliminated?
    iv. How soon must the problem be reduced/eliminated?

2. *Identifying the Requirements.* This amounts to specification of the *ideal* goal. Here are some questions to ask:

    i.   Which statistics are relevant to the solution of the subject-matter problem? The answer should specify the population to observe, the concepts to use, etc.
    ii.   Are the statistics to be used in order to take action on a given finite population, or on the mechanism (cause system) that generated that population? Technically speaking: Which is the prevailing inference situation? (Compare the discussion in section III-A).
   iii. Which statistics (information) are already available which would be helpful to cope with the subject-matter problem?

iv.   How is the survey expected to improve the situation
      with respect to access to relevant statistics
      (i.e. not merely increase the volume of
      statistics)?

   When these and other questions have been fully answered,
it may prove helpful to summarize the answers by producing a
set of 'dummy tables' covering a wide range of possible outcomes of a hypothetical survey carried out to provide the
relevant statistics. If an analysis of these outcomes shows
that the same action would be taken for a wide variety of outcomes, this should be viewed as a signal that it may be too
early to start developing the survey design, if one should be
developed at all!

   3.   The Survey Design.   Here are some questions to ask:

   i.   Does the frame to be used comprise (virtually) the
         whole target population?
   ii.   If there is a 'large' discrepancy in terms of
         coverage, what is the likely impact on the
         inferences to be drawn?
   iii. Are the definitions of key concepts adequate?
         It may be reasonable to compare them with the
         corresponding concepts used in some important
         benchmark statistics; if there is a deviation,
         what is the likely impact (for example with
         respect to comparability with previous surveys)?
   iv.   Is the accuracy to be achieved too large? Too
         small?
   v.   Do the interviewers have the training needed to
         apply the measurement instrument to be used?
   vi.   Is the wording of the questions satisfactory?
         It may prove helpful to use questions which
         have proved to work well in previous surveys;
         but if new wordings are used, what is the
         evidence that they are satisfactory?
   vii. Will the data collection provide data which
         may benefit the development of the editing and
         imputation procedure?
   viii. What steps are to be taken to see to it that
         the implementation of the survey design is not
         impaired by e.g. non-response?
   ix.   Does the budget provide resources for an
         'ex post' evaluation of the survey design?

VII. QUALITY CONTROL OF THE SURVEY OPERATIONS

A. The Methodological Approach

The *aim* of this control is an attempt to ensure that
the survey is carried out in satisfactory agreement with its
design: the implementation has to be "faithful to the
design."

It has been said before, and it deserves and may have to
be repeated: it is one thing to give one's verbal support to
the need for control, but an altogether different matter to
exercise control.

1. The Focus of the Control. The ultimate focus of the
control is the survey error:

$$e = y - X.$$

For the control to be efficient, it must be directed at the
various *sources* which contribute to the total error. This
amounts to three control conditions:

   i.   it must be possible to identify *controllable*
        sources of errors;
   ii. it must be known with reasonable accuracy how much
        each source is likely to contribute to the overall
        error; and
   iii. in addition, the cost of controlling a specific
        source must be known sufficiently well.

2. Two Methodological Approaches. Borrowing the terminology from industrial quality control, I will make a distinction between two methodological approaches to quality control
of the survey operations, viz.:

   i.   preventive control, and
   ii. process control.

These approaches supplement each other. I will discuss
preventive control in sections B-D, and process control in
sections E-G.

B.   Preventive Control - An Overview

A program for preventive control typically calls for identifying the major sources of errors in advance of implementing
the survey design and taking the steps needed to keep their
impact on the total error satisfactorily low.   In sections
C-D, I will elaborate on these two aspects.

C.   Identifying the Sources of Errors

The first of the three control conditions listed in section A is that it must be possible to identify controllable
sources of errors.   As a preamble to a discussion of how this
is possible in the survey context, I will briefly review the
classical theory of errors.

Assume that we want to measure the weight of some
object.   To this end we make n measurements:

$$y_1, \ldots, y_j, \ldots, y_n.$$

These measurements exhibit some variation, which suggests
that at best we will be able to derive an approximation to the
'true weight'.   The classical theory addresses the problem of
how good this approximation is.   Thus the theory postulates
that the n measurements are independent observations on a random variable having a normal distribution with mean μ and
variance σ^2.   Under these assumptions, it can be argued that
the arithmetic mean $\bar{y}$ is a best estimate of μ, the 'true
value' of the random variable.   More specifically, $\bar{y}$ is
unbiased and has a variance equal to σ^2/n.   This variance, or
an estimate of it, is then used to derive a measure of error
$e = \bar{y} - \mu$.

It is important to note that μ is a property of the random variable, not of the object to be measured.   In order to
make $\bar{y}$ a practically meaningful approximation to the weight of
the object, there must be a correspondence between the theory
and the real world.   In today's terminology, the model of the
mechanism generating the variations in the measurements must
be realistic.

What has been said above with reference to the n measurements applies in principle to the whole field of statistics

and statistical studies, be they experiments, surveys,[a] or
of some other kind. Thus, in order to measure the error of an
estimate based on a (sample) survey, we need a model of the
mechanism generating the variation between the observations on
the elements selected for the survey. If the scope of the
model is sufficiently broad, it will implicitly provide a
guide to both 'sample design' (including both the sample
selection plan and the estimation procedure) and 'measurement
design.'

By the same token, for the purpose of controlling the
various sources of errors in a survey, we need a model that
makes it possible to decompose the total error as measured by
the mean-square error. Such a model presented in Hansen et
al. (1961) and several subsequent papers from the U. S. Bureau
of the Census make it possible to decompose the mean-square
error as follows:

$MSE(\overline{y})$ = measurement variance + sampling variance +
      covariance of measurement and sampling
      deviations + bias^2.

Thus this survey model allows the identification of what
I will refer to as 'first-order sources of errors': measurement and sampling. The model being referred to here makes it
in fact possible to identify 'second-order sources of errors'
such as variation between and within primary sampling units,
correlated and simple and correlated measure variation, etc.

What has just been discussed may be expressed as follows. The survey model provides the basis for the development

[a]*Much may be said about the existence or non-existence of
'true values' in the context of some surveys, and especially
in the context of surveys of subjective phenomena. A pertinent reference is Turner and Martin (1981).*

*It may be of relevance here to draw attention to the fact
that while there are in the natural sciences generally agreed
upon technical standards (such as the prototypes for meter
and kilogram, respectively), this is not generally true in
the social sciences.*

*Mention should also be made here of the potential use of
'calibration' in the context of survey measurement.*

of a taxonomy of sources of errors, needed for efficient control.

In view of the importance of this characteristic of a survey model, I will dwell on it by way of giving an example. Thus, a survey model having a broad scope will make it possible to identify say the following major sources of errors:

(1) The sample selection plan
(2) The measurement design
(3) The data processing plan
(4) The estimation procedure

The model may also be applied separately to each one of these major operations/sources of errors. If applied to the measurement design, the following sources of errors may be identified:

(1) Question wording
(2) Interviewers
(3) Respondents

Clearly, if a survey model is to provide a basis for control of the survey error, it must be possible to estimate the components, which make up the mean-square error. For a discussion of how this may be done, reference is given to Bailar and Dalenius (1969).

D. *Getting Access to the Information Needed*

In order to work out an efficient program for control of the survey operations, the survey statistician must have some information about these operations, and especially about their roles as sources of errors, *prior* to launching the survey. A pessimistic conclusion may be that the statistician's task is infeasible.

The best must, however, not be allowed to be the foe of the good. Experience has shown that satisfactory programs for control of the survey operations may be based on information about the operations of previous surveys. The statistician's situation is indeed especially satisfactory, if he is dealing with a sequence of surveys of identical surveys (repeated or continuous surveys). The Current Population Survey carried out by the U. S. Bureau of the Census (and similar surveys carried out by other statistical agencies) is an example in kind.

In subsections 1 and 2, I will discuss two strategies for getting access to (some of) the information needed from previous surveys.

1. Total Error Measurement. All too often, efforts to measure the errors of survey statistics are insufficient, and sometimes even misleading, for one or more of the following reasons:

  i.   the objective is too narrow, focusing on the sampling error;
  ii.   the computations are carried out as if the sample were selected by simple random sampling of elements, when in fact some complex design was used; and
  iii. the standard error – while analyzed as a measure of the sampling error – may also include contribution from the measurement process.

It is well known that this practice is unsatisfactory. Especially, the restriction to the sampling error may result in an inefficient allocation of the resources available for quality control of the survey operations.

What is needed is what I will refer to as 'Total Error Measurement,' TEM. This calls for basing the survey design on a proper survey model, i.e., to integrate sample and measurement designs into 'Total Survey Design,' TSD. In addition it may prove desirable to supplement the measurement of the total error and its components by special methodological experiments.

TEM is clearly an ambitious task, which has to be taken into account in the development of the survey budget. Past experience suggests that it is not easy to sell the idea that a budget should be made available for the purpose of error measurement; an explanation may be that the interest of the users focuses on the survey statistics – measuring the errors would not change them! In these times with increasingly strong reductions of the budgets for statistics, the statistician may find it even more difficult than before to sell the idea.

2. Using an Error Profile. As discussed in Dalenius (1978), the preparation of an error profile calls for

  i.   making a systematic and comprehensive account of the survey operations that lead to a survey statistic;

ii.   followed by an assessment – for each operation –
      of the presence or absence of a deviation between
      the design and its execution, the size of any such
      deviation, and – if possible – a measure of its
      impact.

An error profile may guide the survey statistician in his
efforts to identify those survey operations, which need to be
redesigned or controlled better in order to improve the quality of the survey statistics. In addition an error profile
may – by virtue of its intrinsic simplicity and tangibility –
prove useful to the users of these statistics by enhancing
their appreciation of the limitations of the survey
statistics.

The error profile is a recent development. Consequently,
only a few applications are documented as yet. For two examples, reference is given to Beller (1979) and Brooks and
Bailar (1978). A brief summary of the second-mentioned reference is given in Bailar and Brooks (1978). In that paper the
authors report the conclusion that the error profile prepared
for the Current Population Survey "was extremely useful to see
where the gaps in knowledge about the impact of nonsampling
errors occurred".

3. *An Idea by Horvitz*. TEM to be used for the design of
a specific survey may be viewed in a broader perspective.
Thus, in Horvitz (1978) the suggestion is made to establish a
data bank with statistics concerning various aspects (errors,
costs, etc.) of surveys.

E. Process Control

This term – or the alternative 'rectifying control' –
implies that errors are identified, followed by some action
which aims at eliminating the errors.

I will consider two 'levels' of process control, viz.

i.   control of the individual data as collected; and
ii. control of the aggregates of the survey data.

This type of control is usually referred to as 'editing'.

F. *Process Control of the Individual Data*

I will discuss this control with reference to a survey, for which the data have been collected by a schedule or some similar vehicle.

A critical examination of the schedules will reveal three types of problem:

     i.   unsatisfactory format of the data,
    ii.   possibly inaccurate data, and
  iii.   missing data.

I will briefly discuss these three types.

1. *Unsatisfactory Format.* Simple examples of this type of problem are when a weight has been recorded in pounds when it was to be recorded in kilograms, or length in feet when it was to be recorded in meters.

This type of problem is usually easily and adequately coped with by an 'editing *change*'.

2. *Possibly Inaccurate Data.* This type of problem is – as all survey statisticians know from their own experience – very difficult to cope with.

To be sure, the reason for this difficulty is not a shortage of techniques to use. Access to computers has indeed made it possible to develop a sizeable number of techniques for 'automatic editing,' possibly followed by imputation for clearly inaccurate data. It may nonetheless be argued that the situation leaves something to be desired. If we are not to be stricken by 'mechanitis', we must devote more efforts to the development of theory to guide the use of existing and new techniques. It is – to illuminate one important aspect – interesting to note that, unlike the situation in many areas where the classical theory of errors finds successful applications, much remains to be done before we have a theory of 'outliers' applicable to surveys.

3. *Missing Data.* This type of problem is easily discernible. It may be easy to settle, viz., if the schedule carries *redundant* data. In other cases, the problem has to be tackled in a different way: by means of imputation or by going back to the source of the data.

G. *Process Control of Aggregates*

I will consider here a survey, for which (preliminary) aggregates have been produced for n tabulation cells. In a specific instance, these cells may be geographic areas.

Techniques similar to those used for control of the individual data may be used. Thus, consider counts of the number of elements having a specific property. For the current year, these counts are

$$y_1 , \ldots, y_j , \ldots, y_n .$$

Let

$$x_1 , \ldots, x_j , \ldots, x_n$$

denote the corresponding counts for a previous year, known to be satisfactorily accurate. Then a simple technique for control calls for plotting the n pairs of data, y_j, x_j, j=1,...,n, and inspect the plot for y-values, which (when compared with the x-values) appear to be 'very large' or 'very small.' If there is no known reason to assume that a considerable change has taken place, this is taken as a signal that the y-data may be in serious error.

Alternatively, techniques for 'analytic evaluation' may be used. The evaluation may employ the method of comparison (two sets of statistics are compared for consistency), or it may employ the method of relationship. To illustrate this latter method, consider a survey which produced the count y for the current year. If the count for the previous year was x and the volume of change is known, then (at least approximately)

$$y = x + \text{change.}$$

If y does not satisfy this relationship, there are reasons to subject it to an examination for accuracy.

REFERENCES

Bailar, B. A. and Brooks, C. A. (1978). "An Error Profile for the Current Population Survey Employment Statistics," *Statistical Reporter*, 89-91.

Bailar, B. A. and Dalenius, T. (1969). "Estimating the Re-
    sponse Variance Components of the U. S. Bureau of the
    Census' Survey Model," *Sankhyā, Series B,* 341-360.
Beller, N. D. (1979). "Error Profile for Multi-Frame Surveys,"
    Report ESCS-63. Economics, Statistics, and Cooperative
    Service. U. S. Department of Agriculture, U. S. Government
    Printing Office, Washington, D. C.
Brooks, C. A. and Bailar, B. A. (1978). "An Error Profile:
    Employment as Measured by the Current Labor Force Survey,"
    Statistical Policy Working Paper 3. Office of Federal
    Statistical Policy and Standards, U. S. Department of
    Commerce, U. S. Government Printing Office, Washington,
    D. C.
Campbell, A. A. and Katona, G. (1953). "The Sample Survey: A
    Technique for Social-Science Research," In: *Research
    Methods in the Behavioral Sciences,* Festinger, L. and
    Katz, D. (eds.) The Dryden Press, New York.
Connelly, G. M. (1945). "Now Let's Look at the Real Problem:
    Validity," *Public Opinion Quarterly,* 51-60.
Dalenius, T. (1977). "Bibliography on Nonsampling Errors in
    Surveys I, II, III," *International Statistical Review, 45,*
    71-89; 181-197; 303-317.
Dalenius, T. (1978). "Strain at a Gnat and Swallow a Camel: Or
    the Problem of Measuring Sampling and Nonsampling Errors,"
    *1977 Social Statistics Section Proceedings of the American
    Statistical Association,* 21-25.
Dalenius, T. (1981). "The Survey Statistician's Responsibility
    for Both Sampling and Measurement Errors." In: *Current
    Topics in Survey Sampling,* D. Krewski, R. Platek, and
    J. N. K. Rao (eds.), 17-29, Academic Press, New York.
Hansen, M. H., Hurwitz, W. N. and Bershad, M. A. (1961). "Mea-
    surement Errors in Censuses and Surveys," *Bulletin of the
    International Statistical Institute, 38:2,* 359-374.
Horvitz, D. G. (1978). "Some Design Issues in Sample Surveys."
    In: *Survey Sampling and Measurement,* Namboodiri, N. K.
    (ed.), 3-11, Academic Press, New York.
Kendall, M. G. and Buckland, W. R. (1960). *A Dictionary of
    Statistical Terms,* Oliver and Boyd, Edinburgh and London.
Kruskal, W. and Mosteller, F. (1979). "Representative Sam-
    pling, III: The Current Statistical Literature," *Interna-
    tional Statistical Review, 47,* 245-265.
Kruskal, W. and Mosteller, F. (1980). "Representative Sam-
    pling, IV: The History of the Concept in Statistics,"
    International Statistical Review, 48, 169-195.

Neyman, J. (1934). "On the Two Different Aspects of the Repre-
    sentative Method: The Method of Stratified Sampling and
    the Method of Purposive Selection," *Journal of the Royal
    Statistical Society, Vol. XCVII, Part IV,* 558-606, and
    discussion, 607-625.
Sukhatme, P. V. (1966). "Major Developments in Sampling Theory
    and Practice," In: *Research Papers in Statistics
    Festschrift for J. Neyman,* F. N. David (ed.), John Wiley
    & Sons, New York.
Turner, C. F. and Martin, E. (eds.) (1981). *Surveys of Subjec-
    tive Phenomena: Summary Report.* Panel on Survey Measure-
    ment of Subjective Phenomena Committee on National
    Statistics. National Research Council. National Academy
    Press, Washington, D. C.

A FRAME ON FRAMES: AN ANNOTATED BIBLIOGRAPHY

Tommy Wright

Mathematics and Statistics Research Department
Computer Sciences at
Oak Ridge National Laboratory
Oak Ridge, Tennessee

How J. Tsao

Energy Division
Oak Ridge National Laboratory
Oak Ridge, Tennessee

I.   INTRODUCTION AND DEFINITION OF A FRAME

The success or failure of any sample survey of a finite
population is largely dependent upon the condition and adequacy of the list or frame from which the probability sample
is selected. Much of the published survey sampling related
work has focused on the measurement of sampling errors and,
more recently, on nonsampling errors to a lesser extent.
Recent studies on data quality for various types of data collection systems have revealed that the extent of the
nonsampling errors far exceeds that of the sampling errors in
many cases. While much of this nonsampling error, which is
difficult to measure, can be attributed to poor frames,
relatively little effort or theoretical work has focused on
this contribution to total error.

The objective of this paper is to present an annotated
bibliography on frames with the hope that it will bring
together, for experimenters, a number of suggestions for
action when sampling from imperfect frames and that more
attention will be given to this area of survey methods
research.

STATISTICAL METHODS
AND THE IMPROVEMENT OF DATA QUALITY
25

Before continuing with the discussion in these brief
opening sections, it is necessary to suggest a definition of
frame. Lessler (1980) has given considerable attention to
the number of definitions which appear in the literature
along with competing and related terms. We adopt her definition, which appears to contain all the essentials from the
others:

> *Frame*:   The materials or devices which delimit,
>   identify, and allow access to the elements
>   of the target population. In a sample
>   survey, the units of the frame are the
>   units to which the probability sampling
>   scheme is applied. The frame also includes
>   any auxiliary information (measures of size,
>   demographic information) that is used for 1)
>   special sampling techniques, such as,
>   stratification and probability proportional
>   to size sample selections; or for 2) special
>   estimation techniques, such as ratio or
>   regression estimation.

The literature reveals that not only has some attention
focused on defining a frame, determining how a frame should
be constructed, and what properties it should have, but some
have also talked about various types of frames (Jessen,
1978). A frame need not always be in the form of a list.
For example, Jessen (1955) presents an interesting method of
constructing a frame from the branches of a fruit tree.

Before giving the annotated bibliography, we give a
brief overview in the following sections on concerns, problems, and proposed solutions which appear to form the core of
the frame issues to date. Each section that we consider will
be discussed in the context of a major paper or work which is
in the bibliography. Several books have devoted some pages
to a brief consideration of sampling frames. These include
Hansen, Hurwitz, and Madow (1953); Kish (1965); Sukhatme and
Sukhatme (1970); Cochran (1977); and Jessen (1978). We will
simply list each in the bibliography without making an
attempt to outline the specific topic areas of each because
they are general and, in most cases, the material is covered
in the listed papers. Section II presents comments on how
one constructs and maintains a frame, while Section III
focuses on area frames.

In Section IV, we consider problem areas with imperfect list frames and a model for the measurement of their effects on sample estimates. Section V gives the experimenter a number of suggestions for action when sampling from imperfect list frames. In Section VI, we briefly present the significant work on multiple frames by Hartley (1962, 1974). The last section presents the annotated bibliography of frame related papers. The grouping is by year of publication; within each year, the listing is alphabetical by author. (As with all lists, we caution the reader that this bibliography is subject to the very imperfections which are discussed in the papers.)

II. CONSTRUCTION OF THE SAMPLING FRAME

The importance in building a good sampling frame can be seen from comments made by Jessen (1978):

> In many practical situations the frame is a matter of choice to the survey planner, and sometimes a critical one, since frames not only should provide us with a clear specification of what collection of objects or phenomena we are undertaking to study, but they should also help us carry out our study efficiently and with determinable reliability. Some very worthwhile investigations are not undertaken at all because of the lack of an apparent frame; others, because of faulty frames, have ended in a disaster or in a cloud of doubt.

In this section, we will address issues considered important in building a sampling frame. They will be examined in five major steps. For more, see Singh (1975).

Step 1. Determination of Frame Units. In some simple cases frame units can easily be determined. However, in most cases, the determination of appropriate frame units to be used in a survey require much greater effort. It is important to note that frame development studies should be conducted along with their associated survey design activities. It would be most cost effective if the development of the survey frame could be included as a *task* of the survey design project because the contribution of a sampling frame is to *help* carry out the survey efficiently and with determinable reliability.

In practice, issues such as

- (i)   objectives of the survey,
- (ii)   population of interest,
- (iii) data to be collected (actual survey form),
- (iv)   degree of precision desired,
- (v)   point of measurement (corporate headquarters or plant),
- (vi)   sample selection strategy, and
- (vii) methods of estimation

should be studied to guide (1) the determination of key attributes to be collected from members in the frame prior to the survey and (2) the determination of frame structure and type of units in the frame. Conversely, sampling and estimation procedures are designed to make the frame more efficient and adaptable. The intended structure of the frame and the type of frame units to be used in the survey will always determine the kinds of sampling strategies that can be applied to draw samples from the frame. See, for example, Lanphier and Bailar (1978). The condition of a frame may even force the analyst to change the objective or the target population of the survey.

Factors to be considered in the choice of frame units and the determination of the amount of associated auxiliary information required include

- (i)   cost to obtain and maintain the desired identification and auxiliary information,
- (ii)   time required to construct the frame,
- (iii) availability of required information on frame units,
- (iv)   stability of the frame units through time,
- (v)   accessibility of the identification and auxiliary information, and
- (vi)   effectiveness of obtaining reliable information from target population through frame units.

For example, determination of frame units for a survey to collect energy data (or any survey of establishments) is usually complicated by the industry structure, the business relationships between establishments, and the survey design requirements.

In a survey of certain petroleum product sales to a certain state, it is important to review the defined target

universe and the proposed sampling and estimation procedures. Such information is required in establishing criteria
to qualify members in the frame. In view of the high cost in
identifying qualified dealers in the petroleum industry, for
example, samplers often attempt transferring usable data from
other reliable sources. As a result, a preliminary list may
be generated by merging several data bases to serve as an
information source in building the sampling frame. Such an
effort is discussed by Coulter and Mergerson (1978).

Each member in the merged list might be associated with
one or more than one member in the target universe and the
linkages between different data bases may not be easily
determined. See for example Tepping (1968). This deficiency
would make the job of removing duplicates more difficult. Other
problems are discussed under Sections IV and V of this paper.

Step 2. Development of a Frame. This step assumes that
we understand the kinds of frame units we need and that we
know how to collect such information.

In developing the frame we often create an information
data base; the procedures can be as simple as using an
existing list. It can also be as complicated as conducting
a comprehensive survey (or research) in order to collect
identification and auxiliary information about units that
might be qualified in the final frame.

Step 3. Validation of a Frame. This would be the step
to examine the quality of the frame data base constructed
through Steps 1 and 2 (Eckler and Pritzker, 1951;
Boyes and Brown, 1974). It is important, at this stage, to
assess the coverage, duplication, and information adequacy
problems. Sometimes a sample is required to explore these
problems.

Step 4. Administration of a Frame. If a frame is
designed to serve several large-scale surveys, steps may be
taken to put the administration of the frame on a sound
basis. A joint committee may be set up by users of the frame
to meet the users' requirements of the frame. Research may be
conducted to determine sampling errors of the frame with
different methods of estimation and sampling procedures.

Step 5. Frame Maintenance Procedures. A frame, having
been built, requires frequent adjustments to retain its value
in serving the survey needs and to provide reliable informa-

tion to help improve efficiency of the estimators. The
computerized data base management systems should enable the
planner to update information, remove duplicates, improve
coverage, and, it is hoped, provide some linkage to other data
bases that might be used to improve the existing frame.
Maintenance of a central register is considered by Sunter
(1971).

III. AREA FRAMES

King and Jessen (1945) give a little history concerning
early uses of *area sampling*. Their brief account gives early
uses of area sampling in Europe during the 1920s in a number
of purposively chosen samples. A variety of early applications in the 1930s and 1940s are mentioned which occurred in
the United States including area sampling of farms, sampling
crop acreages, and sampling for estimation of labor force.
Perhaps the major hope with area frames is that one will have
improved coverage of the target population. King and Jessen
(1945) note that in area sampling "the sampling units are
small areas and every unit of observation is uniquely
associated with one and only one such area.... Area sampling
may be extended to provide the primary selection of units of
observations, which are then subsampled. The subsampling is
usually accomplished either by a further sampling of smaller
areas or by making a prelist of individuals."

Monroe and Finkner (1959) define an *area frame* as a
"geographic frame of area units (count units) whereby any
element which has an association with a unit of area can be
identified after locating a particular count unit. The count
units may vary in size and shape, as well as the "counts" –
the number of (say) farms and the number of dwellings
indicated on highway maps and aerial photographs. The one
characteristic common to all (area frames) is definable
area. Within the count unit, sampling units can be defined
and identified."

Several advantages and disadvantages of the area sampling method are given as follows:

Advantages:

   (i) With an area frame, travel costs are reduced since,
       within first-stage sampling units, the travel
       distances are shortened.

   (ii) An expansion factor available to the area sampling
        method is known without error because the total
        number of sampling areas in the population may be
        determined by simply counting them on the maps.
  (iii) First-stage sampling units are generally very
        stable through time.
   (iv) Theoretically, one has total coverage of the
        target population.

Disadvantages:

    (i) Area sampling requires maps of detail sufficient
        to allow the delineation of the sample areas which
        may be located easily and accurately by the
        enumerator in the field.
   (ii) It takes time and money to delineate on a map the
        areas that are efficient in size and that are
        bounded by features which can be clearly
        identified in the field.

The handbook by Monroe and Finkner (1959) gives detailed
discussion on how one might actually execute an area survey.
Topics which are discussed in great detail with examples
include preparation of the sampling materials (use of
census data and maps) and use of the materials (size of the
sampling units, number of sampling units, and selection of
the sample).

IV. IMPERFECT FRAMES

This section is centered around a paper by Szameitat and
Schäffer (1963) which addresses the following questions:

    (i)"What types of errors may occur in the frame, and
        how do they influence the results of the (esti-
        mates)?"
   (ii) What "are the possibilities for reducing or
        describing error components?"

Szameitat and Schäffer (1963) find it convenient to look
at the total error of statistical results with the following
breakdown:

    (i)"errors due to deviation of the target population
        from the *sampled population* (the population that
        matches the frame);

(ii) ascertainment and processing errors; and
(iii) errors caused by a restriction to a sample
      survey."

The ways in which the sampled population (frame) can
deviate from the target population are listed as

1. *Deviations in coverage*

   (a) Reporting units belonging to the target
       population are not included in the sampled
       population. (See: Chandrasekar and Deming,
       1949; Marks, Mauldin, and Nisselson, 1953;
       Zarkovich, 1956; Kish and Hess, 1958; Marks and
       Waksberg, 1966; Siegel and Zelnik, 1966; Sen,
       1970; El-Khorazaty, Imrey, Koch, and Wells,
       1977; Bateman and Cowan, 1979; the 1978 report
       of the National Research Council entitled,
       *Counting the People in 1980: An Appraisal of
       Census Plans* (Chapter 5); and the *Proceedings of
       the Conference on Census Undercount* (1980)).

   (b) Reporting units belonging to the target popula-
       tion are several times contained in the sampled
       population. (See: Mosteller, 1949; Goodman,
       1949, 1952; Deming and Glasser, 1959; Rao, 1968;
       Gurney and Gonzalez, 1972; Tarng, 1980; and
       Chapman, 1981).

   (c) Reporting units contained in the sampled popula-
       tion do not belong to the target population.
       (See Cochran, 1977, pp. 36-38 and Drew,
       Choudhry, and Gray, 1978).

2. *Deviations in content*

   (a) The frame provides incorrect auxiliary informa-
       tion on reporting units.

   (b) Auxiliary information for reporting units is
       lacking in the frame.

Seal (1962) notes that time may be one of the major
sources for frame inadequacy because the survey objectives,
the target population, the survey methodology, and the data
collection methods which directly affect the frame will
usually change through time.

The following simple error model is presented by Szameitat and Schäffer as a means of analyzing the errors associated with the above frame imperfections.

Szameitat and Schäffer's Model for Analyzing Imperfect Frames

The basic assumptions:

    (i) There are K exclusive subpopulations of interest in the target population.

    (ii) Sampling units are the reporting units.

  (iii) The frame contains auxiliary information which can be used to stratify the frame into L strata.

With the above assumptions, the authors define another subpopulation of the target population and another stratum of the sampled population (frame). The additional subpopulation of the target population is the set of all units which are in the target population but are not contained in the sampled population. The additional stratum of the sampled population (frame) is the set of all units which are in the frame but are not a part of the target population.

A cross-classification of the units with respect to the frame and the target population is given in Figure 1.
The following notation is used:

$N^*_{k\ell}$ is "the number of sampling units contained in the ℓth part of the sampled population and belonging to the kth part of the target population for k = 0, 1, ..., K and ℓ = 0, 1, 2, ..., L." (This is the number of units which are correctly assigned to cell kℓ.)

$N^*_{0\ell}$ is "the number of sampling units contained in the ℓth part of the sampled population and not belonging to the target population, but wrongly considered as being part of it."

$N^{**}_{(k)\ell}$ is "the number of sampling units which are contained in the ℓth stratum of the sampled population, do not belong to the target population, but are wrongly allocated to the kth part of the target population." (This is the number of units which are incorrectly assigned to cell kℓ.)

Note: $N^*_{00} = 0$ and $N^{**}_{(k)0} = 0$ for k = 0, 1, ..., K .

Sampled Population
(Frame Categories)

	0 = In target population, but not in frame	1	2	...	ℓ	...	L	T O T A L	
0 = In frame but not in target population									} Overcoverage or Duplication
1									
2									
. . .									
k									
. . .									
K									
TOTAL									

Target Population (Subpopulations)

Undercoverage
(Incompleteness)

FIGURE 1. *Cross-Classification of Target Population With the Sampled Population.*

$N_{k\ell}$ is the number of units which are contained in the ℓth stratum of the sampled population and belong to the kth part of the target population or are allocated to this part for $k = 1, \ldots, K$ and $\ell = 0, 1, \ldots, L$. Thus, the total number of units in cell $k\ell$ is

$$N_{k\ell} = N_{k\ell}^* + N_{(k)\ell}^{**}$$

Also, $N_{k.} = \sum_{\ell=0}^{L} N_{k\ell}$; $N_{k.}^* = \sum_{\ell=0}^{L} N_{k\ell}^*$; $N_{k.}^{**} = \sum_{\ell=0}^{L} N_{(k)\ell}^{**}$.

Further let X be the variable of the characteristic of interest. Then the total of the X's for the $N_{k\ell}^*$ units of the $k\ell$th group is $X_{k\ell}^*$, for the $N_{(k)\ell}^{**}$ units of the $k\ell$th group is $X_{(k)\ell}^{**}$, etc. Also, the total value $X_{k\ell}$ of all units of the $k\ell$th group is $X_{k\ell} = X_{k\ell}^* + X_{(k)\ell}^{**}$. Similarly $X_{k.}^* = \sum_{\ell=0}^{L} X_{k\ell}^*$, etc.

Under the above model, the authors first consider *systematic errors* caused by deviations of the frame coverage when estimating $X_{k.}^*$ and $X^* = \sum_{k=1}^{K} X_k^*$. The focus is on $X_{k.}^*$ under the execution of a *complete census*. The results for a census also apply to a sample survey with unbiased estimation. They note, "In a complete census, the units in the first column of the cross-classification table are not covered and instead of obtaining the desired $X_{k.}^* = \sum_{\ell=0}^{L} X_{k\ell}^*$, we obtain

$$\tilde{X}_{k.} = \sum_{\ell=1}^{L} X_{k\ell} = \sum_{\ell=1}^{L} (X_{k\ell}^* + X_{(k)\ell}^{**})$$

$$= \sum_{\ell=1}^{L} X_{k\ell}^* + \sum_{\ell=1}^{L} X_{(k)\ell}^{**}$$

$$= X_{k.}^* - X_{k0}^* + X_{k.}^{**} \; . "$$

Thus the total systematic bias incurred is $-X_{k0}^{*} + X_{k\cdot}^{**}$, where $-X_{k0}^{*}$ is due to incompleteness of the frame and $X_{k\cdot}^{**}$ is due to overcoverage and possibly duplication.

Note: (i)   If $X_{k0}^{*} = X_{k\cdot}^{**}$, then there is no systematic bias.

(ii)   "Units with large X values can have a significant effect if they are incorrectly omitted from the frame or incorrectly included in the frame (including duplication)," according to the authors.

The authors also consider relative systematic error, which in the case of $X_{K\cdot}^{*}$ is given by $\left(\tilde{X}_{k\cdot} - X_{k\cdot}^{*}\right)/X_{k\cdot}^{*}$.

Under the above model, the authors also consider effects on *random sampling error* caused by deviations of the frame coverage when estimating $X_{k\cdot}^{*}$ (and X^{*}). Their analysis shows that imperfect frames can lead to significant increases in sampling error, which are almost always unknown.

The following general principles are given by Szameitat and Schäffer for consideration when sampling from an imperfect frame.

(i)   The frame will rarely agree totally with the target population. Thus we must be content with a best effort.
(ii)   For each survey, we should describe the error components and attempt to reduce them.
(iii)   Area sampling can be of some help in improving coverage, particularly in the multiple frame approach as discussed in Section VI.
(iv)   Beware of changes in the target population over time.

The authors conclude their paper with a number of examples illustrating where they have had to use imperfect frames and how they assessed their results. Kish and Hess (1958) present a model for looking at the effects of non-coverage.

V. SAMPLING FROM IMPERFECT LIST FRAMES

The content of this section is based completely on a paper by Hansen, Hurwitz, and Jabine (1963). This important and significant paper discusses some of the problems encountered when sampling from an *imperfect (list) frame* and gives suggestions and actual documented examples of how the problems have been addressed in practice.

To these authors, many lists are imperfect, but in spite of these faults, there are some advantages of *list samples* over *area samples*, including

- One has more control over the structure of the sampling units when sampling from lists.

- The auxiliary information on a list frame is generally more correlated with the variables of interest than the auxiliary information with an area frame and hence more reliable estimates can result.

- Having a list can lead to a decrease in cost if the list makes it possible to use telephone or mail.

- Lists often cover the larger units and in many cases account for most of an aggregate being estimated.

- Lists are often more suitable than area frames in sampling some subject populations including: residential construction, truck ownership and operation, shipments from manufacturing establishments, sales of wholesalers and many others.

- More improved lists are available.

- Efficient techniques are available for using a combination of list frames and area frames.

Throughout the remainder of their paper, the authors list a number of problems associated with imperfect lists, give suggestions for solving these problems, and give documented examples where some of these solutions have been applied. In the remainder of this section, we will list the problems and make a brief general statement on the suggested solutions, as given by Hansen, Hurwitz, and Jabine.

Problem I. Lists whose units are not necessarily those in the target population.

Solution. The authors say, "Establish *rules of associa-tion* between the listed units and those in the target population in such a way that the selection of listed units with known probabilities leads directly to the selection of reporting units in the target population also with known probabilities." Various types of correspondences between the target population and the sampling frame are summarized by Lessler (1980).

Problem II. Lists containing units not in the target popula-tion. (Such units are called "out-of scope" units).

Solution. The authors say, "As is well known, extraneous units in the list do not cause biases, unless one makes the elementary error of substituting active units directly for those found to be out of scope. The presence of these units in the list to be sampled can, however, increase sampling errors. One should therefore, whenever economically feasi-ble, do one or more of the following:

(1)   Remove units known to be out-of-scope from the list prior to sampling.
(2)   Treat as separate strata groups known to contain high proportions of out-of-scope units...
(3)   Resample periodically from an up-to-date list."

Problem III. Lists containing erroneous and incomplete entries. (Examples of this are "those cases where data recorded on the list are used for stratification or selection with probability proportionate to a measure of size and these data prove to be badly in error. See Hansen, Hurwitz, and Madow (1953, Vol. I, pp. 351-353).")

Solution. The authors say, "There is no entirely satis-factory solution in a one-time survey ... If the list sample we are using is one in which data for successive occasions are to be obtained, rotation of the sample of noncertainty sampling units provides a powerful tool for reducing the sampling error due to poor measures of size... If the list sample is being used jointly with an area sample, or with some other procedure for reaching non-listed units, it may be desirable to treat listed units with incomplete information as out-of-scope, and rely on complementary samples to cover the associated reporting units."

Problem IV. Lists containing duplicates ("Duplication occurs
when more than one unit on a list leads to the same reporting
unit. The listed units which are associated with the same
reporting unit may be identical in all respects, or they may
differ in the way in which they identify the reporting
unit.")

  Solution. The authors say, "... take all feasible steps
to eliminate duplicates before the sample is selected. The
usual procedure is to sort the units on the list in some
specified order and then to look for duplicates among groups
of adjacent units ... When the extent of duplication in the
list is unknown, it is possible to select a sample of moder-
ate size and use this to estimate the extent of duplication
in the complete list. Various estimations for this purpose
are given by Goodman (1949)." The authors briefly mention
three cases for consideration when all duplication can not be
eliminated before sampling. i) If we take a 100% sample, all
"duplication will normally be discovered when we try to get
two (or more) reports from the same reporting unit." ii) It
is also possible to uncover some duplication when duplicate
members are selected in the sample. iii) "There are a few
situations in which if either member of a duplicate is selected we can identify it, on the basis of information obtained
from the reporting unit, as a unit which is duplicated on the
list. In such a case, we can determine the true probability
of selection for each reporting unit in the sample and make
an unbiased consistent estimate with no difficulty." (See
Rao (1968)). On duplication, the authors conclude by saying,
"It may be preferable, if duplication is not too frequent, to
simply ignore the duplicate chance of selection in making
estimates and accept the resulting bias."

Problem V. Incomplete Lists

  Solution. The authors note that incompleteness "is the
one (problem) which requires the greatest ingenuity and
expenditure of resources to overcome." A rather extensive
discussion is given for each of the following possible
approaches to this problem in the paper:

  (i) Redefine the target population to match the
       available incomplete list. They say, "Redefinition
       of the target population should be seriously
       considered whenever there is a class of units which

is hard to get at and whose inclusion will substantially raise the cost of the operation, but should
not be resorted to unless the purposes of the survey
can still be adequately served."

(ii)   Supplement the available incomplete list with other
        lists. They say, "When this is done, two questions
        must be asked: (1) Does the new list account for
        all of the units which cannot be reached via the
        original list? (2) Are there any units which can be
        reached through both lists?" Much discussion fol-
        lows these two questions.

(iii)   Supplement the available incomplete list with area
        samples. When one talks about a joint list-area
        sample design, the authors say that a number of
        items are of "particular importance," including a)
        "The survey design must include a procedure for
        identifying those reporting units that are access-
        ible through both the list and area samples. The
        term commonly used for this process is *unduplication*
        ... b) The unduplication process may be subject to
        bias ... c) The danger of bias is less when all
        units on the list are included in the sample ... d)
        There are advantages (costs) to be gained from
        overlapping of the list and area samples ... e)
        Units in the area sample which are also represented
        by the list sample do not necessarily have to be
        discarded in making estimates. (See Hartley
        (1962))... f) In a survey taken on successive occa-
        sions, using a list sample of large or specialized
        establishments supplemented by a complementary area
        sample, the sampling error component resulting from
        the complementary area sample can often be substan-
        tially reduced by the use of sample rotation."

(iv)   Supplement the available incomplete list by the
        "Predecessor-Successor" Method. This is a tech-
        nique for including units from the population in the
        sample which are not on the available incomplete
        list. The authors describe this technique as fol-
        lows: "Consider a population of reporting units
        divided into two classes, those that are included on
        an available list and those that are not on this
        list. Let us suppose that we can establish, in
        principle, a geographic ordering of the units in

this population; and further, that the rules for ordering are such that given any one unit in the population, we can uniquely determine its successor by following a defined path of travel. Under these conditions, we can select a probability sample from this population in the following way:

(a)   Select a probability sample of units from the list.
(b)   For each unit in the sample from the list, determine its successor and check to see if it is on the list. If the successor is on the list, discard it. If the successor is not on the list, include it in the sample; then identify its successor and proceed in the same way until a successor is found to be on the list.

Thus the sample will consist of those units in the original sample from the list plus all sequences of units not on the list which immediately follow these units on the path of travel. The probability of selection of any unlisted unit is therefore the same as that of the first listed unit immediately preceding it in the path of travel."

VI.   MULTIPLE FRAME SURVEYS

Thinking that two or more frames are better than one, Hartley (1962, 1974) gives some formal theory for sampling from more than one frame. In this section, we present the basic ideas found in Hartley (1962) using two frames.

The setting is as follows. We want to estimate Y, the total of the y_i's, of a target population of size N and are given two frames, A and B, for this target population. A simple random sample (other designs are possible) is drawn from each frame with the following assumptions:

(i)   Every unit in the target population of interest belongs to at least one of the frames.
(ii) It is possible to record for each sampled unit whether or not it belongs to the other frame.

Thus each element in the population is in one of three domains:

> Domain a if the element belongs to Frame A only,
>
> Domain b if the element belongs to Frame B only, and
>
> Domain ab if the element belongs to both frames.

It is further assumed that all domain sizes N_a, N_b, and N_{ab} are known and that the prescribed sample sizes can only be allocated to the two frames. (Other cases are also considered. Note $N = N_a + N_{ab} + N_b$.)

If domain ab were empty, that is if frames A and B were disjoint, then one would proceed as in a stratified situation. A special method of weight variables is used to create the effect of having two separate (disjoint) frames as follows:

for frame A define $u_i = \begin{cases} y_i & \text{if the ith unit is in domain a.} \\ py_i & \text{if the ith unit is in domain ab.} \end{cases}$

for frame B define $u_i = \begin{cases} y_i & \text{if the ith unit is in domain b.} \\ qy_i & \text{if the ith unit is in domain ab.} \end{cases}$

Note that

$$Y = Y_a + Y_{ab} + Y_b = \left(Y_a + pY_{ab}\right) + \left(qY_{ab} + Y_b\right) = U_A + U_B \qquad (1)$$

where Y_a, Y_{ab}, and Y_b are population totals of domains a, ab, and b respectively, and U_A and U_B are the population totals for frames A and B respectively for the variable u_i. Note further that in terms of the variable u_i, the "new population" has $N^* = N_a + 2N_{ab} + N_b$ elements.

To estimate Y under the above assumptions, take simple random samples of sizes n_A and n_B respectively from frame A (with $N_A = N_a + N_{ab}$ elements) and frame B (with $N_B = N_b + N_{ab}$

elements). Using a post-stratified estimator of U_A (and U_B), we obtain as an estimator of Y

$$\hat{Y} = \hat{U}_A + \hat{U}_B = \left(\hat{Y}_a + p\hat{Y}_{ab}\right) + \left(q\hat{Y}_{ab} + \hat{Y}_b\right)$$

$$= N_a\bar{y}_a + pN_{ab}\bar{y}_{ab} + qN_{ab}\bar{y}_{ba} + N_b\bar{y}_b \tag{2}$$

where $\bar{y}_a (\bar{y}_b)$ is the sample mean of the elements selected from frame A(B) which are only in domain a(b), and $\bar{y}_{ab} (\bar{y}_{ba})$ is the sample mean of the elements selected from frame A(B) which are also in domain ab(ab).

The variance of $\hat{Y}$ is approximately

$$\text{Var}(\hat{Y}) \approx \frac{N_A^2}{n_A} \left\{\sigma_a^2(1-\alpha) + p^2\sigma_{ab}^2\alpha\right\} + \frac{N_B^2}{n_B} \left\{\sigma_b^2(1-\beta) + q^2\sigma_{ab}^2\beta\right\} \tag{3}$$

where $\alpha = N_{ab}/N_A$, $\beta = N_{ab}/N_B$, and σ_a^2 , σ_{ab}^2 , σ_b^2 are the "within domain" population variances.

Assuming the linear cost function $C = c_A n_A + c_B n_B$ and using the method of Lagrange multipliers, the optimum values of p, n_A and n_B are determined for minimizing var($\hat{Y}$) as

(i)
$$p = \frac{\alpha n_A}{\alpha n_A + \beta n_B}$$

(ii)
$$\frac{n_A}{N_A} = \delta \left\{ \frac{\sigma_a^2(1-\alpha) + \alpha p^2\sigma_{ab}^2}{c_A} \right\}^{1/2} \tag{4}$$

(iii)
$$\frac{n_B}{N_B} = \delta \left\{ \frac{\sigma_b^2(1-\beta) + \beta q^2\sigma_{ab}^2}{c_B} \right\}^{1/2}$$

where δ is determined to satisfy $C = c_A n_A + c_B n_B$.

Hartley considers the special case in which the A-frame has 100% coverage so that $N_{ab} = N_B$, $\beta = 1$, and $\sigma_B^2 = \sigma_{ab}^2$. For this special case, he compares the $\text{Var}(\hat{Y})$ for the optimum design (given by (4)) with that of

$$\hat{\hat{Y}} = N_a \bar{y}_a + N_{ab} \bar{y}_{ab} , \qquad (5)$$

which is the post stratified estimator computed from a simple random sample of size $n_A^* = C/c_A$ drawn from frame A only and requiring an identical budget C.

It can be shown that

$$\frac{\text{Var}(\hat{Y})}{\text{Var}(\hat{\hat{Y}})} = \frac{\left(1 + \frac{q\alpha}{p\rho}\right)^2}{1 + \frac{\alpha q(1-p)}{\rho p^2}} \qquad (6)$$

where $p^2 = \dfrac{\phi(1-\alpha)}{\rho - \alpha}$, $\phi = \dfrac{\sigma_a^2}{\sigma_B^2}$, $\rho = \dfrac{c_A}{c_B}$ and $\alpha = \dfrac{N_B}{N_A}$.

After the generation of several tables for various values of ϕ, ρ, and α, Hartley notes that the ratio in (6) tends to decrease (and is less than one) when ϕ^{-1} increases, α increases, and ρ increases.

Thus there are cases when it is better to use two frames rather than one even if one of them completely covers the target population.

Hartley also considers an alternate cost function for the above special case where the cost of sampling from frame A is variable depending on whether a sample element is selected from domain a or domain ab. He also considers the general problem for the case when the domain sizes N_a, N_b, and N_{ab} are not known and only the frame sizes N_A and N_B are known.

Hartley (1974) attempts to formalize and generalize the concepts and results of the multiple frame methodology. In this paper, Hartley gives the following definition: "*Multiple frame surveys* may be defined as a set of several (single

frame) surveys whose samples are combined to provide
parameter estimates for the union of the frames."

Hartley also notes that the probable reasons why multiple frame surveys have not been used more extensively in the
past are the operational problems in their implementation.
These are problems beyond those ordinarily encountered in a
single frame survey and some that are discussed by Hartley
are listed below:

   (i) "With a two frame survey, two operations have to be
        set up and administered so that the overhead cost
        will usually be higher than with a single survey,"
  (ii) "The recording of the fractional content items y_a,
        y_{ab} for units in Frame A and y_b, y_{ba} in Frame B not
        only adds to the number of content items, but these
        may be extremely difficult to measure in certain
        cases." Hartley continues, "A particularly attrac-
        tive method of controlling these difficulties is to
        use a Frame A with 100% coverage, a low sampling
        rate and intensive interviewing achieving the split
        of content items into $y_A = y_a + y_{ab}$. For the
        'cheap' Frame B which has not a 100% coverage, only
        the items $y_B = y_{ba}$ need to be recorded."
 (iii) "... The determination as to whether or not a
        sampled unit belongs to the overlap domain or not
        may result in exasperating matching operations."
        A theory for record linkage is given by Fellegi and
        Sunter (1969).

Advantages of using a multiple-frame survey include:

   (i) "... the considerable reduction in survey costs
        that will result in estimates of precision
        identical with those of a single frame survey."
  (ii) "If the only frame which provides 100% coverage for
        the items of interest is an expensive frame to sam-
        ple, but other cheaper frames (B, C, ...) are all
        incomplete, an adequate survey in Frame A may not
        be affordable resulting in strenuous efforts to
        make one of the other Frames B or C or ... complete
        or resulting in efforts of 'sweeping' the incom-
        pleteness of such frames 'under the carpet'. An
        honest two frame approach may provide the solu-
        tion."

(iii) "If a two frame operation involves a direct interview survey in Frame A and a mail survey in Frame
B, the subsampling of the 'hard core' nonrespondents to the mail questionnaire in B may be
operationally combined with the direct interview
operation in Frame A."

Included in the following papers are discussions on
sample allocation, estimation (mean, variances, etc.),
administration, operation, and cost constraints when sampling
from more than one frame: Bershad, 1953; Williams, 1957;
King, 1960; Hartley, 1962 and 1974; Cochran, 1964, 1965 and
1967; Caudill, 1965; Steinberg, 1965; Ali, 1967; Welsh,
Conner, and Balfour, 1967; Lund, 1968; Choi, 1970;
Burmeister, 1972; Fuller and Burmeister, 1972; Moore and
Jones, 1973; Rao, 1973; Vogel, 1975; Kiranandana, 1976;
Huang, 1977; Bosecker, 1978; Hansen and Tepping, 1978;
Armstrong, 1979; Beller, 1979; Gleason and Tortora, 1979;
Casady and Sirken, 1980; Casady, Snowden, and Sirken, 1981;
Huang, Hogue, and Isaki, 1981; Groves and Lepkowski,
1982; and Sirken and Casady, 1982.

THE ANNOTATED BIBLIOGRAPHY

1945

King, A. J. and Jessen, R. J. (1945). "The Master Sample of
Agriculture," *Journal of the American Statistical Association, 40,* 38-56.

A historical account of some recorded early uses of area
sampling starting in Europe during the 1920s is given; a
variety of applications is mentioned. A discussion of
advantages and disadvantages of area sampling is presented along with a detailed description of the
development of an area sample referred to as the Master
Sample (of Agriculture).

1949

Chandrasekar, C. and Deming, W. E. (1949). "On a Method of
Estimating Birth and Death Rates and the Extent of Registration," *Journal of the American Statistical Association, 44,*
101-115.

The purpose of the paper is to present a theory by which
when vital registration is incomplete, an enquiry in the

form of a house-to-house canvas may be used in conjunction with the registrar's list to estimate, i) the total number of births and deaths in an area over a specified period; ii) the birth and death rates, iii) the deficiencies in registration; and iv) the standard errors of all these estimates.

An important plan for estimating undercoverage is discussed and is briefly summarized here as discussed in the NAS 1978 report on *Counting the People in 1980*. "If two independent surveys are made of a population at about the same time, the total population would be composed of those who were counted both times (N_{11}), those who were counted in the first survey but not in the second (N_{10}), those who were counted in the second survey but not in the first (N_{01}), and those who were counted in neither survey (N_{00}). The object is to estimate the unknown number (N_{00}) who were not counted at all. If it can be assumed that the event of being counted the first time with probability $(N_{11} + N_{10})/(N_{11} + N_{10} + N_{01} + N_{00})$ is independent of the event of being counted the second time with probability $(N_{11} + N_{01})/(N_{11} + N_{10} + N_{01} + N_{00})$ and that N_{11} is not zero, then the unknown N_{00} can be derived as follows:

$$\frac{N_{11}+N_{10}}{N_{11}+N_{10}+N_{01}+N_{00}} \cdot \frac{N_{11}+N_{01}}{N_{11}+N_{10}+N_{01}+N_{00}} = \frac{N_{11}}{N_{11}+N_{10}+N_{01}+N_{00}}$$

hence $\hat{N}_{00} = \dfrac{N_{01}N_{10}}{N_{11}}$.

(The assumption of independence is crucial.)"

Chevry, G. (1949). "Control of a General Census by Means of an Area Sampling Method," *Journal of the American Statistical Association, 44*, 373-379.

This paper discusses in detail the use of area sampling applied to industrial and commercial enterprises in urban areas of France to determine the adequacy of the general census in enumerating them. The investigation showed undercoverage by the census of enterprises of all sizes.

Goodman, L. A. (1949). "On the Estimation of the Number of
Classes in a Population," *Annals of Mathematical Statistics*,
20, 572-579.

> The folowing problem is considered: Suppose a popula-
> tion of known size N is subdivided into an unknown
> number of mutually exclusive classes. It is assumed
> that the class in which an element is contained may be
> determined but that the classes are not ordered.
> Assume a simple random sample of n elements is
> selected. Estimates are given for the total number K of
> classes which subdivide the population on the basis of
> the sample results and knowledge of the population
> size. The results can be considered when estimating the
> extent of duplication in a frame.

Mosteller, F. (ed.) (1949). Questions and Answers. *American
Statistician*, *3*, 12-13.

> Mosteller presents a discussion of three letters which
> were written offering solutions to the following prob-
> lem:
>
> > We have k classes of similar objects, with N_1
> > objects in class 1, N_2 in class 2, ..., N_k in class
> > k. The class of an object is readily identifiable
> > when the object is examined, but the classes are
> > not ordered. We know $N = \Sigma N_i$. From a sample of
> > size n drawn from the N objects, we wish to esti-
> > mate k. A fourth solution to a closely related
> > duplication problem is also mentioned.

1951

Eckler, A. R. and Pritzker, L. (1951). "Measuring the Accuracy of Enumerative Surveys," *Bulletin of the International
Statistical Institute*, *33*, Part 4, 7-24.

> Under the general topic of accuracy of enumerative
> surveys, Eckler and Pritzker discuss two general
> approaches. First they discuss three methods for
> studying the accuracy of an estimate of the total number
> of units in a population. The methods considered are
> i) comparison, ii) inflow-outflow technique, and iii)
> expected age distributions. These three methods are
> useful when considering the coverage of a frame.

Secondly, two methods for measuring accuracy by the study of response errors are presented and discussed.

1952

Goodman, L. A. (1952). "On the Analysis of Samples from k Lists," *Annals of Mathematical Statistics, 23,* 632-634.

This paper presents an unbiased estimator of the amount of overlap between two or more lists based on a simple random sample from each of the lists being considered An unbiased estimator of the number of units which are repeated in exactly k (a fixed number) lists is given. Also, an unbiased estimator of the number of units which are repeated in at least k (a fixed number) lists is given. Goodman shows that the estimators are minimum variance unbiased estimators.

1953

Bershad, M. A. (1953). "The Sample Survey of Retail Stores," in Hansen, Hurvitz and Madow, *Sample Survey Methods and Theory, Volume I,* John Wiley and Sons, Inc., New York 516-558.

This case study represents one of the earliest documented examples of the use of two sampling frames. Part of the sample was selected from a list of retail stores based on the 1939 Census of Business. For those retail stores not on the list, an area sample was selected.

Hansen, M. H., Hurvitz, W. N., and Madow, W. G. (1953). *Sample Survey Methods and Theory, Vols. I and II,* John Wiley and Sons, Inc., New York.

Marks, E. S., Mauldin, W. P., and Nisselson, H. (1953). "The Post-Enumeration Survey of the 1950 Census: A Case History in Survey Design," *Journal of the American Statistical Association, 48,* 220-243.

The authors say, "The primary purpose of the present paper is to trace the development of the Post-Enumeration Survey, which was designed to measure error (coverage) in the 1950 Censuses, and to outline the reasons for the decisions made and the alternatives considered in designing this survey." Aside from much discussion which would be useful in any survey, the problem of checking the completeness (and content) of a frame is considered.

1955

Jessen, R. J. (1955). "Determining the Fruit Count on a Tree by Randomized Branch Sampling," *Biometrics, 11,* 99-109.

This paper gives a rather clever scheme for randomly selecting a sample without having a list from which to sample. The scheme is presented in the context of estimating the total number of fruits on a tree. A numerical comparison of three different methods for determining the probability of branch selection at each step is given. Jessen concludes, "A method of selecting branches, wherein each branch at forking is given a probability of selection proportional to its cross-sectional area, was found to be quite efficient."

1956

Zarkovich, S. S. (1956). "Some Remarks on Coverage Checks in Population Censuses," *Population Studies, 9,* 271-275.

Brief comments are given on the limitations of post enumeration coverage checks as measures of accuracy of coverage.

1957

Williams, R. E. (1957). "Estimation of Overlapping Strata Boundaries," Unpublished M.S. Thesis, University of Wyoming, Laramie.

Maximum likelihood estimators are given of the size of the overlapping domains in multiple frame problems where independent samples are drawn from each frame. Variances of the estimators and estimators of the variance of the estimators are also obtained.

1958

Kish, L. and Hess, I. (1958). "On Noncoverage of Sample Dwellings," *Journal of the American Statistical Association,* *53,* 509-524.

    In this paper, Kish and Hess discuss how they were able to reduce noncoverage in some of their surveys which involve dwelling units by use of an area sample. They note that, "The estimation of errors of noncoverage generally entails one of two difficult alternatives. The first calls for a quality check by procedures which are sufficiently better to provide the 'true value' against which the survey results can be compared... The alternative procedure calls for a reliable (comparable) estimate from an outside source."

    After discussions on the estimation of coverage in the largely expository paper, a model for looking at the effects of noncoverage is presented.

1959

Deming, W. E. and Glasser, G. J. (1959). "On the Problem of Matching Lists by Samples," *Journal of the American Statistical Association,* *54,* 403-415.

    This paper presents theory for estimation of the proportions of names common to two or more lists of names, through use of samples drawn from the lists. The theory covers a) the probability distributions, expected values, variances, and the third and fourth moments of the estimates of the proportions duplicated; b) testing a hypothesis with respect to a proportion; c) optimum allocation of the samples; d) the effect of duplicates within a list; e) possible gains from stratification. Examples are given to illustrate some of the theory.

Monroe, J. and Finkner, A. L. (1959). *Handbook of Area Sampling,* Chilton Company Publishers, Philadelphia.

    Aside from defining area frame, this handbook gives detailed discussion on how one might actually execute completely an area survey. Topics which are discussed in great detail with examples include: 1) preparation of the sampling materials (use of census data and maps),

and 2) use of the materials (size of the sampling units,
number of sampling units, and selection of the sample).
Estimates for several designs are given.

1960

King, D. W. (1960). "Variance Estimation in Populations
Identified by Multiple Sampling Frames," Unpublished M.S.
Thesis, University of Wyoming, Laramie.

This paper discusses the multiple sampling list problem
and the development of an estimator for the number in
each domain by the minimum modified chi-square method.
A further modification is presented that relieves the
difficulty produced when very small numbers of responses
appear in the sample.

The variance for this estimator is derived. The
approach given entails expansion of the function of the
sample variables that provides the desired estimates in
Taylor's form with a remainder. This arrangement of the
function leads to a derivation of a variance estimator.

1962

Hartley, H. O. (1962). "Multiple Frame Surveys," *Proceedings
of the Social Statistics Section of the American Statistical
Association*, 203-206.

This is a basic paper on the study of multiple frames.
Hartley shows that one can obtain more efficient
estimates under certain conditions using two or more
frames as opposed to one. The basic ideas are presented
under Secton VI of this bibliography.

Seal, K. C. (1962). "Use of Out-Dated Frames in Large Scale
Sample Surveys," *Calcutta Statistical Association Bulletin*,
11, 68-84.

In planning a large-scale sample survey, it is often
found that the available frame from which the sample
could be drawn is not up to date. In a dynamic population the sample thus drawn does not usually provide
unbiased estimates of the population characteristics
existing during the period of the survey. Unless some

adjustments are made on the data collected during the survey, estimates of any population characteristics would be somewhat biased. Some simple methods are suggested on the basis of a reasonable birth and death process (for taking into account the changing population) which could be easily worked out in most practical situations. Illustrations explaining the suggested methods have also been given.

1963

Hansen, M. H., Hurwitz, W. N., and Jabine, T. B. (1963). "The Use of Imperfect Lists for Probability Sampling at the U.S. Bureau of the Census," *Bulletin of the International Statistical Institute, 40, Book 1,* 497-517.

This important paper discusses some of the problems encountered when sampling from an imperfect (list) frame and gives suggestions and actual documented examples on how the problems have been addressed in practice. For more details see Section V of this bibliography.

Szameitat, K. and Schäffer, K-A. (1963). "Imperfect Frames in Statistics and the Consequences for Their Use in Sampling," *Bulletin of the International Statistical Institute, 40, Book 1,* 517-538.

This paper addresses the following questions:

(i) "What types of errors may occur in the frame, and how do they influence the results of the (estimates)?"
(ii) What "are the possibilities for reducing or describing error components?"

Highlights are given under Section IV of this bibliography.

Following are excerpts from discussions of the papers by Hansen, Hurwitz, and Jabine (1963) and Szameitat and Schäffer (1963), included in the references cited.

Cochran, W. G.

While further research is needed, Cochran feels that the problems of undercoverage, overcoverage, and duplication can already be addressed by existing theoretical work.

He feels that new research in this area (frame research)
should focus on determining when one can "safely" ignore
certain imperfections in the frame. He also comments
that the cost of supplementation needs further study.

Omaboe, E. N.

A number of comments are made, including references to
specific problems with imperfect frames in Africa.

Deming, W. E.

"In my own work, I find that people have been in the
habit, many of them, at least in commercial work, of
spending too much money making lists of dwelling units
... The basic requirement is a definable unit; one whose
boundaries are unmistakable."

1964

Cochran, R. S. (1964). "Multiple Frame-Sample Surveys,"
Proceedings of Social Statistics Section of the American Statis-
tical Association, 16-19.

Cochran compares two estimators for the population total
when sampling from two frames. Both estimators were
introduced by Hartley (1962). Frame A is assumed to
completely cover the target population while Frame B is
assumed to only cover a proper subset of the target
population.

To obtain the first estimator, the experimenter randomly
selects $n_A(n_B)$ observations from frame A(B) at a cost of
$c_A(c_B)$ per observation. The estimator given is
$\hat{Y} = N_a \bar{y}_a + pN_{ab}\bar{y}_{ab} + qN_{ab}\bar{y}_{ba}$. To obtain the second
estimator, the experimenter randomly selects n_A observa-
tions from frame A at a cost of c_1 per observation and
randomly selects n_B observations from frame B at a cost
of c_B per observation. Before proceeding, the
experimenter inspects (screens) each and every sample
element chosen from frame A, at a cost of c_2, to determine if the element selected is also on frame B. If it
is not on frame B, then it is kept and processed with

cost c_3. Otherwise it is tossed out and is not used. The estimator which is used is $\hat{Y}_0 = N_a \bar{y}_a + N_B \bar{y}_B$. (Note $c_A = c_1 + c_2 + c_3$.) In terms of variances, Cochran derives criteria under which one estimator will be more efficient than the other.

1965

Caudill, C. E. (1965). "Joint Use of Different Sampling Frames," *Journal of Farm Economics*, 45, #5, 1534-1539.

This paper is concerned with an experimental application of the multiple frame methodology to a survey of Wyoming livestock producers. The two frames used were (1) a general-purpose area sampling frame, and (2) a list of livestock producers compiled by the Agricultural Research Service and originating from the tax records of the county assessor's offices. The potential problems and improvements which would accompany the initiation of this methodology at the Statistical Reporting Service (USDA) are discussed. (Discussions by V. I. West and H. O. Hartley follow the paper.)

Cochran, R. S. (1965). "Theory and Application of Multiple Frame Surveys," Unpublished Ph.D. Thesis, Iowa State University, Ames, Iowa.

The primary concern of this thesis is to present estimators of the multiple frame type suggested by Hartley (1962), derive their variances and estimates of the variances, find optimal sampling and estimation procedures, and to compare this technique with possible alternate sampling plans.

Kish, L. (1965). *Survey Sampling*, John Wiley and Sons, Inc. New York.

Perkins, W. M. and Jones, C. D. (1965). "Matching for Census Coverage Checks," *Proceedings of the Social Statistics Section of the American Statistical Association*, 122-139.

This paper discusses the methodology used in the coverage evaluation of the 1960 Census and the problems that arose when attempting to match persons in a sample which was "independent" of the 1960 Census with persons enumerated in the 1960 Census listing.

Steinberg, J. (1965). "A Multiple Frame Survey for Rare Population Elements," *Proceedings of the Social Statistics Section of the American Statistical Association,* 262-266.

This is an application paper which discusses some of the many problems in the execution of a multiple-frame survey, including 1) the possibility of screening among frames for discarding duplicates versus use of multiple overlapping frames with optimal weighting and 2) administrative considerations, such as the timing of a variety of activities (i.e., unduplication) as well as the cost factors. Unique problems arose because five out of the six target populations were comparatively rare.

1966

Marks, E. S. and Waksberg, J. (1966). "Evaluation of Coverage in the 1960 Census of Population through Case-by-Case Checking," *Proceedings of the Social Statistics Section of the American Statistical Association,* 62-70.

This paper describes the case-by-case checking procedures which were used in the 1960 Census in an evaluation of coverage. Two subcases, case-by-case evaluation through reinterview and case-by-case evaluation through record checks, are discussed. The advantages and limitations of each are given. The former procedure permits estimates of overcoverage and undercoverage, while the latter process only permits estimates of undercoverage.

Siegel, J. S. and Zelnik, M. (1966). "An Evaluation of Coverage in the 1960 Census of Population by Techniques of Demographic Analysis and by Composite Estimates," *Proceedings of the Social Statistics Section of the American Statistical Association,* 71-85.

This paper presents the results of studies using methods of demographic analysis to evaluate the 1960 Census

Counts. These techniques make possible the comparison of census counts with some expected result or standard usually derived by the manipulation of such demographic data as census counts and birth, death, and immigration. The possible advantages and limitations are cited and a number of references to studies of coverage are given.

1967

Ali, M. A. (1967). "Multiple Frame Sample Surveys Involving Different Units and Nonresponses," Unpublished Ph.D. Dissertation, Texas A & M University Library, College Station.

Certain difficulties arise when one uses multiple frame survey techniques. Ali considers two of those difficulties: (a) the fact that in many situations the units to which the different frames give access differ from frame to frame and (b) the fact that the use of the cheaper frame usually entails use of mail questionnaires and hence consequential problems of nonresponse.

Three cases are considered under (a): i) the case in which one frame consists of "elementary units" which are sampled by either a completely random or more sophisticated design, while the second frame consists of "clusters" of the elementary units; ii) the case in which both frames consist of clusters of a different kind but are made up of the same type of elementary unit (an example would be clusters of schools with children as elementary units versus clusters of households with children as elementary units); iii) the case in which the units in the two frames are completely different and no "elementary unit" can be found to serve as a building block for the units in both frames.

Cochran, R. S. (1967). "The Estimation of Domain Sizes When Sampling Frames are Interlocking," *Proceedings of the Social Statistics Section of the American Statistical Association,* 332-335.

The paper presents an estimator for N_{ab} in the two frame survey design discussed by Hartley (1962) when the size of the overlap domain is unknown. Optimal sampling strategies are given. Estimation of N_{ab}, N_{ac}, N_{bc}, and N_{abc} is considered for the case of three frames where the sizes of the overlap domains are unknown.

Welsch, D. E., Conner, J. R., and Balfour II, B. B. (1967). "Use of a Special List of Livestock Producers in a Two Frame Survey: The Beef List Survey," Technical Report to U.S.D.A., Texas A & M University.

The authors describe a survey which is the second phase of a three-phase project supported by the Statistical Reporting Service, U.S. Department of Agriculture. The overall objective of the three-phase project is to "study the operational, statistical, and analytical problems arising in a two-frame survey based on an area-enumerative survey and special lists of farm operators." Seven specific objectives of the second phase of this project are given. The estimators discussed in Hartley (1962) and Rao (1968) are used.

A great deal of the report discusses the many operational problems which occurred during the execution of the multiple frame survey which used a list and an area frame. The authors note, "The importance of both the quality of the list (frame) and the absolute coordination of the area frame survey with the list frame survey cannot be over-emphasized."

1968

Lund,, R. E.(1968). "Estimators in Multiple Frame Surveys," *Proceedings of the Social Statistics Section of the American Statistical Association,* 282-288.

One can show that the optimal p for the estimator of the total presented by Hartley (1962) is $p_0 = \alpha n_A/(\alpha n_A + \beta n_B)$ where $\alpha = N_{ab}/N_A$ and $\beta = N_{ab}/N_B$ whenever n_A and n_B is the optimal allocation of samples selected from the two frames. Lund considered the same estimator of the total but proposed using $p_L = n_{ab}/(n_{ab} + n_{ba})$ instead of p_0. The estimator $\hat{Y}(p_L)$ of the total using p_L has the property that for $n_{ab} > 0$ and $n_{ba} > 0$;

$$\text{Var}\left(\hat{Y}(p_L)\,\big|\,n_{ab},n_{ba}\right) = \min_{p} \text{Var}\left(\hat{Y}(p)\,\big|\,n_{ab},n_{ba}\right)$$

$$\leq \text{Var}\left(\hat{Y}(p_0)\,\big|\,n_{ab},n_{ba}\right) .$$

Rao, J. N. K. (1968). "Some Nonresponse Sampling Theory When the Frame Contains an Unknown Amount of Duplication," *Journal of the American Statistical Association, 63,* 87-90.

> Rao presents an unbiased estimator of the population total and an unbiased estimator of the variance of the estimator when there is an unknown amount of duplication in the frame and there is nonresponse. The estimator is based on the estimator proposed by Hansen and Hurwitz (1946). An estimator of the population mean is also given.

Tepping, B. J. (1968). "A Model for Optimum Linkage of Records," *Journal of the American Statistical Association, 63,* 1321-1332.

> A model is presented for the frequently recurring problem of linking records from two lists. The criterion for an optimum decision rule is taken to be the minimization of the expected total costs associated with the various actions that may be taken for each pair of records that may be compared. A procedure is described for estimating parameters of the model and for successively improving the decision rule. Illustrative results for an application to a file maintenance problem are given.

1969

Fellegi, I. P. and Sunter, A. B. (1969). "A Theory for Record Linkage," *Journal of the American Statistical Association, 64,* 1183-1210.

> A mathematical model is developed to provide a theoretical framework for a computer-oriented solution to the problem of recognizing those records in two files which represent identical persons, objects, or events (said to be matched).

A theorem describing the construction and properties of
the optimal linkage rule and two corollaries to the
theorem which make it a practical working tool are
given. (A number of other computer-oriented record
linkage operations are given in their bibliography.)

1970

Choi, C-H. (1970). "A Bayesian Estimation of Unobserved
Vital Events," Unpublished Ph.D. Dissertation, University of
Michigan, Ann Arbor.

The objectives of this thesis are to find a method for
Bayesian estimation of unobserved vital events and to
compare the estimates of two-frame surveys and three-
frame surveys by a simulation study.

There is evidence that the Bayesian estimation with two-
frame surveys has smaller mean square error than the
maximum likelihood estimation (the Chandrasekar - Deming
method), and that the Bayesian estimation with three-
frame surveys has smaller bias and mean square error
than the estimation with two-frame surveys.

Sen, A. R. (1970). "On the Bias in Estimation Due to
Imperfect Frame in the Canadian Waterfowl Surveys," *Journal
of Wildlife Management,* 703-706.

A technique is described for estimating the bias caused
by undercoverage of a frame used in a survey of Canadian
waterfowl hunters.

Sukhatme, P. V. and Sukhatme, B. V. (1970). *Sampling Theory
of Surveys with Applications* (2nd Revised Ed.), Iowa State
University Press, Ames.

1971

Sunter, A. B. (1971). "On the Construction and Maintenance
of a Central Register for Business," *Bulletin of International Statistical Institute, 44, Part 1,* 701-721.

This paper discusses the basic concept of a Central
Register which can be developed for the control and

coordination of the collection and processing of
statistical data relating to business, government, and
institutions.

The first part of the paper is concerned with the
logical structure of the Central Register, the second
with the operations required to construct and maintain
it, while in the third is given an example of its use
for a survey which must, because of the range of
information required, use two different sets of
reporting units.

1972

Burmeister, L. F. (1972). "Estimators for Samples Selected
From Multiple Overlapping Frames," Unpublished Ph.D.
Dissertation, Iowa State University, Ames.

The primary concern of this thesis is the estimation for
two overlapping frames. Estimators are developed for
two cases: domain sizes, N_a, N_{ab} and N_b, known and
and unknown. When the domain sizes are known, it is
shown that the estimator $\hat{Y}_d = N_a \bar{y}_a + N_{ab} \bar{y}_{ab} + N_b \bar{y}_b$ is
the most efficient of the estimators considered when

costs are ignored. Since $\hat{Y}_d$ is a function of the
distinct elements included in the sample, its use
requires the identification of duplicated elements.
Therefore the cost structures that would lead one to
choose an alternative estimator are investigated.

Estimators of N_{ab} are developed for the two cases:
duplicated elements identified and duplicated elements
not identified. The estimators of N_{ab} are then utilized
in estimators of the total, Y. These estimators of the
total are shown to be more efficient than previously
suggested estimators.

Optimal allocation of the sample subject to cost
constraints is also considered.

Fuller, W. A. and Burmeister, L. F. (1972). "Estimators for
Samples Selected From Two Overlapping Frames," *Proceedings of
the Social Statistics Section of the American Statistical
Association,* 245-249.

The setting is the same as in the paper by Hartley
(1962), except the authors assume N_a, N_b, and N_{ab} are
unknown while N_A and N_B are known. Two problems are
considered: i) The estimation of the number of elements
in the overlap domain, N_{ab}, and ii) the estimation of
the population total. Four estimators of N_{ab} are given
and compared, and two estimators of the population total
are given and compared.

Gurney, M. and Gonzalez M. E. (1972). "Estimates for Samples
from Frames when Some Units Have Multiple Listings,"
*Proceedings of the Social Statistics Section of the American
Statistical Association*, 283-288.

This paper considers the problem of estimation of a
population total when there is an unknown amount of
duplication of elements in the sampling frame. For
various cases, several estimates of the totals are
introduced and compared (mostly empirically) using mean
square error.

1973

Moore, R. P. and Jones, B. L. (1973). "Sampling 17-Year-Olds
Not Enrolled in School," *Proceedings of the Social Statistics
Section of the American Statistical Association*, 359-364.

This paper discusses the application of a multiple frame
survey design for estimating a number of parameters for
the population of 17-year-olds not enrolled in school.

Rao, J. N. K. (1973). "Maximum Likelihood and Bayesian Estimation in Multiple Frame Surveys," Unpublished paper
presented at the International Association of Survey Statisticians Meeting, Vienna.

Using the Hartley (1962) model, a maximum likelihood
estimator of the population total is proposed which is
shown to be more efficient (having smaller variance)
than the estimates of Hartley (1962) and Lund (1968).
The proposed maximum likelihood estimator is also shown
to be a Bayes estimator.

1974

Boyes, B. and Brown, R. (1974). "Quality Measurement and Quality of Sampling Frames," *Proceedings of the Business and Economic Statistics Section of the American Statistical Association*, 162-166.

> This paper gives a discussion of the problems relative to construction, maintenance, and updating of frames and the updating of the auxiliary information which they contain.

Hartley, H. O. (1974). "Multiple Frame Methodology and Selected Applications," *Sankhyā, 36, Series C, Pt. 3*, 99-118.

> In this paper, Hartley attempts to formalize and gener- alize the concepts and results of the multiple frame methodology as presented by such authors as Hartley (1962), Cochran (1965 and 1967), Lund (1968), Ali (1967), and Fuller and Burmeister (1972). He formally defines *multiple frame survey* "as a set of several (single frame) surveys whose samples are combined to provide parameter estimates for the union of the frames." He considers the problems of record matching, frame updating and list maintenance. He also gives a listing of advantages and disadvantages of multiple frame surveys.

1975

Singh, D. (1975). "Establishment of Sampling Frames to Increase the Efficiency and Reliability of Agricultural Census with Special References to India," *1975 Proceedings of the International Statistical Institute, 40, #2*, 70-82.

> In an agricultural census, the basic frame is determined by the list of all operational holdings. Such an up-to- date list of operational holdings hardly exists in any country. An accurate list of operational holdings prepared once becomes outdated after some time. In India, because of the system of maintenance of up-to- date land records, the preparation of an accurate list is much easier. In the present paper, a method of prepara- tion of a list of operational holdings is described. The method depends on the system of maintenance of land

records. Suggestions are given for keeping the frame of
operational holdings up-to-date. Methods to detect
errors in the listing and also to improve the estimates
are discussed.

Vogel, F. A. (1975). "Surveys with Overlapping Frame-
Problems in Application," *Proceedings of the Social Statistics Section of the American Statistical Association*, 694-
699.

Multiple frame surveys are subject to all operational
problems that plague single frame surveys. However, by
their very design, problems unique to multiple frame
surveys also occur. These problems arise from the basic
assumptions involved in a multiple frame sample design
(see Hartley (1962)):

a. Every element of the survey population must be
included in at least one of the frames.
b. It must be possible to determine for every
selected sample unit whether or not it belongs
to any other sample frame.

The latter assumption leads to one of the most critical
aspects of a multiple frame survey. Sometime during the
survey process it is necessary to determine for every
sampled unit whether it could have been selected from
another frame also being used. The available theory
does not tell how this determination is to be made.

This paper examines problems involved in the overlap
determination, and how they can be considered in the
estimation process.

1976

Kiranandana. S. S. (1976). "Imperfect Frames In Sample
Surveys," Unpublished Ph.D. Dissertation, Harvard University,
Cambridge.

This dissertation focuses on 1) noncoverage, 2) duplication, and 3) use of multiple frames. In each case, a
review of the literature is given, and new techniques
are suggested which lead to improved estimates of totals
and means when the frame is found to be imperfect due to
noncoverage or duplication.

1977

Cochran, W. G. (1977). *Sampling Techniques* (3rd ed.) John
Wiley and Sons, New York.

El-Khorazaty, Nabil, M., Imrey, P. B., Koch, G. G., and
Wells, H. B. (1977). "Estimating The Total Number of Events
with Data from Multiple-record Systems: A Review of Methodological Strategies," *International Statistical Review, 45,*
129-157.

> This paper includes a review of the multiple-record sys-
> tem techniques which involve data collection from two or
> more recording systems which cover the same sample or
> subsample of areas at the same time period. This tech-
> nique attempts to give adjustments for the incomplete
> coverage of single systems. The review includes partic-
> ular references to the effects of violations of the
> Chandresekar-Deming (1949) four assumptions and to
> recently developed methods which avoid or ameliorate
> such effects.

Huang, H. (1977). "Relative Efficiency of Some Two-Frame
Estimators," *Proceedings of the Social Statistics Section of the
American Statistical Association,* 793-797.

> This paper illustrates through numerical comparisons the
> relative efficiencies of Hartley's (1962) estimator of the
> population total and an estimator of the population total
> proposed by Fuller and Burmeister (1974). Both estimators
> are written in terms of $\hat{N}_{ab} - \hat{N}_{ba}$ and $\hat{Y}_{ab} - \hat{Y}_{ba}$ which are
> unbiased estimators of zero. For some estimators of the
> population total, empirical results suggest higher effi-
> ciency with an increase in the number of estimators of
> zero used.

1978

Bosecker, R. R. (1978). "Evaluating Alternative Methods for
Determining Overlap Domain In Multiple Frame Surveys," *Pro-
ceedings of the Survey Research Methods Section of the
American Statistical Association,* 325-330.

This paper discusses the results of a numerical evaluation of three alternative methods for determining
membership in the overlap domain in multiple frame
surveys. The three methods are partial nonoverlap
procedure, maximum overlap procedure, and exact match
procedure.

Coulter, R. and Mergerson, J. (1978). "An Application of a
Record Linkage Theory in Constructing a List Sampling Frame,"
*Proceedings of Computer Science and Statistics: Tenth Sympo-
sium on the Interface 1978,* 416-420.

The development of an automated record linkage system
which formats and standardizes several lists is
discussed. An overview of the system is presented with
a brief explanation of the functions of the subsystems
involved. A discussion of the mathematical model
employed to detect duplication and the computer
processing used to implement this model is also given.

Drew, J. D., Choudhry, G. H., and Gray, G. B. (1978). "Some
Methods for Updating Sample Survey Frames and Their Effects
on Estimation," *Survey Methodology, 4, #2,* 225-263.

Frames designed for continuous surveys are sometimes
used for ad hoc surveys which require selection of
sampling units separate from those selected for the
continuous survey. This paper presents an unbiased
extension of Keyfitz's (1951) sample updating method to
the case where a portion of the frame has been reserved
for surveys other than the main continuous survey. A
simple although biased alternative is presented.

The scope under Platek and Singh's (1975) design
strategy for an area based continuous survey requiring
updating is then expanded to encompass rotation of
first-stage units, establishment of a separate special
survey sub-frame, and procedures to prevent reselection
of ultimate sampling units.

The methods are evaluated in a Monte Carlo study using
census data to simulate the design for the Canadian
Labour Force Survey.

Hansen, M. H. and Tepping, B. J. (1978). "Variance Estima-
tion for a Specified Multiple-Frame Survey Design,"
Contributions to Survey Sampling and Applied Statistics, (H.
A. David, ed.). Academic Press, New York, 57-67.

This paper is concerned with the estimation of the variance of estimates based on a multiple-frame sample design in which alphabetic clusters of elements have been sampled from different lists, and where elements selected from different lists may correspond to the same element of the population of interest. A nesting procedure is used to assure that clusters selected from any one of the lists are also in the sample for any other list in which an equal or greater sampling rate has been specified.

Jessen, R. J. (1978). *Statistical Survey Techniques*, John Wiley and Sons, New York.

Lanphier, C. M. and Bailar, B. A. (1978). "A Survey of Surveys: Some Sampling Frame Problems," *Survey Sampling and Measurement*. (N. K. Namboodiri, ed.), New York: Academic Press, 69-85.

This application paper presents the many considerations for the development of a sampling frame for a survey which was proposed to study survey practices in the United States.

National Research Council (1978). *Counting the People in 1980: An Appraisal of Census Plans*. (Chapter 5) Washington, D.C.: National Academy of Sciences.

Chapter 5 of this report compares three possible techniques for adjusting the counts of the U.S. Census: synthetic method, demographic method, and matching method. The report admits that undercoverage in large enumerative surveys is guaranteed and encourages further research for improved adjustment methods.

1979

Armstrong, B. (1979). "Test of Multiple Frame Sampling Techniques for Agricultural Surveys: New Brunswick, 1978," *Proceedings of the Survey Research Methods Section of the American Statistical Association*, 295-300.

This is an application paper which presents the results
of an experiment to determine the usefulness of multiple
frame sampling in the Agriculture Enumerative Survey in
New Brunswick (1978) Canada. In the past, area samples
had been used to obtain estimates. This had been unsatisfactory since the sample size allocated to smaller
provinces, like New Brunswick, had been insufficient to
produce good provincial estimates. The two frames used
were an area frame and a list frame. Three estimators
are compared.

Bateman, D. V. and Cowan, C. D. (1979). "Plans for 1980
Census Coverage Evaluation," *Proceedings of the Section on
Survey Research Methods of the American Statistical Associa-
tion,* 20-28.

The purpose of this paper is to present the objectives
and methodology of the 1980 Census coverage evaluation
program. The emphasis is on issues pertaining to the
estimation of the census undercount of persons. In
particular, two methods for obtaining these data are
discussed: demographic analysis and a postcensus
sample survey. Since a demand now exists for census
undercount estimates for relatively small geographic
areas, a section of this paper discusses regression
synthetic estimation techniques that could be employed
in providing these estimates.

Beller, N. D. (1979). "Error Profile–Multiple Frame
Designs," *Proceedings of the Survey Research Methods Section
of the American Statistical Association,* 221-222.

This paper is a very brief commentary which makes the
following point of the existence of a paradox for statisticians: "Continued efforts to decrease sampling
error (improve precision) often involve greater survey
design complications which can increase the nonsampling
error (decrease accuracy) and, in turn, may result in a
greater total error ... Our (USDA) studies have
provided ample evidence that there are nonsampling
errors associated with domain determination ... It is
probably a safe assumption that the magnitude of errors
arising from domain determination are positively correlated with the proportion of the universe operations
covered by the list frame. If this is true, a relevant
question becomes, how much of the universe should one
attempt to cover with a list frame?"

Gleason, C. P. and Tortora, R. D. (1979). "Successive Sampling of Two Overlapping Frames," *Proceedings of the Survey Research Methods Section of the American Statistical Association,* 320-324.

> This paper presents the theory for estimating the population total using successive sampling with two overlapping frames. An example is also given.

1980

Casady, R. J. and Sirken, M. G. (1980). "A Multiplicity Estimator for Multiple Frame Sampling," *Proceedings of the Social Statistics Section of the American Statistical Association,* 601-605.

> The purpose of this paper is twofold. First, the definitions and notation which have been utilized in the literature to develop the theory and methods of multiple frame sampling and network sampling are to be consolidated and unified.

> Secondly, the multiple frame estimator proposed by Hartley (1962, 1974) is extended to include the situation in which the data for at least one of the sampling frames is collected via a multiplicity counting rule. This generalized Hartley estimator is analytically compared to the stratified sampling multiplicity estimator proposed by Sirken (1972).

Lessler, J. T. (1980). "Frame Errors." Phase I Taxonomy Report, Project, Research Triangle Institute 1791/00-01I.

> Lessler considers the various definitions of frame and related terms which occur in the literature. This paper also presents a rather informative and extensive classification of frame errors. The classification is an outline which considers: "1) the source of frame errors, 2) the terminology employed, 3) the models and measures for the extent of the error and the impact of the error, 4) the procedures for estimating the values of the error measures, and methods for conducting surveys in the presence of error."

Proceedings of the 1980 Conference on Census Undercount (1980). U.S. Department of Commerce, Washington, D.C.

This volume contains over twenty papers with discussion
on the problem of the census undercount. The papers
include such topics as (a) methods of measuring the
undercount for subnational areas, including the quality
of the estimates of undercount in relation to the size
and other characteristics of the area, and the feasibility of providing accuracy checks or confidence
intervals; (b) the timing of the adjustment(s) for
undercount; (c) measuring and adjusting for the undercount and misreporting for factors other than total
population, such as social and economic characteristics;
(d) the use of adjusted figures in federal programs and
the impact of adjustments on the federal statistical
system; (e) political and legal issues in making adjustments to the census counts; (f) the effects of
adjustments on equity in the distribution of federal
funds; and (g) decision theory and theoretical aspects
of adjustments.

Tarng, S. H. (1980). "Estimation of the Population Total
When the Sample is Taken from a List Containing an Unknown
Amount of Duplication," Unpublished Ph.D. Dissertation,
Oregon State University, Corvallis.

A frame contains a known number, N, of units, but the
units are grouped into an unknown number of M distinct
classes. A measurement y_i is associated with each
class, and based on the information obtained from a
simple random sample of units from the frame, the goal
is to estimate the population total, $\sum_{i=1}^{M} y_i$ without
knowing M. Five different estimators of M are presented
and compared.

1981

Casady, R. J., Snowden, C. B. and Sirken, M. G. (1981). "A
Study of Dual Frame Estimators for the National Health Inter-
view Survey," *Proceedings of the Survey Research Methods
Section of the American Statistical Association*, 444-447.

This is an application paper on dual frames where one of
the frames is a telephone frame and the other is an area
frame. Using self weighting cluster sampling in both
frames, the paper uses a Lund-like estimator of the

population mean. The initial studies showed potential
gains using the incomplete telephone frame with the area
frame.

Chapman, D. W. (1981). "Estimation Equations for the Number
of Duplicate Housing Unit Listings in the 1980 Census, Based
on a Sample of Enumeration District Clusters," *Proceedings of
the Section on Survey Research Methods of the American Statistical Association,* 556-561.

> This paper presents the results of an empirical study
> using three hypothetical populations with known levels
> of duplication. The object of the study was to obtain
> some comparison of the precision of four estimators of
> the level of duplication.

Huang, E.T., Hogue, C. R., and Isaki, C. T. (1981).
"Comparisons of Multi-Frame with Single-Frame Sample Designs
using Registration and Voting Survey Data," *Survey
Statistician, 6,* (International Association of Survey
Statisticians), 8-9.

> This application paper describes the results of a study
> which was proposed to compare the cost efficiency of a
> two-frame sample design to a single-frame sample design
> for estimating minority registration and voting rates.
> Five models are considered in the comparison of the
> approaches.

1982

Groves, R. M. and Lepkowski, J. M. (1982). "Alternative Dual
Frame Mixed Mode Survey Designs," *Proceedings of the Section
on Survey Research Methods of the American Statistical
Association* (to appear).

> The lower costs of telephone surveys makes them very
> appealing. However, their disadvantages are higher
> rates of noncoverage and nonresponse. On the other
> hand, area surveys have good coverage and good response
> with personal visit interviews, but they cost more.
> This paper seeks a methodology which combines the cost
> advantages of a telephone sample survey with the better
> coverage and response rate properties of an area proba-
> bility sample and personal visit interview survey. A
> multiple frame sampling design (telephone survey and
> area survey) is considered.

The purpose of this paper is to review and explore the
cost and allocation issues of designing dual frame,
mixed-mode surveys. Two estimators for dual frame
designs, Hartley (1962) and Lund (1968), are reviewed
and alternative administrative structures are explored.

Sirken, M. G. and Casady, R. J. (1982). "Nonresponse in Dual
Frame Surveys Based on Area/List and Telephone Frames,"
*Proceedings of the Section on Survey Research Methods of the
American Statistical Association* (to appear).

This paper presents some empirical results on the
effects of various nonresponse rates and different
sample allocation schemes (n_A, n_B) on the sampling error
in the National Health Interview Survey.

DATA COLLECTION FOR DETAILS OVER SPACE AND TIME*

Leslie Kish

University of Michigan
Ann Arbor, Michigan

I. INTRODUCTION

It dawned on me only recently that several topics that
have both involved and interested me greatly during the past
few years all have a common framework; a framework described
by the above title. I would now try to convince you that such
a framework can also serve to organize your thoughts about
sample designs and about methods for collecting data.

We begin by considering that our variables and populations can vary over space and over time. Hence continuous or
periodic censuses or samples or registers could be posed as
ideals for collecting all the information we could desire.
But all those would be unrealistic. To borrow from a great
American: You can poll all of the people some of the time and
you can poll some of the people all of the time, but you cannot poll all of the people all the time. Especially not about
everything. So we must face the conflict and look for compro-
mises. We must choose between statistical designs, and for
that task we need statisticians.

Right here I would avoid the dichotomous form into which
this conflict is often cast: one-time cross sections versus
longitudinal studies that are narrowly restricted in space.
That kind of choice may be forced by practical cost considerations, but the restriction to one of the dimensions should be
recognized as a serious sacrifice. It is seldom that strong
models can cover the sacrificed dimension confidently.

*Talk given after conference dinner on November 11, 1982.

II. SAMPLES AND CENSUSES

Sample surveys can be designed to obtain wide varieties
of complex data, rich and deep in content. They can be tai-
lored flexibly to fit a variety of needs and methods of collection. Such data are not gathered with complete censuses;
attempts to do so would result in very high costs and also in
low quality. Even less should one try to stretch the scope of
administrative registers to those tasks. The observational
procedures in sample surveys can be directed to obtain data
which are relevant and pertinent to research and for decisions and which are reasonably accurate for defined aims in
many situations.

That small samples can be made inexpensive is well appre-
ciated, but we should also stress that samples are and can be
much more timely and repeated more often -- yearly, monthly,
even weekly--if planned. For rapidly changing or fluctuating
variables this can more than make up for their small sizes; I
note epidemics as one example and seasonal crops as another.
Flexibility in timing, in spacing, and in methods can be had
in samples. They can meet the needs for timing in seasonal
activities in crops, employment, etc. that censuses cannot.

Because they are large and complete, *censuses* are precise
and detailed. Precision refers to the inverse of sampling
variability; but censuses may be more inaccurate than samples
due to biases of measurement. Censuses give data in great
detail for small domains and especially for local areas, which
samples fail to provide; this is probably their principal
continuing utility. Even here we sound several cautions.
First, detail and precision are both lost in trends over time,
especially for unstable variables and populations (Waksberg,
1968). (Consider epidemics, industrial output, and fertility
in these times of changing birth rates!) Second, precision
for small local areas is subject to random fluctuations over
time (i.e., when based on small populations we expect great
variations of births, deaths, disease, crime, etc.). In addition censuses of small areas are also subject to relatively
large correlated errors of enumerators.

Censuses seem often (though not always, nor necessarily)
to obtain better coverage than sample surveys. Thus they tend
to be more inclusive in population extent than sample surveys. This is partly because it is less difficult to check
complete rather than sample coverage but mostly because of the
credibility aroused by the public relations campaigns for

TABLE 1. *Eight Criteria for Comparing Three Sources of Data*

Criteria	Samples	Census	Adm. Registers
Rich, Complex, Diverse, Flexible	* * *		
Accurate, Relevant, Pertinent	*		?
Inexpensive	*		* * *
Timely, opportune, seasonal	* *		*
Precise (large and complete)		*	*
Detailed		* *	*
Inclusive (coverage), credible, P.R.		*	?
Population content	* *	*	

*Denotes advantages

censuses. These can greatly improve coverage in censuses. But the needed campaign of the propaganda can also have undesired effects on variables -- and even on some census counts (this has happened in some countries). The content -- as distinct from the extent -- of the survey population can be controlled and directed toward survey aims better in specialized surveys than in complete censuses, which must have more general aims. The definition of the population can be made to suit the survey's aims, but this flexibility may be prohibited by the public aspects of the census. These points are developed elsewhere (Kish, 1979; Kish and Verma, 1983).

III. SAMPLES CONNECTED WITH CENSUSES

Methods of survey sampling have a large literature that needs no summary here. The methods are oriented to designs for distinct and separate surveys, but those methods have general applicability. Yet the applications of those methods to samples connected with censuses deserve some special attention; these samples differ from surveys because of their double roots. They share methods, techniques, and theory with the survey samples, but their connection with censuses gives them both special functions and special advantages in funds and in resources. Hence they often have large sizes, especially those used to obtain supplementary data. They also share with censuses some inflexibilities in timing, also in the contents of their populations, and especially in the restrictions

on data that official censuses can afford to collect without
jeopardizing the wide cooperation they need and get (Kish,
1979 and Kish and Verma, 1983).

IV. DATA FROM REGISTERS

     Data from registers, like censuses, are detailed and pre-
cise. However, their accuracy varies greatly: electric bills
and reported wages may or may not be more accurate than interviews, but birth and death registers are known to be woefully
inaccurate in many countries. The data are often timely and
up to date. The population coverage may be good or poor, and
'compulsory' reporting does not mean good coverage. Think of
school records and of the history of establishing compulsory
education in many countries. Many registers (like utilities)
may have high coverage or low, and their contents may also
differ greatly from the populations one needs. Primarily, data
from registers differ from other sources in being far from
rich, but very inexpensive.

     That leads to an attractive prospect: to utilize regis-
ters, especially registers with good coverage, to obtain
richer data. Registers are financed to serve the needs of
individuals (like medical and utility lists) or of society
(like taxes and military service); it seems attractive to
obtain statistical data for 'little' extra cost. Without
those registers we would not have historical demography,
because budgets just for statistical data are not old.

     However, we should be more careful with our enthusiasm:
how good and how cheap are the data? It should be noted that
these two qualities may well conflict. Obtaining and keeping
data involves administrative costs, plus social burdens on the
respondents. The richness of the data should be severely
limited, because their quality would suffer from being a
fringe activity for both clerks and respondents, whose
interests are elsewhere.

     I believe we should separate personal data from
statistical data. Personal data are needed for the
individual's own use; should be confidential; need individual
identification; and can have individualized form and content.
In full contrast, statistical data are needed for population
aggregates and averages, for public use, should be anonymous,
and must be standardized in form and content. Because of
these conflicts I believe that sampling should be used to

collect the statistical data which are not needed for personal
data on registers. Sampling should get better and richer data
from specially trained personnel, and cheaper data because of
great reductions in size of the effort.

V. A BRIEF HISTORICAL OVERVIEW OF CENSUSES

A cautious statistician does not undertake lightly the
task of comparing samples with censuses, and, especially, he
does not suggest lightly the possibility of substituting one
for the other. There are heavy stakes involved with each
census -- financial, legal, constitutional, professional and
emotional stakes. We do not wish to interfere with the noble,
difficult, and serious work of the U. S. Census Bureau and of
the U. N. Statistical Office. Let me make the usual
disclaimer: I am not now talking about the U. S. Census of
1980 or 1985 or 1990 - nor any other actual Census, living or
dead.

However, it is desirable to look objectively and
historically at the role that censuses have played in
history. They constitute a great and ancient invention that
is still to come into full use in all countries in our 20th
Century. Yet it may be disappearing already in one corner of
the world, in Scandinavia, and getting critical reviews elsewhere.

I would just add that censuses have increased and multi-
plied though their roles have changed considerably. In early
times they chiefly served to distribute onerous duties on to
diverse portions of nations: duties like taxes and soldiers to
be levied against provinces. Later came scientific and statistical curiosity. Very recently the census has become the
basis for distributing money from the nation to small domains,
and this raises new problems.

VI. POSTCENSAL ESTIMATES FOR DOMAINS

Estimates for local areas and other small domains have
been of general interest for a long time, but have been un-
available except for estimates from population censuses, special surveys, or administrative registers. These interests,
however, have been superseded by increasing demands for more
diverse, rich, and current data for small domains, which are

required for the planning of reforms, welfare and administration in many fields.

Estimates for small domains have been largely neglected until recently by statistical and sampling theory. As exceptions, we note that for population counts of local areas statistical demographers have developed several competing methods, but these methods have been essentially accounting procedures specialized for population counts, with the notable addition of the ratio-correlation method, which has wider application. Generally, statistical theory has been concerned with the estimation of overall means based on the entire sample. At the other end, some statistics exist for predictions (and related decision functions) for individual cases. However the problems between the two extremes, estimates for subpopulations (especially small domains), has been largely neglected.

Only in recent years have estimates for small domains become an active area for research. This has resulted in investigations of a variety of statistical techniques for application to problems of estimation for small domains; it has become perhaps the most active and productive field of investigation in survey sampling today. Purcell and Kish (1979, 1980) give several references.

TABLE 2. *Sources of Data for Postcensal Estimates (Kish and Purcell, 1979; Kish and Verma, 1983.)*

Methods	Census	Sample	Register
1. Symptomatic Accounting	*		*
2. Regression-Symptomatic	*		*
3. Synthetic (Ratio) Estimates	*	*	
4. James-Stein, Bayesian, Shrinkage	(*)	*	
5. Sample-Regression	*	*	(*)
6. Synthetic-Regression	*	*	(*)
7. Base Unit Methods	*	*	(*)
8. Categorical Data Analysis	(*)	(*)	(*)

*   Sources needed.
(*) Sources useful but not needed.

VII. DESIGN AND ESTIMATION FOR DOMAINS

Domains and *subclasses* are terms used similarly in the literature of survey sampling to denote divisions, usually partitions, both of the population and of the sample for separate estimation. Let us take advantage of that redundancy: let domains denote subpopulations, and let subclassses refer to their reflected subdivisions in the sample.

Estimates are required for a diversity of domains and the types of domains should influence the choices both of *design* and of *estimation*. A classification of three *types* of domains is therefore desirable, and I suggest the following terminology for them (Kish, 1981).

(a) There are *design domains* for which separate samples have been planned, designed, and selected; their combination forms the entire sample, usually as a weighted sum of independent samples. For example, major regions or urban and rural domains, where these are composed of entire strata of primary sampling units; also geographical or alphabetical divisions, when names are so selected individually from appropriately ordered listings.

(b) At the other extreme are *cross-classes* which cut across the sample designs, across strata, and across sampling units. These are the most commonly used kinds of domains and subclasses (e.g., age, sex, occupation, education and income classes, behaviour and attitude types, etc.). They have not been separated into design domains because information was not available on these variables, or because they seemed less important than others, or because they were forgotten.

(c) Between the two extremes, but less commonly used than the two dominant types, are *mixed domains* of diverse kinds; they have not been separated by the design, but they tend to concentrate unevenly in the sampling units or in strata. For example, occupations such as fishermen, farming specialties, miners and lumberjacks, which are segregated by natural forces or ethnic groups segregated by social forces. In both cases the segregation may be prevalent but neither complete nor available as auxiliary data for design.

The sizes of domains also influence the choice of methods

for design and estimation; hence a cross-classification of the
above types with *classes* based on sizes of domains also seems
useful. This classification is stated roughly to orders of
magnitude, with descriptive names assigned for ready reference.

(1) *Major domains* comprise perhaps 1/10 of the population or more. Examples: major regions for design domains, and 10-year age groups or major occupational
categories for cross-classes. For major domains reasonable estimates can be produced from probability samples
with standard methods and essentially without bias; but
variances are increased for cross-classes, and their estimation requires special attention. Furthermore designing adequate sample sizes for them may lead to conflicts.

(2) *Minor domains* comprise perhaps from 1/10 to 1/100 of
the population. Examples: populations of the 50 states
of the USA or the 63 counties in the UK, or single years
of age or twofold classifications of major domains, like
occupation by education, or regions (designed) by education (cross class).

(3) *Mini-domains* comprise perhaps from 1/100 to 1/1,000
or even to 1/10,000 of the population. Examples: populations of the over 3,000 counties of the USA, or the 625
parliamentary districts in the UK, or a threefold classification of age by occupation by education. For mini-
domains usually (and often for minor domains also)the
sample bases are too small for any usable reliability,
hence standard methods of estimation are inadequate. New
methods are needed and these are mentioned in Section VI.

(4) *Rare types*, comprising less than 1/10,000 in the
population, are problems for which samples of an entire
population are useless, and separate lists and methods
are needed (Kish, 1965, Section 11.4).

VIII. PURPOSES AND DESIGNS FOR PERIODIC SAMPLES

This all too brief treatment must be organized around
designs, but we should think of purposes first and then find
the design that suits them best. We discuss here chiefly the
proportion P of overlaps between the periods of the samples.
We concentrate on the case of positive correlations R between

periods of measurements for individuals and for sampling
units. (See Cochran, 1977, Sections 12.10-12.13; Hansen,
Hurwitz and Madow, 1953, Section 11.7; and Kish, 1965, Sections 12.4-12.6.)

1. *Nonoverlapping* samples (P=0) are best for cumulating
data because variances are reduced in proportion to the cumu-
lation, without increases due to the correlations. They can
also be used for covering seasonal variations and trends in
the variables. This design has been neglected by theory.

2. *Partial overlaps* (0<P<1) on the contrary have received most theoretical attention. They offer some practical
flexibilities and advantages. For static (cross-section) estimates of current levels they offer modest reductions of the
variance for high levels of R in modest overlaps P. Their
chief advantages come in reducing the variance of net changes
between periods. The variance is reduced by 1-PR for simple
estimates, and for weighted estimates it can be reduced by
$(1-R)/\left[1-(1-P)R\right]$. The Current Population Survey operates with
an overlap of 7/8 between successive months, but less or zero
for other gaps.

3. *Complete overlaps* (P=1) would have the lowest variance for measuring net change of means. The value of R is
less than 1 not only because variables change for individuals,
but also because individuals move between sampling units (area
segments) in practical area samples.

4. *Panels* are complete overlaps of individuals. Following panels of people as they move, emigrate, or die becomes
difficult, costly, and impossible. But panels have been man-
aged with diverse successes because they are needed for measuring "gross" changes of individuals.

5. *Combinations* of the above may be designed to fit the
diverse purposes of surveys. See Section X.

IX. ROLLING SAMPLES

The economic solution to the seemingly conflicting demands of timeliness and detail may come from cumulating rolling samples. We and others have designed cumulating samples,
but the outstanding example may come from the Health Interview
Surveys (HIS) of the National Center for Health Statistics.
Weekly non-overlapping samples of about 1,000 households are

cumulated into monthly, quarterly and yearly samples of 4,000,
13,000 and 52,000 households respectively, and about three
times as many persons (NCHS 1958). These surveys demonstrate
the practicality and the desirability of cumulating data for
variables, such as health conditions, which lack stability
over time.

For the sake of clarity I must now create the missing
terminology. *Cumulating* samples, like the HIS surveys, are
designed for the purpose, and thus are a step beyond being
merely *non-overlapping* samples. The next step would be to
design *rolling samples* designed deliberately and skillfully to
cover the entire population in geographic detail. I called
these "rotating samples" earlier but that term means partial
overlap to some people. Finally *rolling censuses* would cover
the entire population in a specified period.

For example in the USA, a 1 percent yearly sample could
be based on weekly samples of 1/5200 for 15,000 households.
It would yield monthly and quarterly samples of 65,000 and
195,000. The yearly samples of 1/100 would be 780,000 and
cumulate to 5 percent samples of 3.9 millions, quinquennially
(Kish, 1981a).

Cumulating samples seems to run up against psychological
blocks based on traditional methods of thinking. However,
consider three kinds of fluctuations over time: secular
(smooth and long term), periodic (similar to seasonal over the
years), and irregular (haphazard, random, unpredictable). It
seems clear to me that sampling and cumulating over time
should be preferable on statistical grounds to accepting any
arbitrarily chosen "typical" period. This would be also true
of other cyclical variations if they occur to any extent. It
seems to me paradoxical that judgmental selection is still
accepted meekly in the time dimension although it is on the
run in area sampling.

X.   PANELS WITH ROLLING SAMPLES

Split panel design (SPD) is the name I propose for a combination of panels with cumulating samples (Kish, 1981b). It
has a future though it has no past, I believe, and a distinct
name should reduce its being confused with other designs. The
notion is simply to add to a panel p a series of rolling samples. Thus in symbols we have pa-pb-pc-pd etc. The design
may be generalized so that p is a complete overlap rather than

a true panel. There is even greater flexibility in the other
portion which may be a partial overlap, for example
pab-pbc-pcd. The nonoverlaps may also vary in size to fit
both changing budgets and changing needs. The overlap portion
p would remain constant but its relative size can be varied
greatly. The advantages of overlaps are insensitive to
changes in the relative sizes of overlaps in the range of 1/4
to 1/2.

The symmetrical design of partial overlaps in use today
have elegance and tradition, but the split panel design will
have several advantages. First come the data that only continuing panels can yield. Of course this must be balanced
against the costs and biases of panels. These could be investigated in an SPD sample and also reduced with modified designs in which only portions of the panel appear in some of
the samples and other portions get a rest; in other words, the
panel can be made rotating.

A second advantage of the SPD design is its flexibility
of periods for measuring net change. Symmetrical designs provide overlaps only for gaps prespecified in the original design. However it is common experience to discover critical
comparisons in later waves that differ from those prespecified
originally. The SPD provides overlaps for *all* comparisons of
net change.

For static (current) estimates, SPD may be a little less
efficient than a symmetrical design because this gets partial
overlaps linked to more samples. But this effect diminishes
pretty fast with time even for high correlations.

Thus, a split panel design may be used to satisfy all
five purposes of periodic samples discussed in Section VIII.
Hence, I foresee a good future for them, especially in connection with rolling samples (Kish, 1981a).

XI. SUMMARY

We made a brief attempt to take a combined view of two
aspects or dimensions of variations in variables, in statistics, in parameters of models: variation over space and over
time. A combined view is useful and justified philosophically
and theoretically. But it has been neglected and the two
aspects have been put in opposition in data collection. Thus
cross-section surveys have been opposed to longitudinal

studies, and censuses with details over space have been contrasted to samples for obtaining data that are timely and detailed over time.

The contrast and conflict of the two methods and of the two aspects, though unjustified in theory and philosophy, have practical basis in cost, in difficulties for covering large populations, and for detail in both aspects. Sections VI, VII, VIII, IX and X refer to diverse attempts to deal with these problems.

REFERENCES

Cochran, W. G. (1977). *Sampling Techniques*, 3rd ed., John Wiley and Sons, New York.

Hansen, M. H., Hurwitz, W. N., and Madow, W. G. (1953). *Sample Survey Theory and Methods, Vol I*, John Wiley and Sons, New York.

Kish, L. (1965). *Survey Sampling*, John Wiley and Sons, New York.

Kish, L. (1979). "Samples and Censuses," *International Statistical Review*, 47, 99–109.

Kish, L. (1980). "Design and Estimation for Domains," *The Statistician (London)*, 29, 209–222.

Kish, L. (1981a). *Using Cumulated Rolling Samples*, Congressional Research Office, U.S. Government 80-5280, 78 pp.

Kish, L. (1981b). "Split Panel Designs," *Survey Methods Newsletter*, London: SCPR, Spring 1981.

Kish, L. and Verma, V. (1983). "Censuses Plus Samples," *Proceedings of the 44th Session of the International Statistical Institute*, (to appear).

Purcell, N. J. and Kish, L. (1979). "Estimation for Small Domains," *Biometrics*, 35, 365–384.

Purcell, N. J. and Kish, L. (1980). "Postcensal Estimates for Local Areas," *International Statistical Review*, 48, 3–18.

National Center for Health Statistics (1958). *Statistical Design of the Health Household - Interview Survey*, Public Health Services, 584-A2, 15–18.

RESPONSE EFFECTS TO BEHAVIOR AND ATTITUDE QUESTIONS

Seymour Sudman
University of Illinois at Urbana–Champaign
Urbana, Illinois

I. INTRODUCTION

The improvement of data quality is essential, given the ever-increasing demands put on the data. The U.S. Population Census, for example, has been attacked, not because the quality of the data is poor or declining, but because the uses of Census data for revenue sharing and other purposes has intensified. The key question in a census is usually one of coverage; have all units in the population been included? Statisticians think first of sample bias. Has the sample been selected in a way which gives some units no probability of selection? Sample bias issues are of great importance, but in many applications they are far less important than the other major difficulty in both censuses and surveys--response effects. In this review paper, I attempt to summarize what we know about response effects for both behavior and attitude questions. I shall primarily concentrate on the effects that are caused by question wording and the order of questions in the questionnaire. It is my belief, and that of most of my colleagues, that these are critical elements in determining the validity of the data in a system.

There have been several recent reviews of response effects. Norman Bradburn and I have attempted to summarize our research on behavioral topics in a series of three books. The most recent, *Asking Questions* (1982), has just been published by Jossey-Bass. The two earlier and more technical books were *Response Effects in Surveys* (1974), which attempted to develop a model of the causes of response effects and *Improving Interview Method and Questionnaire Design* (1979), which described a series of experimental treatments that we used to reduce response effects.

In this review, the majority of the discussion is on behavioral rather than attitude questions. This is not

intended to reflect any judgments about the relative impor-
tance of these types of questions but simply indicates that
we know more about response effects to behavior questions.
The major work on attitude questions has been by Schuman and
his colleagues at the Survey Research Center, University of
Michigan. Much of this work has been summarized in the
recent book by Schuman and Presser, *Questions and Answers in
Attitude Surveys* (1981). Another review by Schuman and
Kalton will be found in the *Journal of the Royal Statistical
Society* (1982). Of course, a major source of research on
response effects is the U.S. Bureau of the Census. Barbara
Bailar will discuss their activities in her paper that
follows.

     In discussing behavior questions, it is useful to dis-
tinguish between threatening and non-threatening questions.
For non-threatening questions, issues of self-presentation
become most important. For attitude questions, not only are
question wordings vital, but the context in which the question appears may have an important effect. After discussing
the nature and magnitude of response effects for each of
these types of questions, I offer some suggestions on how the
quality of the data can be improved.

II. NON-THREATENING BEHAVIOR QUESTIONS

     There are three major kinds of memory error that affect
non-threatening behavior questions:

     1. Omissions
     2. Telescoping
     3. Errors in details

     Omissions – We are aware, unless it has slipped our
minds, that forgetting is a fact of life for most individuals
and on most subjects. As an illustration, Table 1 shows the
average number of purchases of durable goods per household
for periods prior to the interview, ranging from one to twelve
months. It can be seen that reported purchases decline
steadily as the length of the recall period increases. Many
experiments as well as some analysis of survey data have
suggested that the fraction of all events remembered can be
well fitted by a negative exponential function of time:

$$r = ce^{-b_1 t}$$

where

      r is the fraction of all events reported,

      c is a non-time-related factor caused by such things as the threat of the question and whether or not the respondent is aware that the event has ocurred,

      b_1 reflects salience of the topic to the respondent as well as the time period used for t.

To give some illustrations from work by Sudman and Ferber (1971) and Neter and Waksberg (1964) for t measured in months, values of b_1 range from 0 to 0.1 for large expenditures of durable goods or services and from 0.05 to 0.15 for smaller expenditures.

Table 2 shows the reduction in fraction of events remembered over a 12-month period for values of b_1 ranging from 0.01 to 0.15. It may be seen that for values of b_1 around 0.05, there is a loss of about 15 percent in three months, about 25 percent in six months and of 45 percent in twelve months. As events become less salient and b_1 becomes larger, recall becomes very unsatisfactory. One can see from the table why the current Consumer Expenditure Surveys conducted quarterly should yield substantially better data than earlier studies that used 12-month recall.

Telescoping – Telescoping is misremembering the date an event occurréd so as to bring it into the time period being discussed. It results from the demand characteristics of the interview and is not simply random error. Unlike omissions, telescoping problems are relatively most severe for the shortest time periods. Thus, in some earlier work we found that reports of purchases of grocery products such as margarine or coffee or frozen orange juice were likely to be overreported by about fifty percent when people were asked to report their purchases in the previous seven days. Based on work by Weber, it is reasonable to assume that the error in dates is a function of log b_2t. The relative overstatement is then expressed by:

$$o = \frac{\log b_2 \, t}{t}$$

Again from the work of Sudman and Ferber and Neter and Waksberg, values of b_2 range from 2.5 to 3.5 for large expenditures for durable goods and services and from 4 to 5 for

TABLE 1. *Average Number of Purchases of Durable Goods Reported Per 100 Households by Months Prior to Recall^a*

		Month prior to recall					
Product Class	1	2	3	4	5	6-8	9-12
Total	1132.6	1003.1	578.1	612.9	556.6	443.2	342.2
Furniture	34.7	23.7	16.4	21.1	19.1	17.2	9.6
Appliances	16.4	11.2	9.3	8.7	7.1	6.9	4.8
Household goods	65.7	31.5	23.8	23.5	25.0	25.7	18.6
Clothing	746.0	637.9	446.2	526.3	476.8	362.3	286.8
Gifts	245.2	276.0	73.0	25.0	20.7	22.7	16.6
Miscellaneous	24.6	22.8	9.4	8.3	7.9	8.4	5.8

^{a}Source: Sudman and Ferber (1971).

TABLE 2. *Percent Remembered for Various Values of b_1 and t^b*

			b_1	
t	.01	.05	.10	.15
1	99	95	90	86
2	98	90	82	74
3	97	86	74	64
6	94	74	55	41
9	91	64	41	26
12	89	55	30	17

^{b}Source: Sudman and Bradburn (1974).

smaller expenditures. Table 3 shows the relative overstatement for various time periods for values of b_2. It can be
seen that for long periods of six or twelve months, the over-
statements caused by telescoping are small, although they do
not vanish. The greatest effects of telescoping for durables
are observed in the first three months.

Error in Details - Not only are there errors of omission
and telescoping, respondents may also forget the details of
the event, especially if the event or the details are not
very salient. Just a couple of examples. In our recent work
we have observed that respondents tend to misremember whether
something purchased for medical purposes was a prescription
or not; some purchases of over-the-counter drugs are reported
as prescriptions. In earlier work, it was found that there
was a strong tendency in recall surveys for respondents to
misremember the brand of groceries they bought. Overstatements of more than fifty percent were observed in the brand
shares of nationally advertised brands, while chain store and
local brands were underreported by an equal amount. Here,
the impact of advertising seems clear.

*TABLE 3. Relative Percent Overstatements Caused by
Telescoping for Various Values of b_2 and t^a*

	b_2			
t	2	3	4	5
1	30	48	60	70
2	30	39	45	50
3	26	32	36	39
6	16	21	23	25
9	14	16	17	18
12	12	13	14	15

[a]Source: Sudman and Bradburn (1974).

It is, of course, obvious that these types of memory
errors may all be occurring at the same time and that the net
effect may either be substantial, if the errors are additive
or may be small if some of the errors cancel each other.

III. REDUCING MEMORY ERROR

While memory error can never be totally eliminated,
there are some procedures that can help reduce memory error.
The procedures include aided recall, deciding on the appropriate time period, the use of bounded recall and records,
the use of diaries, and the length of questions.

Aided Recall - In its most general sense, an aided
recall procedure is one that provides one or more memory cues
to the respondent as part of the question. Thus, rather than
asking an open question, "What do you do, for recreation or
to relax?" questions are asked about specific activities and
sports.

Similarly, respondents may be shown a card with a list
of books, magazines, and newspapers and asked which they have
read in the past month. A final form of aided recall are
household inventories conducted jointly by the respondent and
interviewer. These household inventories can be used to
determine the presence of furniture and applicances and books
and magazines as well as nondurable goods such as food, soap
and cleaning products. Unless the product has been totally
consumed, its presence is a memory aid.

There is no doubt that aided recall procedures produce
higher levels of reported behavior than do unaided procedures
(Table 4). To the extent that this is caused by remembering
events that would otherwise be forgotten, that is obviously
desirable. There are, however, some precautions to observe
when using aided recall.

The first concern is that the list provided be as
exhaustive as possible. Behaviors not mentioned in the question will be substantially underreported relative to items
that are mentioned specifically. This follows from general
research on memory and has been demonstrated in studies of
readership of newspapers and magazines and the viewing of TV
programs.

TABLE 4. *Comparison of Publications Looked At "Yesterday" Named Using a Check-List System and Using an Open Response System*[a]

Publications in the check-list (test items)	Comparative percentage yield when "yesterday" was a Sunday (Group 1)			Comparative percentage yield when "yesterday" was a weekday (Groups 2, 3, 4)		
	Check list (CL)	Open response (OR)	Recall[b] ratio (OR:CL)	Check list (CL)	Open response (OR)	Recall[b] ratio (OR:CL)
Number of cases	99	110		448	415	
Daily						
Daily Mail				16	12	0.78
The Times				4	3	0.70
Daily Herald				9	5	0.54
Evening News				39	27	0.70
Daily Mirror				46	39	0.85
Star				21	12	0.56
Daily Telegraph				17	13	0.77
Average number of these endorsed per·person				1.52	1.12	0.73
Sunday						
News of the World	46	35	0.74			
Sunday Times	5	3	0.54			
Sunday Express	28	21	0.74			
Sunday Pictorial	42	34	0.79			
Sunday Dispatch	18	7	0.40			
People	26	23	0.87			
Empire News	6	1	0.15			
Average number of these endorsed per person	1.72	1.23	0.71			
Weekly and monthly						
Radio Times	41	5	0.13	38	7	0.17
John Bull	2	0	NC	5	1	0.31
Woman	12	8	0.67	20	10	0.47
Illustrated	2	0	NC	3	0	NC
Weekend	7	1	0.13	6	2	0.27
Readers Digest	5	2	0.36	7	3	0.39
Ideal Home	0	0	NC	3	*	0.17
Practical Householder	6	1	0.15	4	*	0.06
Practical Motorist	2	0	NC	4	0	NC
Average number of these endorsed per person	0.78	0.17	0.22	0.90	0.23	0.25

[b]Based upon percentage figures before rounding.
* < 0.5 percent
NC, No calculation
[a]Source: Belson and Duncan (1962).

To have an exhaustive list may become impossible if the
number of alternatives is too great. In this case, the list
may be restricted to only a limited number of most likely
alternatives. It is then, however, not possible to make an
estimate of the excluded behaviors. Some researchers include
an "All Other" category in such aided recall questions. This
is useful for rapport building because it provides the opportunity for some respondents to answer who otherwise would not
have been able to respond positively. Note, however, that
the data from this "All Other" category cannot be combined
with the listed data for exactly the same reason that aided
recall was used. It is also not possible to make an estimate
of total behavior if the list is not exhaustive, although it
is possible to make a minimum estimate, by summing over only
the listed behavior.

When a list becomes large, the order of the list may
become important, especially when the list is read by the
respondent. Items at the top of a long list will be read
more carefully than items in the middle and at the bottom and
will receive more positive responses. For long lists, careful researchers use two or more different forms and randomize
the order of the items.

In another procedure, the interviewer reads all items to
the respondent and obtains a yes or no answer to each one
separately. This procedure is now widely used in telephone
interviewing where it is not possible to have the respondent
read from a card. It also has the advantage of removing or
reducing list orders effects, although both the interviewer
and respondent may become bored if the list is too long.

Problems with Aided Recall - Imagine a respondent given
a list of 50 behaviors and asked which of these he or she has
done in a specified time period. If the respondent has done
none of these activities, the question is likely to make the
respondent uncomfortable, even if the topic is non-threatening. The respondent will feel that the interviewer expects
at least some "yes" answers from among a long list of activities. Such a respondent is likely to report some activities,
either by deliberately fibbing or by unconsciously misremembering the date when a behavior occurred.

The researcher should attempt to anticipate this problem
and avoid it, in one of two ways. The first is to make the
list so extensive that virtually all respondents will be able
to answer "yes" to some items. The other alternative is to

start with a screening question such as "Do you happen to
have read any magazines in the past two weeks, or not?"
before showing the respondent a list of magazines.

The long list example, however, typifies the most serious problem with aided recall--the implicit demand by the
researcher for positive responses from the respondent. In
situations where omissions of behavior are not frequent,
because of the salience of the event and the shortness of the
time period, aided recall procedures may lead to substantial
over-reporting. In such situations, aided recall procedures
should not be used, or should be used only in conjunction
with other procedures that reduce over-reporting.

Deciding on the Appropriate Time Period - Events that
occur rarely in one's life such as graduation from high
school, marriage, buying a house, having a baby, a serious
automobile accident or surgery are likely to be remembered
almost indefinitely. Historical events can have the same
saliency. Almost anyone, who was old enough can remember
exactly what he or she was doing when World War II started or
ended. On the other hand, habitual events such as all the
things that one did at home and work would be difficult to
remember for even a day or two earlier.

Holding uniqueness constant, the greater the cost or
benefit of an activity, the more one is likely to remember
it. Winners of $10,000 in a lottery will remember the
details better than the winners of $5. For purchases, the
larger the cost of the purchase, the more likely it is to be
remembered. The purchase of a $500 microwave oven is easier
to remember than the purchase of a 69¢ potato peeler. The
juvenile shoplifter will remember the time he or she was
caught when the details of the successful shoplifting efforts
have long been forgotten. Finally, some events result in
continuing reminders that the event happened. The presence
of a house, car, or major appliance is a reminder that the
purchase was made. The presence of children is a reminder of
their births. A continuing disability is a reminder of an
illness or accident.

Many behavioral events are salient along two or three
dimensions. Thus, buying a house is a unique event, requires
payment of a very large sum of money, and the presence of the
structure acts as a continuing reminder. On the other hand,
the purchase of a food item is a low-cost, habitual act with
no continuing consequences. Using this framework, memory

about highly salient events is satisfactory for periods of a
year, or possibly more. Unfortunately, little work has been
done on periods much longer than a year, but for highly
salient events such as major accidents or illnesses, periods
of two or three years appear to be possible.

Periods of two weeks to a month seem to be appropriate
for low salience events. For behaviors of intermediate saliency, periods of one to three months are most widely used.
Choosing an optimum time period does not mean that the data
will be error-free, but only that errors will be minimized
using recall procedures.

If the behavior is highly salient so that the percentage
of omissions is small, substantial over-statements will occur
if the time period is too short because of telescoping. In
this case, the researcher's desire for a longer time period
to obtain more data coincides with the selection of a time
period to get the most accurate recall.

Since both telescoping and omissions are occurring
simultaneously, and since the effects of time work in the
opposite directions for these two forms of forgetting, there
is some time period at which the opposite biases cancel and
the overall levels of reported behavior are about right.
For many kinds of behavior, such as grocery shopping, leisure
activities, and routine medical care, this period appears to be
between two weeks and a month. Note, however, this does not
mean that the details of the behavior are correct at any
individual level. The next two sections suggest methods for
reducing telescoping and improving information on details.

Use of Bounded Recall - Bounded recall procedures as
developed by Neter and Waksberg (1964) involve a series of
interviews with a panel of respondents. The initial interview is unbounded, and the data are not used for this period,
but at all subsequent interviews the respondent is reminded
of behaviors that were reported previously. The interviewer
also checks new behaviors reported with those reported earlier to make sure that no duplication has occurred. Thus the
earlier interviews bound the time period to prevent errors on
dates.

Bounded interviews have been used successfully in a wide
range of applications. Note, however, that the effects of
bounding are just the opposite of those for aided recall.
Bounding will have no effect on omissions and, if omissions

are the more serious problem, may even cause larger errors since compensating biases are eliminated.

The joint use of both aided recall and bounding procedures, if possible, should result in low actual and net biases. The major problem with the bounding procedures now in use is that they require a multiple interview panel and may be too costly for most researchers. An alternative is to use bounding procedures in a single interview. This is possible by starting with questions about an earlier time period and using the data from that period to bound the reports of the current period. Thus, for example, a respondent might first be asked about clothing purchases during the month of June on an interview conducted in the middle of July. Questions would then be asked about clothing purchases in July with the June date being used for bounding.

Records - The use of household records, where available, should always be considered as a method of eliminating date errors that cause telescoping as well as providing more accurate information about other details. It may be seen in Table 5 that respondents who consulted records were substantially more accurate in reporting savings accounts balances than those who did not when the data were validated in a Dutch study. Searching for records, as with a household inventory, is best accomplished in a face-to-face interview.

TABLE 5. Effect of Record Consultation on Accuracy of Reports of Savings Accounts Balances[c] (January balances, as reported in October)

Actual balance (guilders)	Number of cases	Mean reported balance (guilders)	Mean actual balance (guilders)	Difference in means[a] as percentage of mean actual balance	Percentages of respondents in each group reporting balance correctly[b]
Record Consulters					
Under 1,000	354	469	373	26	51
1,000-2,499	370	1,565	1,546	1	45
2,500 or more	323	3,288	3,452	-5	45
Total	1,047	1,726	1,737	-1	47
Non-Consulters					
Under 1,000	191	529	340	56	7
1,000-2,499	214	1,528	1,575	-3	5
2,500 or more	248	2,940	3,569	-18	6
Total	653	1,772	1,971	-10	6
All cases— recorded consulters and non-consulters	1,700	1,744	1,827	-5	31

[a]Reported minus actual.
[b]A report is correct if it lies within one guilder of the balance, as shown in POSB records.
[c]Source: Maynes (1965).

A search for records is not impossible in a telephone interview, but both respondent and interviewer are likely to feel nervous during the search since neither can see what the other is doing. If the search takes too long this could have an adverse effect on the subsequent flow of the interview. An alternative that has been used with phone surveys is to mail the respondent a questionnaire in advance that indicates the types of records it would be useful to consult. Thus, the search is usually conducted before the interview. Where records are available, it is useful for the interviewer to note whether or not they were used, since the more accurate reporting will come from the respondents who used records. On mail surveys, respondents can be asked to use records, but there is no strong motivation for them to do so, nor any way of knowing if they did.

There are many kinds of records available. We list a few types here:

    bills,
    checkbook records or cancelled checks,
    titles and leases, and
    other financial records.

All records are likely to be considered somewhat personal by respondents, especially those dealing with financial assets. While the respondent's use of records should be encouraged, it should not be insisted upon if the respondent is reluctant or the records cannot be located.

The Use of Diaries - An alternative procedure that reduces reliance on recall and thus provides more accurate information about behavior is the use of diaries. The respondent or diary-keeper is asked to record events immediately after they occur, or at least on the same day. Diaries have been used for a variety of topics including consumer expenditures, food preparation, automobile use, and television viewing. These are all examples of frequent non-salient events that are difficult to recall accurately.

Diaries have been used primarily in panel studies where households or individuals report their behavior over time. This then makes it possible to measure change at an individual level. Note, however, that some panel studies such as most voting studies, use repeated interviews and not diaries; some diary uses are only to obtain reliable information for a single time period, such as menu studies and the U.S. Bureau of Labor Statistics Consumer Expenditure Surveys. The major reasons that diaries have not been used more often are that they are costly and require survey techniques that are not familiar to many researchers. Readers who wish to learn more about procedures for using diaries should consult Sudman and Ferber (1980). The reasons for the increased costs are that diary-keepers are usually compensated for their record-keeping activities, while respondents to most other studies are not compensated. It is necessary to use both personal (face-to-face or telephone) recruiting and extensive personal follow-up activities to obtain the same levels of cooperation when using diaries as on other careful personal interviews. This makes the cost of data gathering greater than for one-time interviews, although the cost per unit of information obtained is lower. Some researchers have used less expensive mail procedures for recruiting and collecting diaries, but cooperation with these procedures is much lower.

Although it is not possible to give an extensive discussion of diary formats here, some of the major findings of Sudman and Ferber (1980) are

1. Ledger diaries where events are entered by category yield slightly more accurate information and are easier for the diary-keeper to fill out and for the researcher to process than are journal diaries where events are entered in the sequence in which they occur. This is because different types of events require different details. Also the type of headings act as reminders to record-keepers of what is required.

2. Diaries should be kept relatively short--10 to 20 page diaries have been successfully used. Longer diaries with more items cause underreporting, particularly on items in the center of the diary.

3. Diaries should ask for reports of several items rather than a single type of behavior or purchases of a single product. Otherwise, the recordkeeper will focus on this behavior and is likely to change. A diary study that asks only for reports of purchases of cereal is likely to lead, at least in the short-run, to increased purchases and consumption of cereal.

This brief discussion of the costs and difficulties associated with diaries suggests why diaries have not been used to solve all the memory problems discussed in the earlier sections. Diaries should be considered, however, if one is attempting to obtain accurate, detailed information about frequent, low-salience behavior.

IV. THE LENGTH OF QUESTIONS

Until recently, it has generally been the practice to make questions as short as possible. This was based on research on attitude questions that indicated that response reliability declined as the length of the question increased. Recent research on behavior questions, however, indicates that the findings for attitude questions do not apply to behavior questions. For behavior topics, longer questions can help reduce the number of omitted events and thus improve recall.

There are three reasons why longer questions improve recall. First, the longer questions provide memory cues and act as a form of aided recall. Second, the longer question takes more time for the interviewer to read and gives more time for the respondent to think. All else equal, the longer time the respondent spends on the memory task, the more that will be recalled.

Finally, there have been many psychological experiences which indicate that the length of the reply is directly related to the length of the question. If the interviewer talks more, the respondent will also talk more. While length of response is not necessarily a direct measure of quality of response (particularly on attitudinal questions), longer responses will often lead to remembering additional events, cued by the respondent's own conversation.

Longer questions have the same possible disadvantages as the use of aided recall. While longer questions reduce omissions, they have no effect, or may actually increase telescoping, because of the implicit demand for a positive response. Thus, as we shall see later, long questions are useful for behavior that may be socially undesirable, but may increase over reports of socially desirable behavior.

V. THREATENING BEHAVIORAL QUESTIONS

Threatening behavioral questions are those where there is broad societal agreement that there is a right or wrong answer. Behaviors that are perceived as socially desirable will be over-reported, while those perceived as socially undesirable will be under-reported. The extent of over-work or under-reporting will be a function of perceived desirability or undesirability. Some examples may be useful:

Over-reported behavior:

Being a good citizen
Registering to vote and voting

Interacting with government officials

Taking a role in community activities

Knowing the issue

Being a well-informed and cultured person
Reading newspapers, magazines, books, and using libraries

Going to cultural events such as concerts, plays,
   museum exhibits

Participating in educational activities

Fulfilling Moral and Social Responsibilities
Giving to charity and helping friends in need

Active participation in family affairs and childbearing

Being employed

Under-reported behavior:

Illnesses and Disabilities
Cancer

Venereal diseases

Mental illness

Illegal or Contra-Normative Behavior
Commiting a crime including traffic violations

Tax evasion

Drug use

Consumption of alcoholic products

Sexual practices

Financial Status
Income

Savings and other assets

VI. THE MAGNITUDE OF ERRORS IN THREATENING QUESTIONS

We have no general model that relates level of threat to
level of over- or under-reporting. Nevertheless, there is a
strong relation between these two variables. Table 6 summarizes over- or under-reports for eight behavioral items where
it was possible to obtain this validation information. It
should, of course, be pointed out that memory errors are also
a function of the question wording and the time period, since
threatening questions are subject to exactly the same kinds
of memory errors as are non-threatening questions. For
moderately threatening questions, question wordings may
improve reporting, but for very threatening questions one
must recognize that no question wording will provide anything
near the true response, even though people may answer the
question.

VII. DETERMINING THE PERCEIVED LEVEL OF THREAT

One of the most useful tactics that can be taken with
threatening or potentially threatening questions is to determine the respondent's perception of these questions after the
main part of the interview is completed.

Such questions provide information at the aggregate
level about the perceived threat of questions. Thus, Table 7
gives the percentage of respondents who feel that most people
would be very uneasy or not at all uneasy about a group of
topics that we included in an experimental study.

In the absence of additional validation or comparison
data, one can still assume that the behaviors perceived as
most threatening by respondents will be the most under-
reported if socially undesirable. That is, these questions
are an indirect measure of response validity, or a check if
other measures are also available.

The projective question that asks the respondent about
most people is better than a question that asks directly
"Which questions, if any, were too personal?" This is
because direct questions about threat may themselves be
threatening to respondents.

TABLE 6.   *Level of Over- and Under-Reporting*
for Selected Behaviors[a]

	Percent Over-or Under-reported
Socially Desirable	
Voting in primary	+35
Have a library card	+19
Registered to vote	+11
Socially Undesirable	
Bankruptcy	−31
Wine consumption	−33
Arrest for drunken driving	−49
Beer consumption	−49
Liquor consumption	−64

TABLE 7.   *Percentage of Respondents Who Feel Most People*
Would Be Very Uneasy or Not at All Uneasy about Topic[a]

Topic	Very uneasy	Not at all uneasy
Masturbation	56.4	11.8
Marijuana	42.0	19.8
Intercourse	41.5	14.5
Stimulants and depressants	31.3	20.2
Intoxication	29.0	20.6
Petting and kissing	19.7	26.3
Income	12.5	32.7
Gambling with friends	10.5	39.7
Drinking	10.3	38.0
General leisure	2.4	80.8
Sports activity	1.3	90.1

[a] Source: Bradburn, Sudman and associates (1979).

Questions about perceived threat also provide the researcher with an additional variable that may be used to adjust data for under-reporting. Although adjustments cannot be made at an individual level, it is possible to consider the group who think that most people would be very uneasy about a topic. Controlling for other variables, this group is typically observed to report lower levels of the threatening behavior than do respondents who think that the topic would make most people only moderately uneasy. This would not appear to reflect actual behavior since respondents who do not engage in a behavior such as smoking marijuana are usually less threatened by a question on marijuana smoking since it is not a salient topic to them.

It seems reasonable to assume that the "very uneasy's" are reporting lower levels of threatening behavior but actually doing as much as other respondents. If so, then adjusting the level of the "very uneasy" group's reported behavior upward to the level of the "moderately uneasy" group's seems justified and even conservative. Where validation information has been available, such adjustments improve the overall estimates.

VIII.   METHODS FOR IMPROVING THE QUALITY OF REPORTING OF
        THREATENING QUESTIONS

A. *The Use of Open Questions for Obtaining Frequency of*
   Socially Undesirable Behavior

As a general rule survey researchers prefer closed questions because they are easier to process and reduce coder variability. In this application, however, there is no difficulty in coding since the answer is a frequency. Thus, a question which asks "how often did you drink beer" can be answered daily, several times a week, weekly, monthly, etc. All of these answers can easily be converted to number of days per month of year.

It may be seen in Table 8 that reports of threatening behavior are substantially higher on open questions. For beer drinking, respondents reported drinking 300 cans of beer per year on the open question as compared to 171 cans on the closed question. The same large differences are observed for all the behaviors reported in Table 8. It may not be obvious why the open question here is superior to a closed question that puts the possible alternatives on a card and asks the respondent to select one. The reason is that the closed question must arrange the alternatives in a logical sequence, from most frequent to least frequent, or the reverse. In either case, the most frequent use, "daily," would be at either the extreme top or bottom of a list provided on a card. Heavy drinkers who drank beer daily would need to select the extreme response if they reported correctly. Since there is a general tendency among respondents to avoid extreme responses on a list, whether the questions are attitudinal, knowledge, or behavioral, some of these daily drinkers would choose a less-extreme response, such as several times a week or weekly, causing a substantial understatement.

B. *The Use of Long Questions For Obtaining Frequency of Socially Undesirable Behavior*

The advantages and possible disadvantages of longer questions about behavior have already been discussed and that discussion need not be repeated. When asking questions about frequency of socially undesirable behavior, over-reporting is not a problem and longer questions help to reduce the tendency to under-report. One should try to make the additional material useful in itself. Thus, on questions dealing with use of alcohol, the introduction points out the popularity of beer and wine and lists examples of their uses. It does not seem appropriate to list all the locations or occasions where sexual activity could occur. Rather, the introduction would stress the fact that while this was once a taboo topic, most people are now willing to talk about their sexual activities.

Longer questions increased the reported frequencies of socially undesirable behavior about 25-30 percent as compared to the standard short question (Table 8). Longer questions, however, had no effect on respondent willingness to report ever engaging in a socially undesirable activity such as drinking liquor or getting drunk.

IX. THE USE OF FAMILIAR WORDS

Some critics of survey research procedures claim that the use of standardized wordings makes the interview situation artifical and inhibits the respondent. On the other

TABLE 8. *Annual Means for Drinking and Sexual Activity Frequency Items, by Question Form*[d]

	Open-closed ended		Long-short question		Familiar-standard wording		Long, open (familiar)	Short closed (standard)
Cans of beer								
All drinkers	301 (437)[c]	171 (476)[c]	267 (438)	204 (475)	a	a	320 (208)	131 (246)
Drank in past year	300 (356)	186 (368)	257 (342)	229 (482)	a	a	286 (167)	147 (186)
Glass of wine								
All drinkers	97 (453)	57 (475)	92 (463)	61 (465)	a	a	116 (222)	45 (234)
Drank in past year	95 (361)	68 (377)	94 (375)	69 (363)	a	a	108 (179)	55 (181)
Drinks of liquor								
All drinkers	168 (460)	119 (486)	160 (461)	127 (485)	152 (477)	134 (469)	204 (110)	80 (121)
Drank in past year	143 (374)	108 (392)	127 (373)	133 (393)	141 (382)	119 (87)	175 (87)	78 (98)
Petting or kissing[b]	223 (405)	196 (430)	220 (417)	198 (418)	a	a	232 (206)	184 (219)
Intercourse[b]	124 (348)	107 (369)	123 (352)	108 (365)	116 (364)	112 (353)	137 (93)	91 (100)
Masturbation[b]	102 (43)	49 (61)	82 (56)	58 (48)	77 (58)	63 (46)	182 (11)	49 (14)

[a] Not manipulated.
[b] Question asked only of respondents who reported engaging in activity in past month.
[c] Sample size.
[d] Source: Bradburn, Sudman and associates (1979).

hand, survey researchers are aware that varying the question
wording from respondent to respondent introduces uncontrolled
method variability that may make the responses meaningless.
A middle position is to have the respondent (not the interviewer) make the decision on the word to use, when the
standard words such as sexual intercourse and masturbation
may be too formal.   Thus, most respondents preferred the word
"loving" or "love making" instead of sexual intercourse, and
some used even more direct colloquialisms.

The interviewer would then use the respondent's words in
all subsequent questions on that topic.   The use of familiar
words increased the reported frequencies of socially undesirable behavior about 15 percent as compared to use of standard
wording (Table 8).

There seem to be no major advantages in using this
method for socially desirable or non-threatening behavior
since there are no improvements in reporting to compensate
for the increased complexity.   It is also the case that slang
and colloquialisms are most likely to be used in normal conversation when the behavior being discussed is socially
undesirable.

The Use of Informants - For non-threatening questions,
there are cost efficiencies in using household informants but
at the cost of some loss in quality of information.   For
threatening questions, however, informants may provide more
reliable information than the respondents about themselves.
It is, of course, necessary to ask about behavior that the
informant might know about others, either from observation or
through conversations (Table 9).

X.   DELIBERATELY LOADING THE QUESTION

It has frequently been observed that changing the
wording of attitude questions changes the distribution of
responses.   Some researchers have attempted to improve the
reporting of threatening topics by deliberately loading the
question so that the probability of reporting desirable
behavior is increased.

For undesirable behavior, the following loading techniques have been used:

TABLE 9. *Reported Behavior for Self and Three*
Closest Friends[a]

	Percentage			N
	(I) Self	(II) Three closest friends	(III) Ratio (II)/(I)	
Ever intoxicated past year	31.4	34.5	1.10	1054
Ever smoked marijuana	21.6	19.7	0.91	1088
Smoked marijuana past year	11.6	15.5	1.34	1091

[a]Source: Bradburn, Sudman and associates (1979).

1. *Everybody does it* - The introduction to the question indicates that the behavior is very common so as to reduce the threat of reporting it. For example:

"Even the calmest parents get angry at their children some of the time. Did your child(ren) do anything in the past seven days, since (date), to make you yourself angry?"

2. *Assume the behavior, ask about frequencies or other details* - Usually, it is undesirable to make an assumption that a person is doing something without asking the question first, since this leads to over-reporting of behavior. For behavior that is under-reported, however, this may be what is needed. For example:

"How many cigarettes do you smoke each day?"

For financial questions, assuming the presence of assets and asking about details improves reporting with no effect on respondent cooperation. Thus, instead of asking, "Do you or members of this household have any savings accounts?" the question is asked:

"Turning to savings accounts – that is, accounts in banks, savings and loan associations, credit unions – are there separate accounts for different family members or do you have different accounts in various places under the same names, or what? Since I have several questions on each account, let's take each one in turn. First, in whose name is this account? Where is it? . . . " (Ferber, 1966).

3. *Use of authority to justify behavior* – It has been observed that favorability to a statement can be sharply increased if that statement is attributed to someone whom respondents like or respect. An example might be the following introduction to a question on wine drinking:

Many doctors now think that drinking wine reduces heart attacks and improves digestion. Have you drunk any wine in the past year?

It is probably better to use group designations such as doctors or scientists or researchers and not the names of particular persons since some respondents will not know of the person or may not consider that person to be an expert.

Note that all of these suggestions to load the questions towards reporting of socially undesirable behavior would have undesirable effects on response if the behavior were either socially desirable or non-threatening. Similarly, the following suggestions for reducing over-reporting of socially desirable behavior should not be used with socially undesirable topics.

4. *The casual approach* – The use of the phrase "Did you happen to . . ." is intended to reduce the perceived importance of a topic. This casual approach may help in reducing over-reporting of socially desirable behavior. This method, does not, however, increase reporting of socially undesirable behavior, and may even have the reverse effect. This is illustrated in an example which asks about gun ownership. Fewer respondents report owning a gun when asked "Do you happen to own a gun?" than when asked "Do you own a gun?" People do not just happen to own guns or to smoke marijuana or to murder their wives. Adding the words "happen to" makes such questions sound unnatural and may even increase the respondent's perceived threat. On the other hand for some cultural activities, such as reading a book or attending a concert, the question "Did you happen to attend any concerts this month?" seems natural and threat-reducing.

5. Reasons why not - If respondents are given reasons
for not doing socially desirable things such as voting or
wearing seat belts, they should be less likely to over-report
such behavior. A Gallup question gives one illustration of
this by asking "... did things come up that kept you from
voting, or did you happen to vote?" Even more explicitly one
might use the following introduction to a question on seat-
belt usage:

> Many drivers report that wearing seat belts is uncom-
> fortable and makes it difficult to reach switches such
> as light and windshield wipers. Thinking about the last
> time you got into a car, did you use a seat belt?

Although the suggestions on loading seem reasonable,
they are based on current practices of careful survey research organizations and not on controlled experiments.
Thus, it is not possible to predict how effective these
methods are.

XI. TIME FRAME FOR SOCIALLY UNDESIRABLE AND DESIRABLE
     BEHAVIOR

All else equal, questions about events that have
occurred in the past should be less salient and less threatening than questions about current behavior. Thus, when
asking about socially undesirable behavior it is better to
start with a question that asks "Did you ever, even once ..."
rather than asking immediately about current behavior.

For socially desirable behavior, however, just the
reverse strategy should be adopted. It would be very threatening for the respondent to admit that he or she never did
something like wearing a seat belt or reading a book. Thus,
a question on seat-belt usage using the time frame, "The last
time you got into a car, did you wear a seat belt?" is superior to a question that asked "Do you ever wear seat belts?"

As indicated in the example, this wording works only for
fairly common behavior. For less common behavior, the same
effect may be obtained by asking about the behavior over a
relatively short time period. Thus, instead of asking "Do
you ever attend concerts or plays?" the question would be
asked "Did you happen to attend a concert or play in the past
month?"

XII. NON-INTERVIEW METHODS

Several alternative methods have been suggested for
determining threatening behavior that do not involve standard
questionnaires. The rationale behind these alternatives is
that the more anonymous the respondent feels, the better will
be the reporting of threatening behavior. Especially as
behavior becomes very threatening, none of these methods can
ensure error-free reporting although they may help reduce
threat.

A. *Anonymous Forms*

Self-administered forms may be used either by mail, in
group interviews, or in the usual interview setting. The most
anonymous setting is the large group interview since there is
no way that individual responses can be traced to specific
respondents. Surveys of school or college classrooms or at
meetings of organizations provide this setting. Of course,
responses are not obtained from students who are absent or
members who are not present at the meeting of the organization.

Mail surveys are the next most anonymous procedure. The
respondent does not see the researcher, but at least some
respondents will think that the researcher knows who they
are, even if the questionnaire is anonymous. Finally, on a
personal interview, a researcher may attempt to provide
anonymity to the respondent by having the respondent put a
self-administered form into a sealed envelope so that the
interviewer cannot see the answers. The respondent may
perceive, however, that the answers to the items in the
sealed envelope can be traced back.

The effects of anonymity are not symmetric for socially
desirable and socially undesirable behavior, but seem to work
better for socially desirable behavior. In a personal situation, respondents will feel a need to impress the interviewer
by reporting behavior such as voting, giving to charity and
attending cultural events. Respondents do not feel the same
need to impress anonymous researchers.

The major use of anonymous forms, however, has been in
an effort to increase reporting of socially undesirable
behavior. Here, when comparisons have been made to other
methods or to validation information, the results have generally indicated no major improvements. Evidently, even in the

absence of an interviewer, some respondents are reluctant to
report undesirable behavior to a researcher or to anyone.

Group interviews have been used in only a few situations
and the results have not been compared to validating data or
other methods at an aggregate level. Thus, while we believe
that group interviews are the most effective form of anonymity for undesirable behavior, the research to verify this
has not yet been done.

B. Card Sorting

A procedure that has been used in Great Britain to
measure crime and juvenile delinquency (Belson et al., 1968)
is to hand respondents a set of cards on which are printed
various behaviors, including threatening ones. Respondents
are asked to place each card into a "Yes" or "No" box. After
this has been done, it is possible to go back at later points
in the interview and ask that the respondent reconsider the
cards in the "No" box and re-sort the cards as necessary.
Some respondents will find it easier to admit a socially
undesirable behavior (or not to claim a socially desirable
behavior) when the response is non-verbal. As far as we
know, however, this method has not been validated or compared
to alternative procedures.

C. Randomized Response

The rationale for randomized response is to provide a
method that ensures respondent anonymity by making it impossible for either the interviewer or researcher to know what
question the respondent was answering. This is done by
asking two questions, one threatening and the other completely innocuous. Thus, the following example of a very
threatening question and a non-threatening question:

> (Red) During the last twelve months have you been
> charged by a policeman for driving under the
> influence of liquor?
> (Blue) Is your birthday in the month of September?

Both of these questions have the same possible answers,
"Yes" and "No". The respondent decides which question to
answer on the basis of a probability mechanism. We and
others have used a 3" × 5" plastic box containing 50 beads,
70 percent red and 30 percent blue. The box was designed so
that when it was shaken by the respondent a red or blue bead

would appear in a window of the box that could be seen only by the respondent. If the bead is red, the threatening question is answered, if blue, the innocuous question.

While the researcher has an estimate of the undesirable behavior of the group the respondent's anonymity is fully protected. There is, however, a cost paid for this method. It is not possible to relate individual characteristics of respondents to individual behavior. That is, standard regression procedures are not possible at an individual level. It is possible if one has a very large sample to relate group characteristics to the estimates obtained from randomized response. For example, one could look at all the answers of young women and compare them to all the answers of men and older age groups. In summary, much information is lost by using randomized response.

The accuracy of information obtained by this method depends on respondent willingness to be truthful in exchange for anonymity. Unfortunately, for very threatening behavior such as drunken driving, a validation study we conducted indicated that there was only a slight improvement using randomized response; 35 percent of persons known to have been arrested for drunken driving still refused to admit it under this condition of complete anonymity.

Randomized response is also not an appropriate procedure for asking questions about socially desirable behavior, where it may lead to even higher levels of over-reporting than do standard methods. Randomized response procedures seem to work best, as do anonymous forms, for behavior such as abortions and bankruptcies where the respondent may not personally be ashamed of the action but may not know how the behavior is viewed by the interviewer. In such cases, the improved reporting may compensate for the reduced power of the sample.

XIII. ATTITUDINAL QUESTIONS

For the sake of completeness, I attempt a brief summary of the work of Schuman and his associates. If anything, the magnitude of response effects caused by wording and context is as large for attitudinal as it is for behavioral questions, although for different reasons.

A. *Context Effects*

A major problem arises in the use of attitude questions as indicators of social change. If different earlier questions change the context, then change measures will be distorted, even if the question wording remains constant over time. It is obvious that context effects occur when two or more questions deal with aspects of the same issue or related issues. The more general the question, the more likely it is that respondents will look to earlier questions for clues as to what frame of reference to use.

A useful distinction may be made between part-whole constrast and part-whole consistency. As an example of contrast, favorable responses to a question asking whether legal abortions should be possible drop about 13 percentage points if that question is asked after a more specific question asking about abortion in the case of a defect in an unborn child. Here, one speculates that respondents are answering the general question excluding consideration of those cases where there is a defect, since they have already answered that question. On the other hand, an example of part-whole consistency is found when a question on general happiness is asked after a question on marital happiness. In this case the percentage of respondents saying "very happy" rises by 14 percent. What seems to be happening here is that general happiness is being defined in terms of marital happiness.

Questions considered simultaneously may create or emphasize a norm that is not obvious when the questions are considered separately. The famous two questions "Do you think the United States should let Communist newspaper reporters from other countries come in here and send back to their papers the news as they see it?" and "Do you think a Communist country like Russia should let American newspaper reporters come in and send back to America the news as they see it?" have substantially different responses depending on which question is asked first. It is clear that a norm of reciprocity or even-handedness is at work.

Unfortunately, context effects are of many different types and it is not always possible to predict whether there will be effects, or the direction of these effects. One example is the decision in the National Crime Study to place attitude items before behavioral items so that the attitude items would not be affected by the behavioral answers. The outcome was that the attitudinal questions produced important changes in response to the behavioral questions.

Another form of context effect is the order in which answers are given on a closed question. With long and complex questions, it is sometimes observed that the last alternative receives more support simply because people can remember it best. On the other hand, this does not always occur and in a few cases it is even the first item that is mentioned most. The reasons for these differences are not well understood. Researchers who suspect context effects should use split sample procedures to determine if these effects exist and what their magnitude will be.

B. *Open Versus Closed Attitude Questions*

When questions are asked about broad values and problems and multiple answers are possible, a standard procedure is to start with an open question in a pilot study and then to use a closed question for convenience in processing. Unfortunately, results between the open and closed versions usually differ substantially, although it is not clear which method is superior. The exclusion of important alternatives from the closed question will certainly result in these alternatives being omitted or substantially understated by respondents. On the other hand, closed questions can guide the respondent and provide the frame of reference that the researcher wants.

C. *Balance and Imbalance in Questionnaires*

A standard procedure in questionnaires is to formally balance an attitude question by adding words such as "or oppose" to questions that ask whether the respondent favors a given position. Experiments show that this formal balancing has little or no effect on the responses. Substantive arguments or counter-arguments do, however, change the distribution toward the direction of the argument. While the shift is not massive, it ranges from 4-13 percent in the Schuman experiments.

D. *Salience and Crystallization*

On many topics, respondents will have given little or no thought to the issues before they are asked questions.

Nevertheless, many will express opinions. These opinions are not stable and are highly subject to change with different question wordings or contexts. On the other hand, for salient topics, respondents may have already given a lot of thought to the issues and discussed them with others until their attitudes become crystallized. Such attitudes are highly reliable and resist changes caused by question wording or context. It is possible to discover by asking a few questions just how much thought has been given to an issue and how strongly respondents feel about their attitudes.

Another way of estimating salience is to ask respondents knowledge questions before asking about attitudes. It is then possible to see if there are differences between the attitudes of those who are best and least informed. Generally, global questions asking about broad concepts are non-salient to many respondents and are most prone to the problems of question wording.

XIV. SUMMARY

For both behavioral and attitudinal questions, response effects may be much larger than those caused by sampling variance or even sample biases. These effects cannot be ignored if one wishes high quality survey data. At the least, one should attempt to measure these effects through split-sample procedures and to adjust results accordingly. Even better is to find question wordings that produce accurate results, but, as has been shown in this review, this will often not be possible.

REFERENCES

Belson, William and Duncan, J. A. (1962). "A Comparison of the Checklist and the Open Response Questioning Systems," *Applied Statistics 11*, 253-60.

Belson, William, Millerson, G. L., and Didcott, B. A. (1968). *The Extent of Stealing by London Boys and Some of its Origins.* Survey Research Centre, London School of Economics, London.

Bradburn, Norman and Sudman, Seymour and associates (1979). *Improving Interview Method and Questionnaire Design*, Jossey-Bass, San Francisco.

Ferber, Robert (1966). *The Reliability of Consumer Reports of Financial Assets and Debts.* Studies in Consumer Savings No. 6. Bureau of Economic and Business Research, University of Illinois, Urbana, Illinois.

Maynes, E. Scott (1965). "The Anatomy of Response Errors: Consumer Saving," *Journal of Marketing Research, 2,* 378-87.

Neter, John and Waksberg, Joseph (1964). "A Study of Response Errors in Expenditures Data from Household Interviews," *Journal of the American Statistical Association, 59, 18-55.*

Schuman, Howard and Kalton, Graham (1982). "The Effect of the Question on Survey Responses: A Review," *Journal of the Royal Statistical Society, Series A, 145, 42-57.*

Schuman, Howard and Presser, Stanley (1981). *Questions and Answers in Attitude Surveys,* Academic Press, New York.

Sudman, Seymour and Bradburn, Norman (1974). *Response Effects in Surveys,* Aldine, Chicago.

Sudman, Seymour and Bradburn, Norman (1982). *Asking Questions,* Jossey-Bass, San Francisco.

Sudman, Seymour and Ferber, Robert (1971). *Experiments in Obtaining Consumer Expenditures of Durable Goods by Recall Procedures,* Survey Research Laboratory, University of Illinois, Urbana, Illinois.

Sudman, Seymour and Ferber, Robert (1980). *Consumer Panels,* American Marketing Association, Chicago.

ERROR PROFILES: USES AND ABUSES

Barbara A. Bailar

U. S. Bureau of the Census
Washington, D. C.

I. INTRODUCTION

The Office of Management and Budget oversees the Federal Committee on Statistical Methodology, which considers questions of methodology that may have important effects on the quality of statistical data produced by the federal government. The Committee divides into subcommittees, delving into such concerns as: questionnaire design, contracting for statistical surveys, disclosure practices, telephone data collection, statistical matching, time-series revision policies, and the effect of nonsampling errors. The Subcommittee on Nonsampling Errors was concerned about the difficulty of quantifying the amount of nonsampling errors in surveys. Sampling errors are usually produced and are taken into account in the design of surveys. Usually surveys are designed to minimize the sampling variance for a given cost. Nonsampling errors are not explicitly taken into account, though survey procedures are often designed with the hope that nonsampling errors are minimized. The Subcommittee had many long and heated discussions about the approach to take to obtain an overall evaluation of both sampling and nonsampling errors in survey results. Finally, the Subcommittee decided to prepare an error profile, a systematic and comprehensive account of survey operations that yield survey results.

Ideally an *error profile* would not only list the survey operations and the potential sources of error, but also the impact of the error in each operation on the total survey error. This ideal is rarely, if ever, possible because the measurement of nonsampling errors is rarely undertaken. Another reason it is as yet impossible to get a measurement of total survey error is that we do not yet have a mathematical model that adequately reflects the interaction of the errors

117

from different sources. For example, nonresponse and imputation may both be thought of as potential sources of error,
even though imputation is looked upon as a partial curative
for nonresponse. However, values imputed may frequently be
incorrect, no matter what the method of imputation. But if
nonresponse is more likely among groups with certain characteristics and this is not recognized in the imputation process, then the imputation process may increase, not decrease
the potential error. No model of survey error has yet taken
these interactions into account.

The benefits of error profiles are many, both to data
producers and to data users. Some of these are as follows:

o   to minimize total error, not just sampling error,
    within given cost constraints,
o   to force a thorough documentation of the survey
    process,
o   to guide a user on the effects of possible errors
    and their impact on specific uses,
o   to develop a sound quality control program,
o   to use in training programs for new staff persons
    in either the operational or research phases, and
o   to use as the foundation for a sound research and
    analysis program.

With all of these benefits, one would think that the idea
would have caught on and there would be several error profiles
in existence. The Office of Management and Budget encourages
agencies to prepare error profiles, at least for the major
statistical series. Seminars were held on why and how to do
this. Yet four years after the preparation of all illustrative error profiles only two are in existence. They are

*An Error Profile: Employment as Measured by the
Current Population Survey* by Camilla Brooks and
Barbara A. Bailar.

Error Profile for Multiple-Frame Surveys by Norman
Beller.

There seem to be four main themes that come through over
and over again in discussions of preparing error profiles.
Basically, they are not produced because:

The staff resources that would go into producing an error

profile are too great and are in competition with other, more urgent needs.

Producing a report which tells about errors in the surveys would lead to less credibility in the statistics produced.

Admitting that there are errors is admitting that we haven't done our jobs well.

Calling a report on a survey an "Error Profile" gives many negative connotations.

All of these things can and have been refuted. A year's staff time identifying what is known and unknown about the quality of a survey can pay for itself. Usually, describing possible sources of error and what has been done about them increases rather than decreases credibility. Anyone who knows anything about surveys realizes that there are survey errors. Coping with difficult data design, collection, and analysis problems is an important part of the job. And, finally, one can change the name from "Error Profile" to "Quality Profile." Even with these refutations, there seems to be a reluctance to expose areas of difficult methodology or concepts to the world at large, though there is much less reluctance, even great enthusiasm, to expose methodology which has overcome serious problems. Maybe the problem is simply one that we all have-- we like people to comment on the things we do well and right and we could do without comments on things we do less well and sometimes even poorly.

II. HOW TO DEVELOP ERROR PROFILES

The development of an error profile parallels the survey process. In the error profile for the Current Population Survey (CPS) we listed the following elements:

1. Objectives and specifications of the survey.
2. Sampling design and implementations.
    The frame.
    Procedure for sample selection.
3. Observational design and implementation.
    Basic data collection procedure.
    Questionnaire design and instructions.

           Data collection staff.
4.   Data processing.
      Microfilming and input to computer.
      Editing and weighting.
5.   Estimation.
      Weighting.
      Composite estimation.
      Seasonal adjustment.
6.   Analysis and publication.

These are sufficiently broad that the entire range of survey
activities should be encompassed. A problem is that some
things still tend to get left out. For example, the CPS error
profile never addressed the length of the interviewing period
--one week in a month--to provide a monthly estimate.

Beller included the following elements in the error profile on multiple-frame concepts:

1.   Questionnaire and survey concepts.
2.   Domain determination.
3.   Size of list and proportion to sample.
4.   Estimation.
5.   Nonresponse and data imputation.

An error profile can start to go wrong when the steps of
the survey are listed. Here, a detailed listing of the steps
of the survey will vary from one survey to another. There is
a tendency to leave processes out. For example, in the CPS
error profile, we did not discuss the concept of employment
and the way conceptual problems might lead to nonsampling
errors. As Kruskal (1979) said, "The concepts of membership
in the labor force, employment status, racial or ethnic identification, etc. are, as you know better than I, ambiguous,
difficult, and shifting with time. Most of the study is on
more technical, more properly statistical, issues, but surely
conceptual problems are in a sense primary. Why worry about
measuring carefully the height of someone when you really want
the weight?" Obviously, conceptual problems are basic to survey error, but the decision was made by the authors not to
discuss these issues because they were under discussion by a
Presidential Commission, the Levitan Commission. We decided
to take the concepts as previously stated, accept their translation into definitions, and go from there.

A second thing that can go wrong is that survey processes
get omitted because the data available to assess them looks

bad. Thus, the end result is an error profile that is incomplete and presents, on the whole, only results that show that
all processes are either of high quality or are not discussed.
This is more likely to happen if an error profile is compiled
in an operating area which usually does not have a very objective view about the survey limitations.

Another problem, and this is probably the most pervasive
problem in compiling an error profile is that very little research on nonsampling errors has been done in a systematic
way. The error profile outlines the sources of error, but no
evidence can be presented to give any quantifiable estimate of
the error. Usually in the absence of data indicating a problem it is assumed that all is well. One basic assumption in
constructing an error profile is that there is a common understanding of what the underlying concepts and models are. For
example, a common problem discussed in survey methodology is
what we have come to call recall "errors". But I think this
term now includes at least three different kinds of errors
which probably do not tend to work in the same direction. Let
me illustrate this with some data from the National Crime
Survey given in Table 1.

TABLE 1. *Victimization Rates for Each Month of the
Recall Period, June 1973 - September 1974*

Types of Crime	Number of Months Prior to Interview					
	One	Two	Three	Four	Five	Six
Personal crimes[a]/						
Crimes of violence	72.46	46.77	41.91	37.20	31.11	26.19
Assault	58.91	35.79	32.47	27.02	23.29	17.87
Personal theft	189.15	137.03	120.66	101.94	93.58	74.19
Household crimes[b]/						
Burglary	185.44	135.27	127.75	112.16	100.77	81.17
Larceny	264.43	183.81	162.79	138.45	126.00	100.45
Motor vehicle theft	35.30	28.55	25.98	23.41	22.44	19.28

[a]/ Rates per 1,000 persons age 12 and over.

[b]/ Rates per 1,000 households.

The phenomenon illustrated by these data occurs for most panel

surveys. First of all one could explain the reduction in
number of crime victimizations from the month immediately
preceding the interview to later time periods by saying that
respondents forget. The longer the time from the occurrence
of the event to the reporting of the event, the less likely
people are to remember an event. Though this seems reasonable
when thinking about such events as buying household equipment,
it seems less reasonable about such events as criminal
assaults. Another explanation is the displacement of events
in time, and this can happen in two ways. Perhaps some of the
heaping of events in some time periods is caused by the bring-
ing in of events from another reference period. In the NCS,
respondents are asked about criminal victimizations that
occurred in the last 6 months. Perhaps some events are
brought in from 7 months or 8 months or even longer ago. This
isn't supposed to happen because part of the procedures call
for matching events for previous time periods. This works
well for people who have been in the sample before, but for
the 8-10 percent of people who have just moved into the sample
addresses, there could be problems.

The second way displacement in time occurs is after a
respondent says that he or she was subjected to criminal victimizations. Then the interviewer asks the respondent in what
month the victimizations occurred. It seems to be fairly
common that more events are placed closer to the interview
period.

When this whole recall problem is investigated, the three
components must be addressed separately. In a study of a
3-month vs a 6-month recall period, Singh (1982) found that
the 3-month recall period yielded substantially higher victimization rates. Obviously, this shows forgetting is a major
problem. But just a comparison of the yields of two different
reference periods does not shed light on the displacement
phenomenon. For that problem, record-check studies may be
needed. Bailar and Biemer (1983) attempted to model the
recall problem in the NCS. The data in Table 2 show the
effects of fitting a curve of the form $f(t) = ae^{-bt} + c$. One
way of interpreting such a model is to let "a" be the total
number of events which are subject to recall loss, the
"forgettable" events. The parameter "b" corresponds to the
rate of memory loss per unit of time and "c" is the total
number of unforgettable events.

Several peculiarities show in the residuals. The

residuals for the second and sixth month are always negative
with all others being positive, except for motor vehicle theft
for the second month. This is probably an indication that
there is more going on than forgetting. Also, the ratio of
unforgettable events to forgettable events is greatest for
motor vehicle thefts, not crimes of violence. This may be an
indication that displacement is more important than forgetting. In any case, it is obvious that recall is not a simple
concept.

TABLE 2. *Observed and Predicted Values of Victimization
Rates for Each Month of the Recall Period*

| Types of Crime | Number of Months Prior to Interview | | | | | |
	One	Two	Three	Four	Five	Six
Crimes of violence	a = 81.98		b = 0.62		c = 26.93	
Observed	72.46	46.77	41.91	37.20	31.11	26.19
Predicted	71.25	50.89	39.88	33.93	30.71	28.98
Assault	a = 72.76		b = 0.63		c = 19.06	
Observed	58.91	35.79	32.47	27.02	23.29	17.87
Predicted	47.81	39.69	30.50	24.91	22.18	20.72
Personal theft	a = 184.09		b = 0.42		c = 65.58	
Observed	189.15	137.03	120.66	101.94	93.58	74.19
Predicted	186.34	144.80	117.55	99.67	87.94	80.25
Burglary	a = 159.80		b = 0.36		c = 70.07	
Observed	185.44	135.27	127.75	112.16	100.77	81.17
Predicted	181.00	147.08	123.53	107.18	95.83	87.95
Household Larceny	a = 269.29		b =0.50		c = 96.32	
Observed	264.43	183.81	162.79	138.45	126.00	100.45
Predicted	260.31	196.19	157.14	133.36	118.88	110.06
Motor vehicle theft	a = 25.30		b = 0.37		c = 17.50	
Observed	35.30	28.55	25.98	23.41	22.44	19.28
Predicted	34.91	19.49	25.76	23.18	21.41	20.19

Another example of a lack of common understanding occurs
in a discussion of imputation. Jay Waite (1982) in a presentation to the American Statistical Association Advisory

Committee to the Census Bureau on imputation strategies for
establishment and agricultural surveys showed that there was
confusion among the terms "imputations," "edited data," and
"revisions based on external information." All of these
involve either filling in nonexistent data or changing respondent data. Sometimes it is not clear which of these operations has occurred. For example, a respondent may provide the
amount of acreage under different kinds of crops but not give
the total acreage. By adding together the individual amounts,
the total is ascertained. This is usually referred to as
"editing." Sometimes a respondent leaves a blank which is
filled on the basis of reports from other industries of the
same size. This is "imputation." Sometimes it is known from
something reported elsewhere what the missing answer is or
that the reported answer is incorrect, and this is "revisions
based on external information."

At the same session, a comment was made that there was
less imputation for income items in the 1980 census than in
the 1970 census, but there was more editing.

Beller (1979) also refers to editing. In the Error
Profile he states, "The amount of editing on some questions
resulted in changing the level of cattle and calves by an
amount two or three times greater than the error caused by
sampling. This amount of editing is cause for alarm in that
it clearly shows a breakdown in the survey process."

To get around some of these definitional problems, we
have begun talking about missing and murky data.

Another assumption in constructing an error profile is
that there is agreement on the criterion that permits a measure of error. For example, in the comparison of a 3-month
versus a 6-month recall period, it was assumed that the more
criminal victimizations reported, the better the data. This
raises the question, "Is more better?" If you examine the
assumptions used in much of the nonsampling research, you will
find that implicitly, and maybe even explicitly, people are
answering that question, "Yes." It is hard to believe that
every survey estimate -- on crime victimizations, unemployment, rental vacancies, retail sales, visits to the doctor --
are all biased downward. Yet for a few surveys we know that
reports are biased upwards -- voter intentions and voter behavior surveys being cases in point. Also in the Consumer
Expenditure Survey and the National Crime Survey the results
of the first interview at an address are not used in the estimation, because it is claimed that they are biased upward.

Another criterion that is frequently used to estimate a measure of error is administrative records as a standard of "truth." In many income studies, a comparison of reported survey income with income reported to the Internal Revenue Service (IRS) is the basis for estimating a bias in the survey data. Given the indication that there may be a sizeable underground economy, one may look askance at the IRS data as a standard of "truth."

Thus, it is clear that there must be a more careful demonstration of the accuracy of the criterion used to measure error since more isn't always better and records aren't always right.

Finally, another assumption used in constructing an error profile is that the correct model is used to describe the phenomenon. For example, a common problem in panel surveys is what has been described as "rotation group bias" or "time-in-sample" bias. The distinguishing feature of this bias is that the number of times a person is asked to respond in a survey has an effect on the pattern of response. In a survey such as the Current Population Survey where some respondents are in the sample for the first time, some for the second, and, finally, some for the eighth time, respondents are more likely to report that they are employed or unemployed the first time they are in the sample. In the NCS, respondents report more crime victimizations for the earlier times in sample.

Now, the fact that there is a differential bias among the estimates corresponding to different lengths of time in sample is not disputed. The way that bias affects the estimates, of course, depends on the estimation scheme used. In the CPS, a composite estimator is used which takes advantage of the overlap of the sample from month to month. The estimator of level of employed or unemployed is affected substantially by the rotation group bias, assuming that the bias is modeled as a linear effect. That is,

$$E(y_t) = Y_t + \sum_{i=1}^{8} a_i$$

where y_t is the ratio estimator of the population parameter Y_t, and the a_i are the biases associated with the rotation groups in the i-th month in sample. Given that model,

estimates of level are affected, but estimates of change from
month-to-month are not, if one assumes the bias is constant
from month to month. However, McCarthy (1978) pointed out
that if one models the bias as a multiplicative rather than an
additive factor, then estimates of level are unaffected but
estimates of change are affected. McCarthy explained his
model in terms of two rotation groups, letting y_1 and y_2 be
the ratio estimators for months 1 and 2 respectively, where
$y_1 = y_{11} + y_{12}$, the contributions from the 2 rotation groups for
month 1. Suppose

$$E(y_{11}) = \frac{1}{2} Y_1 + a_{11} \left(\frac{1}{2} Y_1 \right)$$

$$E(y_{12}) = \frac{1}{2} Y_1 + a_{12} \left(\frac{1}{2} Y_1 \right)$$

$$E(y_{21}) = \frac{1}{2} Y_2 + a_{21} \left(\frac{1}{2} Y_2 \right)$$

$$E(y_{22}) = \frac{1}{2} Y_2 + a_{22} \left(\frac{1}{2} Y_2 \right).$$

Then

$$E(y_1) = Y_1 \left[1 + \frac{a_{11} + a_{12}}{2} \right]$$

$$E(y_2) = Y_2 \left[1 + \frac{a_{21} + a_{22}}{2} \right] .$$

If $a_{11} = a_{21} = a_1$ and $a_{12} = a_{22} = a_2$, then

$$E(y_2 - y_1) = (Y_2 - Y_1) \left[1 + \frac{a_1 + a_2}{2} \right] .$$

Finally, in constructing an error profile one has to find
data available on the different sources of error. We were
lucky when we constructed the profile for the CPS. There has
probably been more methodological work on that survey than on
any other. However, even where data from experiments on a
given survey are not available, sometimes data from other
sources can be used. For example, up until this last year
the Bureau of the Census had not started research in the use
of random digit dialing (RDD) and had no comparisons of distributions of data based on RDD and personal interviewing.
However, we made extensive use of data from the University
of Michigan and the work of Kahn and Groves (1979) to help us

design our experiments. In the error profile on the CPS, we said there was no evidence that personal interviewing and telephone interviewing yield different results on employment questions. The telephone interviewing mentioned was the kind done by interviewers in their homes. In this next year, we will be comparing distributions of employment by our traditional interviewing methods, which are a combination of personal and telephone interviewing with centralized telephone interviewing and RDD.

The lack of data on nonsampling errors should not be viewed as a reason for not creating an error profile. First, it will serve a function to raise questions and, second, data from other similar surveys can be used.

III. HOW TO USE ERROR PROFILES

Error profiles are going to be used by two different groups of people who have very different agenda. The first group is that of data users. Error profiles should be useful to data users in giving them a greater appreciation of the limitations of survey data. Many data users treat survey results as perfect point estimates. Use of sampling errors is not a common occurrence by many data users. But if data users could get a better appreciation of the effect of question wording, panel effects, processing decisions, and so forth, their uses of the data might be enhanced.

The other group of users of error profiles is data producers, who can use error profiles to improve specific surveys and to gain a better understanding of some of the more common survey problems.

Probably the most immediate benefit of an error profile is to highlight problems that were unknown but could be easily resolved. For example, in compiling the error profile for the CPS, we found that the noninterview adjustment procedure for unit nonresponse did not work according to specifications in some situations for mixed-race households. The documentation showed that the programming for mixed-race households was not consistent and that, though the derivation of noninterview factors for mixed-race households is based on the race of the so-called "principal person," it was applied on the basis of the race of the household individuals. Mixed-race households

are rare. There were only 309 cases in the March 1975 CPS. Of
the 309 cases, 238 had two different noninterview factors
applied within the households. It was not a serious problem
for the employment statistics, but it was corrected.

A second very important use of an error profile is to
serve as the basis for a methodological research program. The
profile shows clearly that certain areas receive a lot of
attention and that other areas receive little attention. Of
course, not all areas deserve equal attention, but many times
we do not understand the possible impact of errors arising
from certain survey procedures. The error profile may show
the need for some creative effort to design controlled experiments that will not only show which treatment produces more,
but what the impact of errors of given kinds is on survey
estimates.

An example of a need in this area is for work on interviewer training. Most survey practitioners would agree that
good interviewer training is important to getting good estimates. Yet how can one measure the impact of training? In
the CPS error profile a study conducted by Rustemeyer (1977)
was discussed in which the difference between visible and
concealed interviewer errors was focused upon. A training
experiment was used in which five scripts covering a variety
of labor force situations were used. The conclusion of the
study, when interviewers filled in the CPS questionnaire based
on interviews from these cases, was that 36 percent of the
experienced interviewers, 67 percent of the inexperienced
interviewers, and 61 percent of the interviewers with 2 or 3
months' experience made errors that resulted in labor force
misclassification. As another part of that study, it was also
shown that there was very low correlation between these kinds
of errors and any other criteria by which interviewers were
evaluated. How does one go from the acknowledgment that
training can make a difference to an ability to measure the
difference in a quantifiable way that can be attached to the
survey estimate?

This is one of the most useful results of an error profile -- the stimulation of creative minds to designing a
solidly based research program.

Another way data producers can use an error profile is in
the design of new surveys or the redesign of existing surveys.
Instead of optimizing only for minimizing sampling variance,
one hopes that with the additional information provided in an

error profile there would be an optimization for the reduction of total survey error.

In using an error profile to design a new survey, there is an implicit understanding that many problem areas are common across subject matter. Thus time-in-sample bias exists for every panel survey for which survey practitioners have tabulated the data in order to see if there is such a bias. Recall problems exist for most surveys. Methods to cope with item nonresponse are common across surveys. Each of these problems is tempered by the particular subject matter, but an error profile will alert the survey designer to the need to address the problem.

Finally, the frustration that exists among many data producers and data users after they finish reading an error profile can be severe. We want to be able to put all the information together and come out with one number that mea-sures the total survey error. So far, we have been unable to do so. At the Bureau we use a model of survey error developed by Hansen, Hurwitz, and Bershad (1961) that splits out some forms of measurement error and sampling error but lumps the remainder into a bias term. It does not adequately reflect the interaction of different sources of error. Perhaps the production of more error profiles will be the stimulus needed to develop a model that will enable us to estimate a mean-square error in which the contribution from different sources of error are identifiable and their interactions shown.

REFERENCES

Bailar, B. A. and Biemer, P. (1983). "Some Methods for
    Evaluating Nonsampling Error in Household Censuses and
    Surveys," to be published in a volume dedicated to William
    G. Cochran.
Beller, N. D. (1979). "Error Profile for Multiple-Frame
    Surveys," Economics, Statistics, and Cooperatives Ser-
    vices, Department of Agriculture.
Brooks, C. A. and Bailar, B. A. (1978). "An Error Profile:
    Employment as Measured by the Current Population Survey,"
    Statistical Policy Working Paper 3, Department of
    Commerce.
Hansen, M. H., Hurwitz, W. N., and Bershad, M. A. (1961).
    "Measurement Errors in Censuses and Surveys," Bulletin of
    International Statistical Institute, 38, Pt 2, 359-374.

Kahn, R. L. and Groves, R. M. (1979). *Surveys by Telephone: A National Comparison with Personal Interviews*, Academic Press, New York.

Kruskal, W. (1979). Letter to Joseph W. Duncan.

McCarthy, P. J. (1978). "Some Sources of Error in Labor Force Estimates from the Current Population Survey," National Commission of Employment and Unemployment Statistics.

Rustemeyer, A. (1977). "Measuring Interviewer Performance in Mock Interviews", *Proceedings of the Social Statistics Section of the American Statistical Association*.

Singh, R. P. (1982). Memorandum on "Investigation to Determine the Best Reference Period Length for the National Crime Survey," to Gary M. Shapiro.

Waite, P. J. (1982). "Imputation Methodology: Economic Censuses and Surveys," prepared for the Census Advisory Committee of the American Statistical Association, October 7-8, 1982.

PRINCIPLES AND METHODS FOR HANDLING OUTLIERS IN DATA SETS

Vic Barnett

University of Sheffield
Sheffield, England

I. INTRODUCTION

In looking through the literature I recently came across the following remarks.

> In almost every true series of observations, some are found, which differ so much from the others as to indicate some abnormal source of error not contemplated in the theoretical discussions, and the introduction of which into the investigations can only serve...to perplex and mislead the inquirer.

The subject matter is, of course, *outliers*– or 'spurious', 'unrepresentative', 'rogue', 'maverick' sample values. The remark embodies much of the basic character and many of our grounds for concern about the presence of outliers in a set of data. It is interesting that the source of the remark is a paper by Benjamin Peirce published over 130 years ago (Peirce, 1852) which refers to *previous* practice in handling outliers.

The topic is thus a very ancient one in the historical perspective of statistics. Indeed it predates by a substantial period of time what most would regard as the origins of organised study of statistical methods. Inevitably, the proposals of the time were ill-formulated; often ill-based. Even today attitudes still range from the one extreme of never daring to cast doubt on the integrity of a data set to an almost indiscriminate discarding of any observations which do not seem to fit some tidy pattern which the data are expected to observe. But we now have a substantial middle ground of theory and practice to support a rational approach to the handling of outliers, and the daunting task of this review is to summarise the complex assortment of aims and methods in this field.

The magnitude of this task is apparent if we begin to draw some basic distinctions. Data may be univariate or multivariate, one-off or routinely generated, unstructured or highly constrained (from a random sample of unknown origin to the outcome of a regression, designed experiment or time series model). Outliers may arise from assorted causes (from deterministic gross errors of measurement to random mixing of diverse populations). Aims can range from outlier *rejection* (the earliest pre-occupation) to 'clean-up' the data, through *identification* of the outliers and their source mechanism for separate specific study, to the adoption of robust methods of inference about the predominating (uncontaminated) data source which *accommodates* the outliers without the need for their separate isolation and study. Some practical illustrations of data exhibiting the different sources of outliers, and a discussion of the various aims and models, are given by Barnett (1978a).

A comprehensive study of the range of methods for handling outliers is given by Barnett and Lewis (1978). Space does not permit any thorough representation of the current state of knowledge about aim, model, method and application. Detailed study is best approached through Barnett and Lewis (1978) and its extensive References and Bibliography section, which records nearly 400 published sources. We shall concentrate on two aspects of the topic: some of the basic definitions, distinctions, and aims and some references to new work which has appeared in this still rapidly developing field over the last 4 years or so. In the latter respect the paper serves as an updated bibliography for the period 1978-1982.

II. SOME BASIC CONSIDERATIONS FOR UNIVARIATE SAMPLES

There are some fundamental questions which need to be asked. Firstly, what is an outlier? It is an observation (or subset of observations) which *appears to be inconsistent with ('deviates markedly from') the remainder of the sample in which it resides.* For univariate samples this is straightforward. Let the sample be

$$x_1, x_2, x_3, \ldots, x_n ;$$

we can order this as

$$x_{(1)}, \ x_{(2)}, \ x_{(3)}, \ldots, \ x_{(n)}.$$

Any outliers are bound to appear among the extremes e.g. as $x_{(1)}$, or $x_{(n)}$, or the outlier-pair $(x_{(n-1)}, \ x_{(n)})$ - they 'stick out at the ends of the sample'. (For *multivariate* data this detection process is less obvious in form!)

Of course, *any sample has extremes* and we would not wish to automatically reject or react specifically to *any* extreme. The outlier is not only an extreme but is extreme to a surprising extent: 'it appears inconsistent with the remainder of the sample.' Thus the declaration of an outlier involves a *subjective* element which must be acknowledged.

Let us go back to the Peirce (1852) paper. He presents data in the form of 30 residuals of measurements by Professor Coffin and Lieutenant Page in Washington in 1846 of the vertical semidiameter of the planet *Venus*.

FIGURE 1a.   The First Peirce Data Set.

Another data set on the same theme is presented: this for data collected by Lieutenant Herndon in Washington in 1846. The 15 residuals appear thus:

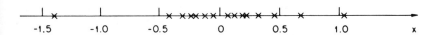

FIGURE 1b.   The Second Peirce Data Set.

Notice the qualitative difference in the two data sets in
Figures 1a and 1b. In the first we *might* choose to declare
$x_{(30)}$ = 0.83 an upper outlier. In the second we almost
certainly *would* declare $x_{(1)}$ = -1.40 a lower outlier and
$x_{(15)}$ = +1.01 an upper outlier.

Now consider our aims! If we want to estimate location
and dispersion relatively free of the influence of outliers, we
might choose to use some *robust estimators* e.g. the *median*, m,
and *median deviation*

$$s = median\{|x_j - m|\} ,$$

which are relatively unaffected by (thus '*accommodate*') any
outliers. But I must express a rather blunt view on this
matter. Until very recently there did not seem to be any
substantial body of work which was concerned with *robustness
in the face of outliers*. Much robustness work, implicitly
directed to variations in tail behaviour for a homogeneous
sample, claims protection against outliers without any real
justification beyond a mild degree of intuitive appeal!

In the last few years however a few proposals have been
made which are more directly concerned with robustness in the
presence of outliers. Some relevant references (mainly for
univariate samples) are Brown and Kildea (1979); Campbell
(1980); Chikkagoudar and Kunchur (1980); Dallal and Hartigan
(1980); David (1979); David and Shu (1978); Guttman and Kraft
(1980); Guttman and Tiao (1978); Iman and Conover (1977);
Johnson, McGuire, and Milliken (1978); Lingappaiah (1979);
Marks and Rao (1979); Prescott (1980); Rauhut (1982).

But if accommodation is not our aim, we are lead to ask
a more specific question. Apart from the outlier being an
extreme, indeed extreme to a surprising degree (the stimulus
for its declaration as an outlier), is it also *statistically
unreasonable when viewed as an extreme value?* This is the
basis of a *test of discordancy* which is used to justify *rejection* or *identification of the outlier* (for separate investigation) - leaving aside of course any overt deterministic
explanation of the presence of the outlier. If the outlier is
significant on such a test it is termed a *discordant outlier*
(at the level of the test).

Many additional factors now arise. Consider again the
remark of Peirce: in particular 'differ so much ... as to

indicate ... abnormal ... error not contemplated in the theoretical discussion'. This and the subjective basis for
declaring the outlier and the structure of the test of discordancy all imply that statistical processing of the outlier *can
only be contemplated in relation to a stated basic model* (call
it F) *for the generation of the data in uncontaminated form.*
Thus the null hypothesis for the test of discordancy is that
x_1, x_2,..., x_n arise as a random sample from F. The test then
operates as follows. On such an assumption, is $x_{(n)}$ (or whatever outlier or outlier-subset is declared) significantly
unreasonable in terms of its null-model behavioural characteristics?

Note two points. A null model F must be specified.
Aberrance is assessed relative to the behaviour of *extremes*
under F. It is failure to perceive this second point which
leads to *erroneous* principles for outlier rejection in the
past (Peirce, 1852; Chauvenet, 1863; Stone, 1868) which
persist even to recent times (Calvin *et al.*, 1949; Afifi and
Azen, 1979). The error is essentially that of replacing
$x_{(n)}$ [or $x_{(1)}$, or $(x_{(n-1)}, x_{(n)})$ etc] by x_i (or (x_i, x_j)) in
the discordancy test principle which declares $x_{(n)}$ [or...]
discordant if, under F, it is far out in the tail of the distribution. This can be a costly error. For the Chauvenet
principle it implies almost a 0.50 probability of rejection of
at least one observation in any perfectly reasonable (uncontaminated) large sample from F. On the Afifi and Azen proposal (for multivariate data, further considered in §III-B
below) the error probability approaches 1!

Let us be more specific, using the Peirce data sets for
illustration. Adopting (uncritically) a normal distribution
for F, the Chauvenet criterion shows that there is no reason
to reject any outlier in the first data set, whereas
$x_{(1)}$ = -1.40 is (in our terms) discordant in the second data
set. These conclusions are based on (essentially) the probabilistic behaviour of $(x_i - \bar{x})/s$ (where $\bar{x}$ and s are sample
mean and standard deviation) under F. More appropriately,
however, we should have considered the test statistic
$(x_{(1)} - \bar{x})/s$ in the second data set. From Table VIIa of
Barnett and Lewis (1978) a value of -2.71 is needed for significance at the 1% level. In fact $(x_{(1)} - \bar{x})/s$ = -2.58. This

is significant at the 5% level, but nowhere near as conclusive as using Chauvenet's principle (the 5% points are -2.41 and -2.14, respectively). We could also examine the outlier *pair* $x_{(1)} = -1.40$ and $x_{(n)} = +1.01$. Here we might use the test statistic $[x_{(n)} - x_{(1)}]/s$ and Table XIa of Barnett and Lewis (1978) gives a value 4.17 for rejection at the 5% level; in fact $[x_{(n)} - x_{(1)}]/s = 4.38$ and we thus reject $[x_{(1)}, x_{(n)}]$ at this level.

Let us consider some other possible discordancy tests on the second data set.

TABLE 1.   *Various Tests of Discordancy for the Second Peirce Data Set*

	Outlier	Test Statistic	Value	1% point	5% point	Table of Barnett & Lewis (1978)
i)	lower	$[x_{(1)} - x_{(2)}]/[x_{(n)} - x_{(1)}]$	-0.40	-0.438	-0.339	XIIIa
ii)	lower	$[x_{(1)} - x_{(2)}]/[x_{(n-1)} - x_{(1)}]$	-0.47	-0.487	-0.382	XIIIc
iii)	upper	$(x_{(n)} - \bar{x})/s$	1.80	2.71	2.41	VIIa
iv)	upper	$[x_{(n)} - x_{(n-1)}]/[x_{(n)} - x_{(1)}]$	0.16	0.438	0.339	XIIIa
v)	lower pair	$[x_{(1)} - x_{(3)}]/[x_{(n)} - x_{(1)}]$	-0.46	-0.523	-0.432	XIIIe

We shall come back to these results after making some further general distinctions (§II-E).

A. *Null Model and Alternative Model*

   If in the null case all observations arise from F, what
are we to assume if we reject the null model (find a discordant outlier)? The specification of an alternative (outlier-
generating) model $\overline{F}$ is not needed for conducting the test
of discordancy since only behaviour under F is relevant.
However, to measure the power of a test (or compare two tests)
we need to specify $\overline{F}$, and its form is also relevant to other
basic considerations.

   One possibility for $\overline{F}$ is the *slippage* model in which n–k
observations arise from F, and k from G, where G is a shifted
form of F for a specified value of k (e.g., if k=1 and G is
shifted to the right – see Figure 2 – we have a model for a
simple outlier). See Barnett (1978a) for other classes of
alternative models. If x_j comes from G we call it a *dis-*
cordant value or a *contaminant;* see §II-B.

   Note that $\overline{F}$ does not specify *which* observation comes from
G. Instead of $\overline{F}$:$x_j \epsilon F$ (j≠i), $x_i \epsilon G$ we might consider the more
empirically appealing prospect:

$$\overline{F}' : x_{(j)} \epsilon\ F\ (j=1,\ 2,\ldots,\ n-1),\ x_{(n)} \epsilon\ G.$$

The latter is called a *labelled* alternative model. This takes
us into a new area of statistical inference, where a hypothesis to be tested is *data dependent* ('adaptive'). See Barnett
and Lewis (1978, §3.1) for some further comments on this distinction.

B. *Extremes, Outliers, Discordant Outliers, Discordant Values*
   (Contaminants)

   We need to be quite clear about distinctions here. Consider again the slippage model from §II.A. An outlier shows
itself in the tails of the sample; it may or may not arise
from G (the contaminating distribution). An outlier is an
extreme; not every extreme is an outlier – it depends on the
form of F. A discordant value arises from G; it may or may
not be manifest as an outlier. Indeed, the form of G in relation to F is also crucial. If G were located similarly to F,
but with *lower* dispersion, we would not expect it to throw up
outliers; rather, undetectable 'inliers'. A discordant

outlier is statistically unreasonable as an extreme in a sample of size n from F; even so it is not necessarily from G
i.e. a discordant value or *contaminant*. See Figure 2 for
illustration of these distinctions.

The lack of inevitable coincidence of outlying, and contaminant, behaviour makes it difficult to construct a simple
measure of the 'power' of a test of discordancy. Various
measures have been proposed, including

p{outlier discordant|outlier is a contaminant}

p{outlier discordant|there is a contaminant}

The latter is really the measure of *power*, but is by no means
the only useful measure of test behaviour relative to the alternative hypothesis. See Barnett and Lewis (1978; §3.2).

C. *Subjectivity*

Given the subjective stimulus to the declaration of an
outlier we must note that conventional notions of the meaning
of the significance level of the test of discordancy do not
apply. Consider a level- α test. In the null case (model F)
it is *not* true that we reject with probabiity α, since not all
samples would be subjected to a test: *only those we happen to
distinguish as having an outlier present.* An empirical study
of this effect was made by Collett and Lewis (1976). The im-
precision caused by this effect disappears in regular screening for outliers applied to routinely collected data sets –
since every sample is tested as a matter of course. But it
may not really make practical or statistical sense to test
every sample for discordant outliers.

D. *Inclusive and Exclusive Measures*

Consider a test of discordancy for an upper outlier which
uses the intuitively appealing test statistic

$$T = [x_{(n)} - \bar{x}]/s.$$

If $\bar{x}$ and s are calculated from the whole sample, including the
outlier $x_{(n)}$, the statistic is an *inclusive* measure. Many
might feel that it is illogical, indeed ill-conceived, to

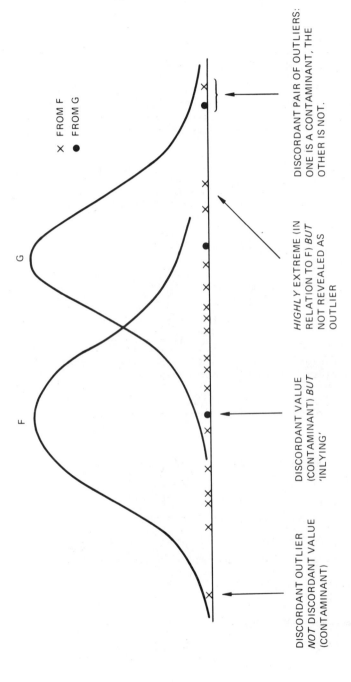

FIGURE 2. Outliers, discordant outliers, and contaminants

include $x_{(n)}$ and that the more appropriate statistic is the *exclusive* measure

$$T' = \left[x_{(n)} - \bar{x}'\right]/s'$$

where $\bar{x}'$ and s' are calculated from the restricted sample which excludes $x_{(n)}$. In fact it is largely irrelevant which is used provided the value is referred to the correct null distribution. Indeed the inclusive and exclusive measures are often functionally related. This is so for T and T' above, where

$$\left(\frac{n-1}{T}\right)^2 - \left(\frac{n-2}{n-1}\right)\left(\frac{n}{T'}\right)^2 \equiv n.$$

E. *Multiple Outliers: Masking and Swamping ('Now you see it, now you don't!')*

Often we may wish to test for *more than one* discordant outlier. For example, we may want to test both $x_{(n-1)}$ and $x_{(n)}$. There are two possibilities: a *block* test of the pair $\left[x_{(n-1)}, x_{(n)}\right]$ or *consecutive* tests of $x_{(n)}$ and then $x_{(n-1)}$. Both have problems, apart from distributional intractabil- ities. Consider the sample configuration:

$$x_{(n-1)} \quad x_{(n)}$$

The consecutive test may fail at the first stage of testing $x_{(n)}$ because of the proximity of $x_{(n-1)}$ which *masks* the effect of $x_{(n)}$. For example, the statistic $\left[x_{(n)} - x_{(n-1)}\right]/\left[x_{(n)} - x_{(1)}\right]$ will be prone to masking for obvi- ous reasons. On the other hand a block test of $\left[x_{(n-1)}, x_{(n)}\right]$ may convincingly declare the *pair* to be discordant.

But for the sample:

$$x_{(n-1)} \qquad x_{(n)}$$

a block test of $\left[x_{(n-1)}, x_{(n)}\right]$ may declare the *pair* to be discordant, whereas consecutive tests show $x_{(n)}$ to be discordant, but not $x_{(n-1)}$. The marked outlier $x_{(n)}$ has 'carried' the innocuous $x_{(n-1)}$ with it in the block test: this is known as *swamping*.

The dangers of these effects (and masking is a problem even for single outliers, of course) can be minimised by appropriate choice of test statistic for one-off samples. Such protection is not so readily available for automated procedures on regularly collected data sets.

The tests in Table 1 for the Peirce data illustrate such effects. Comparison of i) and ii) illustrates the masking effect of the *upper* outlier in test i) on a test of a *lower* outlier. Looking at iii) and iv) we see how much more prone to masking is the Dixon-type statistic $\left[x_{(n)}- x_{(n-1)}\right]/\left[x_{(n)}- x_{(1)}\right]$ than is $(x_{(n)}- \bar{x})/s$. Test (v) clearly illustrates the swamping effect of the highly discordant lower outlier.

Some recent developments on tests of multiple outliers in univariate data appear in Chhikara and Feiveson (1980); Draper and John (1980); Gentlemen (1980); Hawkins (1978, 1979); Jain (1981); Jain and Pingel (1981); Kimber and Stevens (1981) Marks and Rao (1978); Prescott (1978, 1979); Tietjen and Moore (1979).

F. Tests of Discordancy for Specific Distributions

The literature contains a wealth of different situations - too copious to attempt to summarise. There are tests for the normal distribution (with or without knowledge of the values of mean and variance); for exponential, gamma, Pareto, uniform, Gumbel, Frechet, Weibull, lognormal as well as binomial and Poisson. Barnett and Lewis (1978) review the prospects and describe special features of individual tests (e.g., statistical properties such as being a likelihood ratio test, degree of protection against masking, etc.) and tabulate relevant critical values. The scale of the state of knowledge is indicated by the fact that over 40 different tests for the normal distribution are described; approaching 20 for the exponential and gamma.

Some specific results and recent developments in tests of discordancy for univariate samples include the following:

Exponential and Gamma samples. Suppose F is characterised by the probability density function

$$f(x) = \frac{\lambda(\lambda x)^{r-1} e^{-\lambda x}}{\Gamma(r)} , \quad (x > 0)$$

i.e. the gamma distribution (including exponential: $r = 1$, and χ^2_n: $\lambda = 1/2$, $r = n/2$) so widely relevant to practical data. Some existing tests of discordancy for upper outliers have natural form. Thus we might use test statistics $x_{(n)}/\Sigma x_i$ or (with particular relevance to an exponential distribution with shifted origin) $[x_{(n)} - x_{(n-1)}]/[x_{(n)} - x_{(1)}]$. The test statistic $x_{(n)}/x_{(1)}$ provides a test for an upper and lower *outlier-pair*.

Data on excess cycle times in steel manufacture (see for example, Barnett and Lewis, 1978, p. 80) have 131 observations with $x_{(130)} = 35$, $x_{(131)} = 92$ and (omitting $x_{(131)}$) $\bar{x}/s = 1.04$, $m_3/s^3 = 2.09$, $m_4/s^4 = 9.24$: indicative of an exponential distribution. We have $T = x_{(n)}/\Sigma x_i = 0.099$ with critical level <0.0001 making $x_{(131)}$ highly discordant. The test with $T' = [x_{(n)} - x_{(n-1)}]/x_{(n)} = 0.620$ has critical level 0.0013, showing the vulnerability of this test to masking.

Relationships between distributions often enable outlier tests to be developed by means of transformations. Clearly this is possible in an obvious way for the *lognormal* distribution, using tests for the normal distribution. Consider a Pareto distribution with distribution function

$$F(y) = 1 - (a/y)^r \quad (y \geq a).$$

Then $X = \ln Y$ is shifted exponential with origin $\ln a$ and scale parameter $1/r$ and tests for the exponential distribution, which are independent of the origin, as is that based on $[x_{(n)} - x_{(n-1)}]/[x_{(n)} - x_{(1)}]$, can be applied to transformed observations $x_i = \ell n y_i$ (i=1,2,...,n). If a is known, we are better to use $X' = \ell n(Y/a)$. For a Weibull distribution an appropriate *exponential* transformation of the observations again enables tests for the exponential distribution to be employed.

Some recent work on outliers in specific distributions includes Patil, Kovner and King (1977); Rauhut (1982) (for the exponential distribution); Kimber (1979); Lewis and Fieller (1979) (for the gamma distribution); Collett (1980) (for circular data); Mirvaliev (1978) (for angular measurements).

G. *Accommodation: Outlier-Robust Methods*

The gamut of robust methods (though not specific to outliers) can assist in drawing inferences about the basic distribution F, minimising the influence of contaminants. Methods range from uses of trimming and Winsorisation, through general estimators of L-, M- and R- types, to specific proposals of tried worth. A review of the present state of robustness studies is given in the book by Huber (1981); Chapter 4 of Barnett and Lewis (1978) is more specific to the outlier problem but more limited in coverage of the general problem. Recent specific contributions have been listed earlier in this section. Accommodation is a principle of particular relevance to automated data-collecting and screening systems if its general ethos (inference on F) is of prime importance. In this context, outlier rejection and identification is more problemmatical but may be less often relevant.

H. *Slippage Tests*

A highly specific aspect of outlier study is that concerned with *outlying samples* in a *set* of data samples. Slippage tests can play the role of tests of discordancy for this situation.

I. *Other Recent References for Outliers in Univariate Samples*

See: Aitkin and Tunnicliffe Wilson (1980); de Alba and Van Ryzin (1980); Dallal and Hartigan (1980); David, Kennedy, and Knight (1978); Hawkins and Perold (1977); Hoaglin,

Iglewicz and Tukey (1980); Jain (1979); Johnson and Hunt
(1979); Kale (1977); Kitigawa (1979); O'Hagan (1979);
Srivastava (1980); Tiku (1977). Review papers, commentaries
and books (not restricted to the univariate problem alone)
include Hawkins (1980); Good (1978); Kale (1976, 1979);
Neyman (1979).

III. MULTIVARIATE OUTLIERS

For outliers in multivariate samples the same general
principles (and precautions) will apply, but with added complications from the practical viewpoint. Accommodation of
outliers requires suitable robust inference methods which are
less well-developed for the multivariate case (and again not
specific to outliers). We shall concentrate on tests of discordancy (for *rejection* or *identification* - or *incorporation:*
the adoption of an *homogeneous* model, in place of F, to explain the *whole* data set).

A. *Principles of Tests of Discordancy*

The ideas remain essentially the same with the three
stages

b) declare an extreme observation $x_{(n)}$ [or subset
of extreme observations] to be outlying
c) assume a basic model F
d) examine, relative to F, whether $x_{(n)}$ is statistically unreasonable when viewed as an extreme
value; if so, designate it a discordant outlier.

But a major new problem arises. There is no universal
basis for *ordering* multivariate data; so what is meant by an
extreme? Thus we need an extra stage

a) adopt a principle for representing extremeness i.e.
for detecting an outlier.

Various methods of *sub-ordering* might be used (see
Barnett, 1976) and again considerations of test principle and
alternative model, $\bar{F}$, are relevant (Barnett, 1979). The most

appealing prospect is to use a *reduced* measure of sub-ordering in which each multivariate observation $\underset{\sim}{x}$ is ordered in relation to a scalar value $R(x)$. The sample $\underset{\sim 1}{x}$, $\underset{\sim 2}{x}$,..., $\underset{\sim n}{x}$ is then relabelled $\underset{\sim(1)}{x}$, $\underset{\sim(2)}{x}$,..., $\underset{\sim(n)}{x}$ in increasing order of the values $R(\underset{\sim i}{x})$ (i=1,2,...,n). Thus the most 'extreme' observation $x_{(n)}$ has the largest R-value: $R_{(n)}$. Relative to the distribution of $R_{(n)}$ under F, $x_{(n)}$ is discordant if $R_{(n)}$ is sufficiently large. Note that the idea of a *lower* outlier is now more nebulous!

The problem of how to determine what form $R(x)$ should take, and what principles should guide the choice, has no obvious answer. Often the $R(x)$ has only intuitive support, except in rare instances where it arises from some accepted statistical principle applied specifically to F and $\overline{F}$. One such principle might be to declare as an outlier that observation $\underset{\sim i}{x}$ whose omission from the sample most increases the maximised likelihood (or joint probability density) of the remaining data under F. (An extended principle involving the alternative model $\overline{F}$ is described by Barnett, 1979). Such a principle *may* yield a reduced measure $R(x)$, but even if this happens the corresponding distribution theory can be prohibitively complicated.

Relatively little has been published on multivariate outliers; most of the few proposals are *ad hoc* in nature and relate to the normal distribution. Experience suggests that the multivariate normal distribution is of far from universal relevance. So often marginal distributions are skew or even i-shaped. It is ironical that again the normal distribution proves 'too true not to be good' in the sense that it is the sole model where proposed tests are seen to rest on sound statistical principles. We shall consider the normal case briefly and then proceed to a few results for non-normal situations.

B. *The Normal Distribution*

Most proposals here can be seen to rest explicitly or implicitly on use of a quadratic distance measure

$$R(\underset{\sim}{x}) = (\underset{\sim}{x} - \underset{\sim}{a})' \; \Gamma \; (\underset{\sim}{x} - \underset{\sim}{a})$$

for ordering the data (where $\underset{\sim}{a}$ describes location; Γ, inverse covariation). Depending on state of knowledge about the mean $\underset{\sim}{\mu}$ and variance-covariance matrix Σ we may take $\underset{\sim}{a}$ as $\underset{\sim}{0}$, $\underset{\sim}{\mu}$, or $\underset{\sim}{\bar{x}}$ and Γ as I, Σ^{-1}, or S^{-1}. Such a measure is intuitively attractive (consider probability density ellipsoids) but has added support in being implicit in the original Wilks (1963) proposals for the normal case, in arising from the maximum-likelihood principles mentioned above and in forming the basis of optimal tests relative to a reasonable choice of alternative model, $\bar{F}$. See Barnett (1978b) for more detailed discussion; also Schwager and Margolin (1982).

Thus we evaluate $R_j = R(\underset{\sim}{x}_j)$ ($j = 1,2,\ldots,n$) and declare $\underset{\sim}{x}_i$ yielding the maximum value $R_{(n)}$ to be the outlier (if extreme enough). If, relating to the model F: $N(\underset{\sim}{\mu},\Sigma)$, $R_{(n)}$ is significantly large, $\underset{\sim}{x}_i$ is then *discordant*. Distributional results are well-known here, or at least well-tabulated (for all cases of $\underset{\sim}{a} = \underset{\sim}{0}$, $\underset{\sim}{\mu}$, or $\underset{\sim}{\bar{x}}$ and $\Gamma = I$, Σ^{-1}, or S^{-1}).

One of the few references to multivariate outlier testing in basic texts on statistics is the section 5.1 of Afifi and Azen (1979). They propose use of an *exclusive version* of $R(x) = (x-\bar{x})' \; S^{-1}(x-\bar{x})$, where $\bar{x}$ and S are calculated omitting any observation being studied. They proceed to investigate a bivariate data set involving systolic and diastolic blood pressures for 15 patients, as shown in Table 2.

TABLE 2. Afifi and Azen Data on Blood Pressures

Observation	1	2	3	4	5	6	7	8	9	10	11	12	13	14	15
x_1: systolic	154	136	91	125	133	125	93	80	132	107	142	115	114	120	141
x_2: diastolic	108	90	54	89	93	77	43	50	125	76	96	74	79	71	90

Inspection of the scatter diagram reveals x_9 as suspicious; we might also wonder about x_7. Afifi and Azen do not discuss the underlying model. Simple probability plots of the ordered marginal samples $x_{1(k)}$ and $x_{2(k)}$ ($k = 1,2,\ldots,15$) against α_k ($k = 1,2,\ldots,15$) where

$$\alpha_k = E[Z_{(k)}]$$

($Z_{(k)}$ is the kth order statistic for a standard normal sample of size 15) suggest slight negative skewness for X_1 and some 'lumpiness' for X_2, but no strong contraindication of normality.

Suppose we do assume that $X \sim N(\mu,\Sigma)$. The appropriate test of discordancy requires us to consider the quadratic distance measure with μ estimated by the sample mean ($a = \overline{x}$) and Σ by unbiased sample variance-covariance matrix ($\Gamma = S^{-1}$). Thus we seek the observation yielding the largest value of

$$R_j(\overline{x},\ S) = (x_j - \overline{x})'\ S^{-1}(x_j - \overline{x}).$$

This turns out to be x_9, and since $\overline{x}_1 = 120.53$, $\overline{x}_2 = 81.00$ and

$$S = \begin{bmatrix} 435.41 & 389.00 \\ 389.00 & 470.57 \end{bmatrix},$$

we find that $R_{(15)} = R_9 = 11.78$. The appropriate test (see e.g. Barnett and Lewis, 1978, Chapter 6 and Table XXVIII) has 5%, 1%, and 0.1% critical values of 8.02, 9.20 and 10.08, respectively. *Thus x_9 is a highly discordant outlier.*

We could now omit x_9 and repeat the test on the reduced sample of size n'=14. We now have $\overline{x}_1' = 119.71$, $\overline{x}_2' = 77.86$ and

$$S' = \begin{bmatrix} 458.07 & 377.34 \\ 377.34 & 347.21 \end{bmatrix} .$$

Now $\underset{\sim}{x}_7$ yields $R_{(n')}$. In fact $R_{(14)} = R_7 = 2.76$, nowhere near the 5% point for n=14, which is 7.74.

We conclude that the data contain a single discordant outlier, namely $\underset{\sim}{x}_9$. But this is not how Afifi and Azen approached the problem. In fact they used a principle similar to (but even more extreme than) the erroneous one proposed by Chauvenet. They suggest that for each $\underset{\sim}{x}_j$ we determine

$$p_j = P\left[(\underset{\sim}{X}-\underset{\sim}{\overline{X}})' \, S^{-1}(\underset{\sim}{X}-\underset{\sim}{\overline{X}}) > (\underset{\sim}{x}_j-\underset{\sim}{\overline{x}})'S^{-1}(\underset{\sim}{x}_j-\underset{\sim}{\overline{x}}) \right]$$

(but they employ the distribution of the *inclusive* statistic, rather than that of the *exclusive* form which they have calculated). If, for some small value α, $p_j > \alpha (j=1,2,...n)$ we are advised to declare no outliers. If $\min_j p_j < \alpha$, we are told to reject the offending $\underset{\sim}{x}_i$ and repeat this process as long as is necessary on the reduced sample. On this basis $\underset{\sim}{x}_9$ and $\underset{\sim}{x}_7$ are rejected (with $p_9 = 0.0003$, $p_7 = 0.0264$), with the remark that subsequent 'examination of the records' showed that $\underset{\sim}{x}_9$ and $\underset{\sim}{x}_7$ were wrongly recorded – they should have been (132,94) and (93,54)!

Consider the univariate equivalent of this procedure. If x_α satisfies $P(X > x_\alpha) = \alpha$, we have

$$P(\text{reject an 'outlier'}) = P(\text{at least one } x_j > x_\alpha)$$

$$= 1 - (1 - \alpha)^n .$$

Suppose we take $\alpha = 0.05$. For n = 15, there is thus a probability of at least 0.5 of spuriously rejecting an 'outlier'. For other sample sizes we have

n	5	10	15	20	40	60	100
P(reject 'outlier')	0.23	0.40	0.53	0.64	0.87	0.95	0.99

The proper principle should relate to $x_{(n)}$, not to an arbitrary x_j. We should adjudge $x_{(n)}$ discordant if $P(X_{(n)} > x_{(n)}) < \alpha$: that is, if

$$x_{(n)} > x_c \text{ with } c = \{1 - (1 - \alpha)^{1/n}\}; \text{ not if } x_{(n)} > x_\alpha.$$

For obvious reasons, this type of misconception has most serious effects in the case of automated, large-scale, data collection systems; it would change the whole nature of the perceived data generating mechanism.

C. *A Bivariate Exponential Distribution*

Few proposals have been made for outlier tests in non-normal multivariate samples. In this section and the next we consider just two examples of tests of discordancy for non--normal bivariate outliers, proposed by Barnett (1979).

Suppose (X_1, X_2) have a bivariate *exponential* distribution (Gumbel, 1960) with probability density function

$$f(x_1, x_2) = e^{- x_1 - x_2 - \theta x_1 x_2}[(1 + \theta x_1)(1 + \theta x_2) - \theta]$$

with $x_1 > 0$, $x_2 > 0$ and θ in $(0, 1)$. (X_1, X_2) have non-positive correlation in the range $(-0.4037, 0)$ as θ varies from 1 to 0.

A restricted form of the principle of maximising joint probability density described above yields

$$R(\underset{\sim}{X}) = X_1 + X_2 + \theta X_1 X_2$$

for investigating an 'upper' outlier. The distribution of the corresponding $R_{(n)}$ *is* tractable here. Its distribution function is

$$F(r) = \{1 - \frac{e^{-r}}{\theta}[(1 + \theta r)\ln(1 + \theta r) + \theta]\}^n,$$

and the critical value for a level-α test of discordancy is β_α given by

$$F(\beta_\alpha) = 1 - \alpha.$$

This is somewhat (though not entirely) unrealistic in that it assumes θ known. In automated routine data scrutiny θ may indeed be essentially known, but even if θ is not known, a conservative test is available and critical levels β_α are also tabulated (see Barnett, 1979).

D. *A Bivariate Pareto Distribution*

Another case which can be readily handled is that of the positively correlated bivariate Pareto distribution (Mardia, 1962) where (X_1, X_2) has probability density function

$$f(x_1, x_2) = a(a + 1) (\theta_1\theta_2)^{a+1}(\theta_2 x_1 + \theta_1 x_2 - \theta_1\theta_2)^{-(a+2)}$$

for $x_1 \geq \theta_1 > 0$, $x_2 \geq \theta_2 > 0$, with a > 0.

Consider the case where the terminals θ_1, θ_2 and the association parameter a are known, or specified. The same principle as in §III-C now yields (for study of an upper outlier) the measure

$$R(\underset{\sim}{X}) = X_1/\theta_1 + X_2/\theta_2 - 1.$$

We now find that the critical level, γ_α, for a level-α test of discordancy satisfies

$$\delta\gamma_\alpha^{a+1} - (a + 1) \gamma_\alpha + a = 0,$$

where $\delta = 1 - (1 - \alpha)^{1/n}$.

The critical level, γ_α, is tabulated for various values of a in the range (2,40) in Barnett (1979), where the implications of unknown θ_1 and θ_2 are also discussed and a conservative test derived.

E. *Towards a Unified Approach*

The tractability of the test of discordancy for normal data, and its desirable statistical properties, make it tempting to seek a transformation principle through which outliers in non-normal data sets might be examined using the test for the normal case. This is asking a lot, but some progress in this direction seems possible. Consider the bivariate situation.

Suppose that under the null model F, $\underset{\sim}{X} = (X_1, X_2)$ has marginal and conditional distribution functions denoted by $F_{X_i}(x_i)$ and $F_{X_i|x_j}(x_i)(i=1,2,;j\neq i)$, respectively. In particular, consider $F_{X_1}(x_1)$ and $F_{X_2|x_1}(x_2)$. If $G(u_1)$ and $H(u_2)$ are distribution functions, then the transformation

$$F_{X_1}(x_1) \quad = \quad G(u_1)$$

$$F_{X_2|x_1}(x_2) \quad = \quad H(u_2)$$

takes the general bivariate random variable (X_1, X_2) to a pair of independent random varibles (U_1, U_2) with distribution functions $G(u_1)$ and $H(u_2)$, respectively.

If we choose $G(\ ) = H(\ ) = \Phi(\ )$, where $\Phi(\ )$ is the distribution function of a standard normal random variable, $N(0,1)$, then arbitrary $(\underset{\sim}{X_1}, X_2)$ are transferred to *independent standard normal variates*. But for such independent standard normal components the test of discordancy is straightforward being based on $R(\underset{\sim}{U}) = U_1^2 + U_2^2$, and $R_{(n)}/2$ is distributed as the largest order statistic from an *exponential* sample of size n. Thus critical values ξ_α have the simple explicit form

$$\xi_\alpha = -2 \ln\left[1 - (1 - \alpha)^{1/n}\right].$$

Thus we have only to transform the original sample $\underset{\sim}{x_1}, \underset{\sim}{x_2}, \ldots, \underset{\sim}{x_n}$ to an independent normal sample $\underset{\sim}{u_1}, \underset{\sim}{u_2}, \ldots, \underset{\sim}{u_n}$, detect the principal outlier as that observation yielding $R_{(n)} = \max_i (u_{i1}^2 + u_{i2}^2)$, and test discordancy by referring

$R_{(n)}$ to $- 2 \ln \left[1 - (1 - \alpha)^{1/n} \right]$.

It all sounds too simple. What is the catch? Several matters are not as straightforward as they might appear.

   i)   The distribution of (X_1, X_2) is implicitly *fully specified*. Unknown parameter values will necessitate solving some difficult estimation problems.

  ii)   The transformation is not unique. What criteria should be employed to choose from the various possibilities?

 iii)   How do sample characteristics transfer when we go from $\underset{\sim}{X}$ to $\underset{\sim}{U}$? Does the implicit reduced measure on the $\underset{\sim}{X}$-space, induced by $R(\underset{\sim}{U}) = U_1^2 + U_2^2$, make sense as a basis for ordering the original data set?

  iv)   The transformation from $\underset{\sim}{X}$ to $\underset{\sim}{U}$ is unlikely to have a simple explicit form.

All these points need further investigation. Some of them are considered in Barnett (1983).

F. *Some Additional Recent Developments for Multivariate Outliers*

There are few new proposals for unstructured multivariate data (see later for outliers in regression, linear models, designed experiments, etc.). Apart from Barnett (1978b, 1979, 1983) we have Andrews and Pregibon (1978), Garel (1978), and Schwager and Margolin (1982).

IV. OUTLIERS IN LINEAR MODELS

Many of the data sets we have to consider are not in the form of independent random samples. We may wish to use them to estimate or test parameters in a linear model, (either of a general regression type or arising from a designed experiment) or in a time-series model. Outliers can be present in these more structured situations and again we may need tests of discordancy for 'cleaning up the data' prior to fuller analysis, or for identification of discordant values. Alternatively we might like to proceed directly to the full analysis but using robust techniques not seriously influenced by outliers.

Space does not permit any detailed review of this field. Chapters 6 and 7 of Barnett and Lewis (1978) describe and illustrate many of the available techniques, and we shall only consider here an illustrative situation.

A. *Outliers in Linear Regression*

To demonstrate some of the general principles we can take the simplest case. Observations (x_1,u_1), $(x_2,u_2),\ldots,(x_n,u_n)$ satisfy a linear regression model

$$x_j = \theta_o + \theta_1 u_j + \varepsilon_j \quad (j = 1,2,\ldots,n)$$

where the residuals ε_j are uncorrelated with variance σ^2.
The data in Table 3 show the results of an accelerated 'dry-weathering' test on a random sample of 12 pieces of rubber. Tensile strengths (Z) are recorded after u days of weathering. Figure 3 suggests that a linear regression of $X = \ell nZ$ on u is a reasonable model. But we immediately note that the observation at u = 11 days is an outlier. Notice a

TABLE 3. 'Dry-weathering' Test Data

Days (u)	4	5	7	9	11	14	17	20	23	26	30	35
Tensile Strengths (z: oz.)	110	81	90	74	20	30	37	22	38	25	18	9
$x = \ell nz$	4.7	4.4	4.5	4.3	3.0	3.4	3.6	3.1	3.6	3.2	2.9	2.2

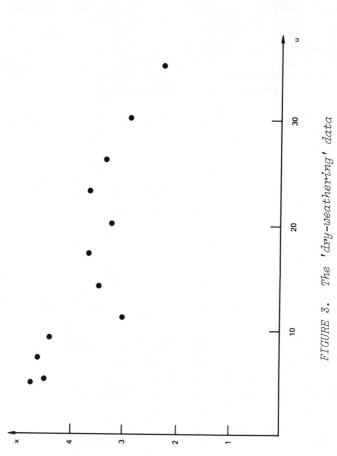

FIGURE 3. The 'dry-weathering' data

crucial distinction here. The outlier is not an *extreme:* it
stands out because of its marked 'pattern-breaking' characteristic. Of course where it may be extreme is in the value of
its associated residual ε_i and much outlier study for linear

models etc. is approached through the estimation of residuals.
Since the true residuals ε_j are unknown, we proceed to esti-

mate them.

If $\tilde{\theta}_o$ and $\tilde{\theta}_1$ are least squares estimators of θ_o and θ_1,
the estimated residuals are

$$\tilde{\varepsilon}_j = x_j - \tilde{\theta}_o - \tilde{\theta}_1 u_j \quad (j=1,2,\ldots,n)$$

with

$$\sigma_j^2 = \mathrm{Var}(\tilde{\varepsilon}_j) = \sigma^2 \{\frac{n-1}{n} - (u_j - \overline{u})^2 / \sum_{k=1}^{n} (u_k - \overline{u})^2 \}.$$

Note the strange 'ballooning' effect in the form of σ_j^2.
Estimated residuals have largest variance in the vincinity of
$\overline{u}$; the variance *decreases* as we approach the extremes of the
data. There are implications here for model validation which
are somewhat counter-intuitive and need to be acknowledged
when we investigate the propriety of the model.(Homoscedas-
ticity is *not* supported by apparently constant variance for
the estimated residuals.)

Thus to compare the estimated residuals we need to 'stan-
dardise' them. Studentised forms

$$e_j = \tilde{\varepsilon}_j / S_j$$

are used, where S_j^2 is the unbiased least squares estimator
of σ_j^2. That is

$$S_j^2 = S^2 \{\frac{n-1}{n} - (u_j - \overline{u})^2 / \sum_{k=1}^{n} (u_k - \overline{u})^2 \} \text{ with } S^2 = \sum_{j=1}^{n} \tilde{\varepsilon}_j^2 / (n-2).$$

We can now detect an outlier as that observation (x_i, u_i),
which has largest studentised residual $t = \max_j (\tilde{\varepsilon}_j / S_j)$. It is

discordant if t is sufficiently large. The observation maximising $\{e_j\}$ may be different from that with largest estimated
residual!

We should also note that the estimated residuals are not
correlated. In fact

$$\text{Cov}(\tilde{\varepsilon}_j, \tilde{\varepsilon}_k) = -\sigma^2 \{\frac{1}{n} + (u_j - \overline{u})(u_k - \overline{u}) / \sum_{\ell=1}^{n} (u_\ell - \overline{u})^2\}$$

Again this varies with the values of u_j and u_k relative to $\overline{u}$.

To test discordancy we need to know the distribution of t
in the null case. This is intractable in exact form even when
$\varepsilon_j \sim N(0,\sigma^2)$, but good approximations have been proposed and
tabulated.

Returning to the dry-weathering data, we see in Table 4
the estimated residuals and the corresponding studentised
values.

TABLE 4.   *Estimated and Studentised Residuals*
            for 'Dry-weathering' Data

u	4	5	7	9	11	14	17	20	23	26	30	35
x	4.7	4.4	4.5	4.3	3.0	3.4	3.6	3.1	3.6	3.2	2.9	2.2
$\tilde{\varepsilon}$	0.30	0.06	0.29	0.22	-0.95	-0.35	0.04	-0.26	0.43	0.22	0.18	-0.19
e	0.85	0.17	0.79	0.59	[-2.50]	-0.91	0.10	-0.68	1.13	0.59	0.51	-0.60

Sure enough, the observation with u = 11 stands out markedly. Reference to Table XXXII of Barnett and Lewis (1978)
shows a 5% critical value of 2.43 for a two-tailed test.
Since $|t|$ = 2.50 here, we have a discordant outlier at the 5%
level.

This approach is readily extended to the general linear
model including designed experiment data. In the latter case
we have special features. Residuals tend to be less accessible and the concept of 'pattern breaking' as a stimulus to the
declaration of an outlier is less immediate in impact. Estimated residuals can have complex intercorrelation, but for a

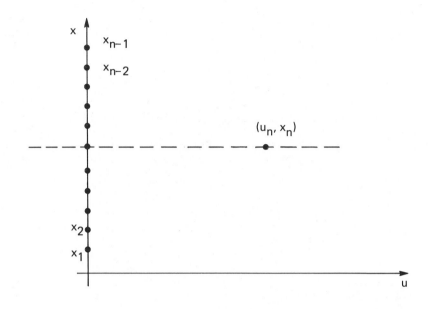

FIGURE 4 a

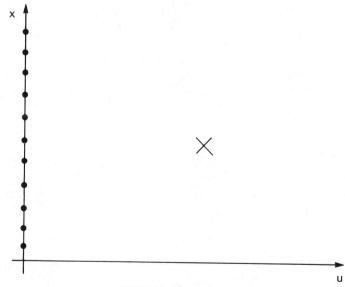

FIGURE 4 b

large class of orthogonal designs they have *constant variance*
under the null model. Methods (and tabulated results) for the
general linear model can be used to test for discordancy.

B. A Paradox?

Use of estimated residuals to examine outliers can sometimes appear superficially perverse. Consider the data set
shown in Figure 4a, and the application of a linear regression
model. The least squares fit to all n observations passes
through (x_n, u_n) where $u_n = n$. If there is an outlier it looks
intuitively as if the obvious candidate is (x_n, u_n), since
omitting this observation we have an exact fit to the remaining n-1 observations. (See Figure 4b). But if we employ the
principle of detecting an outlier from the estimated residuals
we find that $\tilde{\varepsilon}_n = 0$. Can (x_n, u_n) be the outlier?

Notice that the method above involved *studentisation* for
legitimate comparison of estimated residuals. With
$u_1 = u_2 = \ldots = u_{n-1} = 0$ (or any shift or rotation of the data
set) we have

$$\sigma_n^2 = \mathrm{Var}(\tilde{\varepsilon}_n) = \sigma^2 (\frac{n-1}{n} - (u_n - \overline{u})^2 / \Sigma (u_j - \overline{u})^2).$$

But $\overline{u} = 1$ and $\Sigma (u_j - \overline{u})^2 = n(n-1)$; so that $\sigma_n^2 \equiv 0$. Thus although $\tilde{\varepsilon}_n = 0$, the studentised form e_n is indeterminate and
consequently makes sense as an outlier in comparison with the
finite values of the other e_j's$(j \neq n)$.

C. Some Recent Work for Linear Models, Etc.

There has been quite a lot of activity in this field over
recent years. We have the following work.

Time series: Abraham and Box (1979);

Regression and linear model: Abraham and Box (1978); Atkinson
(1980); Belsley, Kuh, and Welsch (1980); Carroll
(1982); Cook (1979); Cook and Prescott (1981);

Cook and Weisberg (1980); Dempster and Gasko-
Green (1981); Doornbos (1981); Draper and John
(1980, 1981); Gentle (1978); Gentlemen (1980);
Joshi (1977); Mirvaliev (1978); Tamhane (1982).

Robustness for structured data: Brown and Kildea (1979);
Carroll (1980, 1982); Dutter and Guttman (1979);
Escoffier and Le Roux (1976); Hill (1982).

Designed experiments: Bradu (1975); Bradu and Hawkins (1982);
Draper and Herzberg (1979); Galpin and Hawkins
(1981); John (1978); John and Draper (1978).

Other (discriminant analysis, contingency tables, etc.)
Campbell (1978); Fuchs and Keneff (1980);
Paulson and Thornton (1975).

V. IMPLICATIONS OF THE DATA COLLECTING MECHANISM FOR THE PROCESSING OF OUTLIERS

Data can be obtained in a variety of ways and forms. We
can distinguish four particularly relevant dichotomies.

Size.　　　Samples may be small (s) or large (S).

Pattern.　　The data may arise as a random sample of independent observations from (on the null model)
a specific distribution (p) or as a structured
data set supported by a soundly based linear or
general linear model (P).

Dimension.　The basic observations (or their response components) may be univariate (d) or multivariate
(D).

Mechanism.　The data may be a single (one-off) sample relevant to a specific isolated situation (m) or one
of a sequence of samples routinely (and perhaps
automatically) generated and processed from an
assumed stable and unchanging source (M).

The effects of many of these distinctions on outlier
methodology have been described throughout this report. This

is particularly true of the differences due to p/P and d/D.
Some reference has also been made to the effects of the distinction m/M. In all cases the effects are subject to the
overriding consideration of the basic aim and purpose of any
investigation.

As far as s/S is concerned the major effect is that the
larger the data set the less embarrassing is lack of knowledge
of basic model or parameter values. This is always true of
course, but it is particularly important with outlier study
where we have the strange combination of features: informality
of purpose (as an initial data-screening process) but in a
highly model-dependent form. But with outlier accommodation,
increasing size of sample is not self-protecting since the
influence of outliers remains acute. For a test of discordancy on the other hand a larger sample size provides protection through greater ease of model choice and validation. For
the case M, an accumulation of small samples provides a similar service with respect to model choice and validation, but
there is an incipient danger. It is tempting to try to auto-
mate the whole process of data generation, data screening, and
data analysis, perhaps with some comprehensive computer package. Such a non-interventionalist programme has an obvious
appeal in cost-efficiency terms and in reducing the need for
constant statistical expertise. But for outlier study (and
other aspects of data screening) we pay the price that the
very type of non-anticipated aberrance of behaviour of the
data is (inevitably) not detected. This is particularly acute
for outlier study due to many of the effects previously described: masking, swamping, and the tendency to unreasonably
homogenize the data sets in order to protect against the relatively rare occasions where modification is genuinely needed.
This is the danger in all automated data handlng systems: we
cannot militate for all prospects. There is no substitute for
professional statistical skill.

REFERENCES

Abraham, B. and Box, G.E.P. (1978). "Linear Models and
    Spurious Observations," *Applied Statistics*, *27*, 131-138.
Abraham, B. and Box, G.E.P. (1979). "Bayesian Analysis of Some
    Outlier Problems in Time Series," *Biometrika*, *66*, 229-236.
Afifi, A.A. and Azen, S.P. (1979). *Statistical Analysis: A
    Computer Oriented Approach* 2nd Ed., Academic Press, New
    York.

Aitken, M. and Tunnicliffe Wilson, G. (1980). "Mixture Models, Outliers and the EM Algorithm," *Technometrics*, *22*, 325-331.

Andrews, D.F. and Pregibon, D. (1978). "Finding the Outliers that Matter," *J. Roy. Statist. Soc. B*, *40*, 85-93.

Atkinson, A.C. (1980). "Use of Two Graphical Displays for the Detection of Influential and Outlying Observations in Regression," *COMPSTAT 1980*, Physica, Vienna.

Barnett, V. (1976). "The Ordering of Multivariate Data (with Discussion)," *J. Roy. Statist. Soc. A*, *139*, 318-355.

Barnett, V. (1978a). "The Study of Outliers: Purpose and Model," *Applied Statistics*, *27*, 242-250.

Barnett, V. (1978b). "Multivariate Outliers: Wilk's Test and Distance Measures," *Bull. Int. Statist. Inst.*, *47*(4), 37-40.

Barnett, V. (1979). "Some Outlier Tests for Multivariate Samples," *South African Statist. J.*, *13*, 29-52.

Barnett, V. (1983). "Reduced Distance Measures and Transformations in Processing Multivariate Outliers," *Austral. J. Statist.*, *25*, 1-12.

Barnett, V. and Lewis, T. (1978). *Outliers in Statistical Data*, Wiley, Chichester.

Belsey, D.A., Kuh, E. and Welsch, R.E. (1980). *Regression Diagnostics: Identifying Influential Data and Sources of Collinearity*. Wiley, New York.

Bradu, D. (1975). "Search and Anova Methods for Interaction Originating in a Small Set of Outliers," *EDV Med. Biol.*, *6*, 93-100.

Bradu, D. and Hawkins, D.M. (1982). "Location of Multiple Outliers in Two-way Tables, Using Tetrads," *Technometrics*, *24*, 103-108.

Brown, B.M. and Kildea, D.G. (1979). "Outlier-detection Tests and Robust Estimators Based on Signs of Residuals," *Comm. Statist. A*, *8*, 257-269.

Calvin, M., Heidelberger, C., Reid, J.C., Tolbert, B.M. and Yankwich, P.F. (1949). *Isotopic Carbon: Techniques in Its Measurements and Chemical Manipulation*, Wiley, New York.

Campbell, N.A. (1978). "The Influence Function as an Aid in Outlier Detection in Discriminant Analysis," *Applied Statistics*, *27*, 251-258.

Campbell, N.A. (1980). "Robust Procedures in Multivariate Analysis I: Robust Covariance Estimation," *Applied Statistics*, *29*, 231-237.

Carroll, R.J. (1980). "Robust Methods for Factorial Experiments with Outliers," *Applied Statistics*, *29*, 246-251.

Carroll, R.J. (1982). "Two Examples of Transformations when There Are Possible Outliers," *Applied Statistics*, *31*, 149-152.

Chauvenet, W. (1863). "Method of Least Squares," Appendix to
    Manual of Spherical and Practical Astronomy Vol. 2. Re-
    printed 5th Ed. (1960) Dover, New York.
Chhikara, R.A. and Feiveson, A.L. (1980). "Value of Extreme
    Studentized Deviate Test Statistics for Detecting Multiple
    Outliers," *Comm. Statist. B, B9*, 155-166.
Chikkagoudar, M.S. and Kunchur, S.H. (1980). "Estimation of
    the Mean of an Exponential Distribution in the Presence
    of an Outlier," *Canadian J. Statist., 8*, 59-63.
Collett, D. (1980). "Outliers in Circular Data," *Applied Sta-
    tistics, 29*, 50-57.
Collett, D. and Lewis, T. (1976). "The Subjective Nature of
    Outlier Rejection Procedures," *Applied Statistics, 25*,
    228-237.
Cook, R.D. (1979). "Influential Observations in Linear Regres-
    sion," *J. Amer. Statist. Assn., 74*, 169-174.
Cook, R.D. and Weisberg, S. (1980). "Characterizations of an
    Empirical Influence Function for Detecting Influential
    Cases in Regression," *Technometrics, 22*, 495-508.
Cook, R.D. and Prescott, P. (1981). "On the Accuracy of
    Bonferroni Significance Levels for Detecting Outliers in
    Linear Models," *Technometrics, 23*, 59-64.
Dallal, G.E. and Hartigan, J.A. (1980). "Note on a Test of
    Monotone Association Insensitive to Outliers," *J. Amer.
    Statist. Assn., 75*, 722-725.
David, H.A. (1979). "Robust Estimation in the Presence of Out-
    liers," pp. 61-74 in Launer, R.L. and Wilkinson, G.N. (Eds.)
    (1979) *Robustness in Statistics*, Academic Press, New York.
David, H.A. and Shu, V.S. (1978). "Robustness of Location
    Estimators in the Presence of an Outlier," pp.235-250 in
    David, H.A. (Ed) (1978) *Contributions to Survey Sampling
    and Applied Statistics, in honour of H. O. Hartley*, Aca-
    demic Press, New York.
David, H.A., Kennedy, W.J. and Knight, R.D. (1978). "Means,
    Variances and Covariances of the Normal Order Statistics
    in the Presence of an Outlier," In Harter, H.L. and Owen,
    D.B. (Eds) (1978) *Selected Tables in Mathematical Statis-
    tics. Vol. III*, Amer. Math. Soc., Providence, RI.
de Alba, H. and Van Ryzin, J. (1980). "An Empirical Bayes
    Approach to Outliers," *J. Statist. Pl. Inf., 4*, 217-236.
Dempster, A.P. and Gasko-Green, M. (1981). "New Tools for Re-
    sidual Analysis," *Ann. Statist., 9*, 945-959.
Doornbos, R. (1981). "Testing for a Single Outlier in a Linear
    Model," *Biometrics, 37*, 705-712.
Draper, N.R. and Herzberg, A.M. (1979). "Designs to Guard
    Against Outliers in the Presence or Absence of Model
    Bias," *Canadian J. Statist., 7*, 127-135.

Draper, N.R. and John, J.A. (1980). "Testing for Three or Fewer Outliers in Two-way Tables," *Technometrics*, *22*, 9-15.

Draper, N.R. and John, J.A. (1981). "Influential Observations and Outliers in Regression," *Technometrics*, *23*, 21-26.

Dutter, R. and Guttman, I. (1979). "Outlier detection. On Estimation in the Linear Model When Spurious Observations Are Present - A Bayesian Approach," *Comm. Statist. A.*, *8*, 611-636.

Escoffier, B. and Le Roux, B. (1976). "Factor's Stability in Correspondence Analysis. How to Control the Influence of Outlying Data," (in French). *Cahiers Anal. Donnees*, *1*, 297-318 (Dunod, Paris).

Fuchs, C. and Kenett, R. (1980). "A Test for Outlying Cells in the Multinomial Distribution and Two-way Contingency Tables," *J. Amer. Statist. Assn.*, *75*, 395-398.

Galpin, J.S. and Hawkins, D.M. (1981). "Rejection of a Single Outlier in Two- or Three-way Layouts," *Technometrics*, *23*, 65-70.

Garel, B. (1978). "Detection Tests for Multidimensional Outliers," (in French). *Ann. Inst. H. Poincare. B.*, *14*, 303-314.

Gentle, J.E. (1978). "Testing for Outliers in Linear Regression," pp. 223-234 of David, H.A. (Ed) (1978). *Contributions to Survey Sampling and Applied Statistics, in honour of H. O. Hartley*. Academic Press, New York.

Gentleman, J.F. (1980). "Finding the k Most Likely Outliers in Two-way Tables," *Technometrics*, *22*, 591-600.

Good, I.J. (1978). "Should Outliers Be Dragged In?" *J. Statist. Comp. Sim*, *7*, 163-164.

Gumbel, E.J. (1960). "Bivariate Exponential Distributions," *J. Amer. Statist. Assn.*, *55*, 698-707.

Guttman, I. and Kraft, H. (1980). "Robustness to Spurious Observations of Linearized Hodges-Lehmann Estimators and Anscombe Estimators," *Technometrics*, *22*, 55-63.

Guttman, I. and Tiao, G.C. (1978). "Effect of Correlation on the Estimation of a Mean in the Presence of Spurious Observations," *Canadian J. Statist.*, *6*, 229-248.

Hawkins, D.M. (1978). "Analysis of Three Tests for One or Two Outliers," *Statistica Neerlandica*, *32*, 137-148.

Hawkins, D.M. (1979). "Fractiles of an Extended Multiple Outlier Test," *J. Statist. Comp. Sim.*, *8*, 227-236.

Hawkins, D.M. (1980). *Identification of Outliers*, Chapman-Hall, London.

Hawkins, D.M. and Perold, A.F. (1977). "On the Joint Distribution of Left-and-Right-Sided Outlier Statistics," *Utilitas Math.*, *12*, 129-143.

Hill, R.W. (1982). "Robust Regression when there Are Outliers in the Carriers: the Univariate Case," *Comm. Statist. Theor. Meth.*, *11*, 849-868.

Hoaglin, D.C., Iglewicz, B. and Tukey, J.W. (1980). "Small-Sample Performance of a Resistant Rule for Outlier Detection," *ASA Proc. Statist. Comp.* 148-152.

Huber, P. J. (1981). *Robust Statistics*, Wiley, New York.

Iman, R.L. and Conover, W.J. (1977). "On the Power of the t-Test and Some Rank Tests when Outliers May Be Present," *Canadian J. Statist*, *5*, 187-193.

Jain, R.B. (1979). "FORTRAN Subroutines to Detect Outliers from Normal Samples," *Ap. Psych M*, *3*, 176.

Jain, R.B. (1981). "Percentage Points of Many-outlier Detection Procedures," *Technometrics*, *23*, 71-76.

Jain, R.B. and Pingel, L.A. (1981a). "A Procedure for Estimating the Number of Outliers," *Comm. Statist. A.*, *10*, 1029-1041.

Jain, R.B. and Pingel, L.A. (1981b). "On the Robustness of Recursive Outlier Detection Procedures to Non-normality," *Comm. Statist. A.*, *10*, 1323-1334.

John, J.A. (1978). "Outliers in Factorial Experiments," *Applied Statistics*, *27*, 111-119.

John, J.A. and Draper, N.R. (1978). "On Testing for Two Outliers or One Outlier in Two-way Tables," *Technometrics*, *20*, 69-78.

Johnson, B.A. and Hunt, H.H. (1979). "Performance Characteristics for Certain Tests to Detect Outliers," *ASA Proc. Statist. Comp.*, 247-249.

Johnson, D.E., McGuire, S.A. and Milliken, G.A. (1978). "Estimating σ^2 in the Presence of Outliers," *Technometrics*, *20*, 441-456.

Joshi, P.C. (1977). "Detection of Outliers in Linear Regression," *Gujarat Statist. Rev.*, *4/1*, 1-16.

Kale, B.K. (1976). "Detection of Outliers," *Sankhyā B*, *38*, 356-363.

Kale, B.K. (1977). "A Note on Outlier Resistant Families and Mixtures of Distributions," *J. Ind. Statist. Assn.*, *15*, 119.

Kale, B.K. (1979)."Outliers - A Review," *J. Ind. Statist. Assn.*, *17*, 51-67.

Kimber, A.C. (1979). "Tests for a Single Outlier in a Gamma Sample with Unknown Shape and Scale Parameters," *Applied Statistics*, *28*, 243-250.

Kimber, A.C. and Stevens, H.J. (1981). "The Null Distribution of a Test for Two Upper Outliers in an Exponential Sample," *Applied Statistics*, *30*, 153-157.

Kitigawa, G. (1979). "On the Use of AIC (Akaike's Information Criterion) for the Detection of Outliers," *Technometrics, 21,* 193-200.

Lewis, T. and Fieller, N.R.J. (1979). "A Recursive Algorithm for Null Distributions for Outliers: 1 Gamma Samples," *Technometrics, 21,* 371-376.

Lingappaiah, G.S. (1979). "Problem of Estimation when the Outliers Are Present," *Trab. Estadist. y Invest. Oper., 30/3,* 71-80.

Mardia, K.V. (1962). "Multivariate Pareto Distributions," *Ann. Math. Statist., 33,* 1008-1015.

Marks, R.G. and Rao, P.V. (1978). "A Modified Tiao-Guttman Rule for Multiple Outliers," *Comm. Statist. A., 7,* 113-126.

Marks, R.G. and Rao, P.V. (1979). "An Estimation Procedure for Data Containing Outliers with One-directional Shift in the Mean," *J. Amer. Statist. Assn., 74,* 614-620.

Mirvaliev, M. (*translated by* Kashper, A.) (1978a). "Rejection of Outlying Results of Angular Measurements," *Theor. Prob. Ap., 23,* 814-819.

Mirvaliev, M. (*translated by* Kashper, A.) (1978b). "The Rejection of Outlying Observations in Regression Analysis," *Theor. Prob. Ap., 23,* 588-602.

Neyman, J. (1979). "Outlier Proneness and Resistance. Developments in Probability and Mathematical Statistics Generated by Studies in Meteorology and Weather," *Comm. Statist. A., 8,* 1097-1110.

O'Hagan, A. (1979). "On Outlier Rejection Phenomena in Bayes Inference," *J. Roy. Statist. Soc. B., 41,* 358-367.

Patil, S.A., Kovner, J.L. and King, R.M. (1977). "Tables of Percentage Points of Ratios of Linear Combinations of Order Statistics of Samples from Exponential Distributions," *Comm. Statist. B., 6,* 115-136.

Paulson, A.S. and Thornton, J.C. (1975). "A New Approach to Goodness of Fit and Outliers," *Proc. 6th Pittsburgh Conf: Modelling and Simulation.* Vogt, W.G. and Mickle, M. H. (Eds) Instrument Soc. Amer., Pittsburgh, PA.

Peirce, B. (1852). "Criterion for the Rejection of Doubtful Observations," *Astr. J., 2,* 161-163.

Prescott, P. (1978). "Examination of the Behaviour of Tests for Outliers when More Than One Outlier Is Present," *Applied Statistics, 27,* 10-25.

Prescott, P. (1979). "Critical Values for a Sequential Test for Many Outliers," *Applied Statistics, 28,* 36-39.

Prescott, P. (1980). "A Review of Some Robust Data Analysis and Multiple Outlier Detection Procedures," *BIAS, 7,* 141-158.

Rauhut, B.O. (1982). "Estimation of the Mean of the Exponential Distribution with an Outlying Observation," *Comm. Statist. Theo. Meth.*, *11*, 1439-1452.

Schwager, S.J. and Margolin, B. (1982). "Detection of Multivariate Normal Outliers," *Ann. Statist.*, *10*, 943-954.

Srivastava, M.S. (1980). "Effect of Equicorrelation in Detecting a Spurious Observation," *Canadian J. Statist. 8*, 249-252.

Stone, E.J. (1868). "On the Rejection of Discordant Observations," *Monthly Notices Roy. Astro. Soc.*, *28*, 165-168.

Tamhane, A.C. (1982). "A Note on the Use of Residuals for Detecting an Outlier in Linear Regression," *Biometrika*, *69*, 488-489.

Tietjen, G.L. and Moore, R.H. (1979). Correction to "Some Grubbs-type Statistics for Detection of Several Outliers", *Technometrics*, *21*, 396.

Tiku, M.L. (1977). Rejoinder to "Comment on 'A New Statistic for Testing Suspected Outliers,'" *Comm. Statist. A.*, *6*, 1417-1422.

Wilks, S.S. (1963). "Multivariate Statistical Outliers," *Sankhyā*, *A.*, *25*, 407-426.

INFLUENCE FUNCTIONS, OUTLIER DETECTION, AND
DATA EDITING

Michael R. Chernick

Aerospace Corporation
Los Angeles, California

I. INTRODUCTION

The influence function was defined by Hampel (1974) as a
tool for assessing robust estimators. Gnanadesikan (1977)
points out the potential value of the influence function for
detecting outliers in multivariate observations, particularly
in the case of bivariate correlation. Chernick (1982) applies
the influence function for bivariate correlation to the detection of outliers in a particular Department of Energy data
base. The use. of an influence function matrix for the autocorrelation function of a time series is given in Chernick,
Downing, and Pike (1982).

Chernick and Murthy (1983) give the influence functions
and sample estimates for the mean, variance and for regression
coefficients. They illustrate the potential for using these
estimates to detect outliers and to assess the effect of data
editing procedures on estimates.

This summary article reviews some of the main results of
Chernick (1982), Chernick, Downing, and Pike (1982), and
Chernick and Murthy (1983).

II. MULTIVARIATE OUTLIERS

In the validation of data, as in the various data evaluation studies done for the Energy Information Administration,
there are usually data sets collected on several related
variables. These data are accumulated in reports which are
used by various organizations for a variety of purposes. Con-

sequently, various types of correlation are of interest.
Users might compute bivariate correlation and in regression,
multiple correlation. Outliers which affect the estimates of
these correlations would be of particular concern to users of
the data.

Multivariate data exhibit structure and, consequently,
special techniques are required to take account of that structure. Univariate outlier techniques are not sufficient as
they cannot take account of the correlation structure in multivariate data. This is illustrated in Figure 1. One observation is clearly an outlier as it falls outside the ellipse.
This observation falls inside the rectangle and hence would
not be detected by univariate tests applied to each component. Several observations fall outside the rectangle but
remain inside the ellipse. These observations are not really
outliers although univariate tests would indicate that they
are.

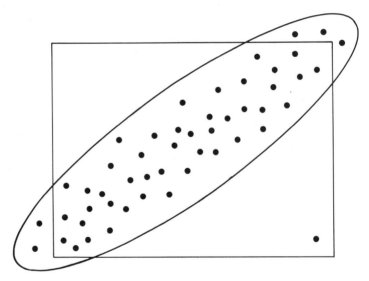

FIGURE 1. Data from a bivariate normal population with
           possible outliers.

For multivariate observations there is not a natural direction to use for defining extreme observations. There are
several ways of defining and testing for multivariate outliers. The method chosen should depend on the importance of
detecting a particular type of outlier.

The influence function approach to detecting multivariate outliers focuses attention on statistics of interest such as bivariate correlation, multiple correlation and regression co-efficients. An influence function is defined which measures the effect particular multivariate observations have on these statistics. Those observations with large influence are con-sidered to be outliers.

III. INFLUENCE FUNCTIONS

To give a formal definition, we point out that the influ-ence function depends on the distribution function F of a ran-dom observation vector, the parameter of interest, which is commonly written T(F), and the observation vector. The para-meter is considered as a functional T(F) of the distribution function F. The influence function is defined by the follow-ing equation whenever the limit on the right hand side exists:

$$I(F, \ T(F), \ \underset{\sim}{x}) \ = \ \lim_{\varepsilon \to 0} \frac{T[(1-\varepsilon)F + \varepsilon \ \delta(\underset{\sim}{x})] \ - \ T[F]}{\varepsilon} \tag{1}$$

where $\underset{\sim}{x} = (x_1, \ x_2, \ \dots, \ x_n)$ is a point of interest in the observation space, ε is a positive real number, $\delta(\underset{\sim}{x})$ is the distribution function with all its probability mass concentrated at the point $\underset{\sim}{x}$, and T(F) is the parameter of interest.

The influence function is approximately equal in large samples to n times the difference between the estimator with an observation at x included and the estimator with the observation at $\underset{\sim}{x}$ excluded where n is the sample size. This can be seen by replacing F with F_{n-1} (the empiric distribution function for a sample of size n-1) and approxima-ting the limit as ε tends to 0 by replacing ε with $\frac{1}{n}$. Since $(\frac{n-1}{n}) \ F_{n-1} + \frac{\delta(\underset{\sim}{x})}{n} = F_n$, we get that the influence function is approximately $n\big(T(F_n) - T(F_{n-1})\big)$ as claimed.

Given a sample of observations, the influence function for a parameter of interest may be estimated for each observation. An observation which has a very large estimated

influence* will deserve particular attention, and we may be
better off to discount it in our estimation procedure. If it
is necessary for such an observation to be replaced, we may
choose a value with small or zero influence on our estimator.

In orbit determination problems, least–squares fitting
methods are used to estimate orbit parameters based on data
such as pseudo–range, delta range, and azimuth and elevation
angle measurements. It is well known that the least–squares
procedure leads to parameter estimates that can be very
sensitive to outlying observations. Consequently, robust
filtering or outlier rejection techniques sometimes need to be
used to obtain good estimates of orbital elements based on
such data. The methodology proposed in this paper can be used
to arrive at more sophisticated outlier rejection and
replacement techniques for the processing of these data.

The details of this concept are illustrated by considering the mean of a distribution. For a univariate distribution
function F, the mean can be written as

$$T(F) = \int_{-\infty}^{\infty} y dF \text{ and the sample mean as } \bar{X} = \frac{1}{m} \sum_{i=1}^{m} X_i = T(F_m),$$

where we assume $|T(F)| < \infty$, $\{X_i\}_{i=1}^{m}$ are the m independent
observations and F_m is the empiric distribution function
based on these observations. In this case

$$I(F, T(F), x) = \lim_{\varepsilon \to 0} \frac{(1-\varepsilon) \int_{-\infty}^{\infty} y dF + \varepsilon x - \int_{-\infty}^{\infty} y dF}{\varepsilon}$$

$$= x - \int_{-\infty}^{\infty} y dF = x - T(F) = x - \mu.$$

Replacing μ by $\bar{X}$, we obtain a sample estimate for I

$$\hat{I} = x - \bar{X}.$$

*What constitutes a large estimated influence depends on what
assumptions are made about the underlying distribution.

TABLE 1. Influence Functions for Various Parameters

T(F)	$I(F, T(F), \underset{\sim}{x})$
1. μ, the mean of a distribution	$x - \mu$
2. σ^2, the variance of a distribution	$(x - \mu)^2 - \sigma^2$
3. β, the slope of a regression line	$\dfrac{\sigma_y}{\sigma_x} I(F, \rho, (x, y)) + \rho \left(\dfrac{I(F, \sigma_y^2, y)}{2\sigma_y \sigma_x} - \dfrac{\sigma_y \, I(F, \sigma_x^2, x)}{2\sigma_x^3} \right)$
4. α, the intercept of a regression line	$y - \mu_y - \beta(x - \mu_x) - \mu_x \, I(F, \beta, (x, y))$
5. ρ, the bivariate correlation coefficient	$\left(\dfrac{y - \mu_y}{\sigma_y} \right) \left(\dfrac{x - \mu_x}{\sigma_x} \right) - \dfrac{\rho}{2} \left(\left(\dfrac{y - \mu_y}{\sigma_y} \right)^2 + \left(\dfrac{x - \mu_x}{\sigma_x} \right)^2 \right)$
6. c, circular error probability	$\dfrac{\sqrt{2\ell n 2}}{2\sigma} \left(\dfrac{x^2 + y^2}{2} - \sigma^2 \right)$

This estimate of I is unbiased and consistent. Large values
of Î correspond to observations which are say 2 or 3 standard
deviations away from the mean. So the influence function for
the mean is equivalent to a 3 sigma outlier rejection rule.
If the observations have a normal distribution, the probability of the influence function estimate exceeding 3 standard
deviations is less than 0.01. Other examples of formulas for
influence functions are given in Chernick and Murthy (1983).
They are given in Table 1.

For the circular error probability, the formula given in
Table 1 is for the case when the components x and y both have
normal distributions with zero mean and common variance σ^2.
Under those assumptions $c = \sqrt{2\ln 2}\ \sigma$ where c is defined to be
the median of the distribution for r, and $r = \sqrt{x^2 + y^2}$. In
the other cases no distributional assumptions are made.

Maximum likelihood estimates for the influence function
at $\underset{\sim}{x}$ can be obtained by replacing the unknown parameters with
their maximum likelihood estimates under a hypothesized multivariate distribution, (e.g., the bivariate normal distribution).

Contours of constant value of the influence function indicate the directions in the observation space for which the
influence increases most rapidly. For example, in the case of
bivariate correlation the contours of constant value of the
influence function are hyperbolic. Examples of superimposed
contours over bivariate scatter plots graphically illustrate
which observations are outliers. Examples are given on p. 277
and p. 280 in Gnanadesikan (1977).

IV. FORM 4 APPLICATION

The influence function for bivariate correlation was
applied to the Form 4 data base of the Energy Information
Administration in order to detect outliers. Details are given
in Chernick (1982). Form 4 is a monthly report containing
consumption and generation data for all the U.S. utilities and
some industrial power plants. For a sample of 36 months of
consumption and generation data, 25 power plants were
selected. For 23 of the power plants the correlation between
consumption and generation was 0.98 or higher. For the other
two plants the sample correlations were 0.4704 and 0.4844.

For both of these cases the influence function indicated that the removal of a single observation would significantly increase the correlation. Follow-up interviews with respondents indicated that there were indeed some errors not previously detected by the Department of Energy's automated data editing routines. Errors were due to a misplaced decimal point and forgetting to convert from gallons to barrels. Another outlier detected by the influence function was not an error but turned out to be due to the closing of a steam plant. This fact was an important piece of information about the plant which should be considered before analyzing the data. It appears that the correlation would not be very meaningful if it were computed combining the data prior to the closing of the plant with the data after the closing.

Since the consumption and generation data are really time series and consecutive observations may be correlated, a procedure for detecting outliers in a time series might be helpful. Chernick, Downing, and Pike (1982) propose an influence function matrix for the autocorrelation function of a time series. They show that outliers can have significant effects on the estimated autocorrelations and consequently on autoregressive parameters in an autoregressive time series model. They apply the influence function matrix to the same set of Form 4 data for which outliers had been previously detected.

The same outliers were detected by the use of the influence function matrix. Correction of an observation led to the discovery of additional outliers which were masked initially by the erroneous observation.

V.   INVENTORY DIFFERENCE DATA APPLICATION

The Nuclear Regulatory Commission has for over thirty years kept an inventory on the various nuclear materials stored and used at various national laboratories and plants. For various reasons described in their report it is difficult to keep accurate account of all the material. Due to these difficulties, computed inventory differences are often negative and the differences must then be satisfactorily explained. Due to concern over the possible theft of nuclear materials, statistical procedures have been devised to determine significant changes in the inventory. Control charts and Kalman filters are two such procedures. Chernick, Downing, and Pike (1982) applied the influence function matrix to seven series of annual inventory difference data. The

results were promising. Most encouraging is the fact that the
technique can detect losses at the time of occurrence. The
control chart and the Kalman filter methods usually require
additional data after the occurrence of the loss of material
in order to detect the change. An account of the problems
involved in nuclear materials data is given by Goldman,
Picard, and Shipley (1982). The paper includes several
discussions.

VI. THE USE OF INFLUENCE FUNCTIONS FOR IMPUTATION

Many data bases require the replacement of outliers or
missing data points with estimates called imputed values. In
some cases these imputation procedures can significantly affect other estimates of interest to users of the data base.
Chernick and Murthy (1983) show how the influence functions
for parameters such as the mean and variance can be used to
assess the effects of imputation schemes. In fact if one
wishes to replace an observation with an imputed value but
wants to have little or no effect on a particular estimate of
a parameter, he can determine a value for which the estimated
influence is zero or nearly zero for that estimate of a parameter.

Chernick and Murthy (1983) show that replacing an outlier
with the sample mean of the remaining observations does not
affect the sample mean, but it does affect the sample variance. On the other hand if one wants to have no effect on the
sample variance, one can replace the observation, say X_n, with
the value

$$\hat{X}_n = \overline{X}_{n-1} + \sqrt{\frac{n}{n-1}}\; S_{n-1}$$

or

$$\hat{X}_n = \overline{X}_{n-1} - \sqrt{\frac{n}{n-1}}\; S_{n-1}$$

where

$$\overline{X}_{n-1} = \sum_{i=1}^{n-1} X_i/(n-1)$$

and

$$s^2_{n-1} = \sum_{i=1}^{n-1} (X_i - \bar{X}_{n-1})^2/(n-1).$$

This estimate will however have an influence on the mean.

If we have two outliers, say X_n and X_{n-1}, we can choose

$$\hat{X}_{n-1} = \bar{X}_{n-2} - S_{n-2}$$

and

$$\hat{X}_n = \bar{X}_{n-2} + S_{n-2}$$

where

$$\bar{X}_{n-2} = \sum_{i=1}^{n-2} X_i/(n-2)$$

and

$$s^2_{n-2} = \sum_{i=1}^{n-2} (X_i - \bar{X}_{n-2})^2/(n-2).$$

The result of this imputation is zero influence on both the sample mean and the sample variance.

In general when we are interested in the effect on more than one parameter a compromise will be required as we will not be able to simultaneously make the influence zero on several parameters.

REFERENCES

Chernick, M. R. (1982). "The Influence Function and Its Application to Data Validation," *American Journal of Mathematical and Management Sciences*, 2, 263-288.

Chernick, M. R., Downing, D. J., and Pike, D. H. (1982). "Detecting Outliers in Time Series Data," *Journal of the American Statistical Association*, 77, 743-747.

Chernick, M. R., and Murthy, V. K. (1983). "The Use of
    Influence Functions for Outlier Detection and Data
    Editing," *American Journal of Mathematical and Management
    Sciences*, to appear.

Gnanadesikan, R. (1977). *Methods for Statistical Data
    Analysis of Multivariate Observations*, Wiley, New York.

Goldman, A. S., Picard, R. R., and Shipley, J. P. (1982).
    "Statistical Methods for Nuclear Materials Safeguards:
    An Overview," *Technometrics, 24*, 267-294.

Hampel, F. R. (1974). "The Influence Curve and its Role
    in Robust Estimation," *Journal of the American
    Statistical Association, 69*, 383-393.

USING EXPLORATORY DATA ANALYSIS
TO MONITOR SOCIO-ECONOMIC DATA QUALITY
IN DEVELOPING COUNTRIES

Paul F. Velleman
David F. Williamson

Cornell University
Ithaca, New York

I. INTRODUCTION

Large data collection systems in developing countries
face special problems maintaining and assessing data quality
(Casley and Lury, 1981). Approaches to these problems that
employ traditional statistical and computing techniques are
often inappropriate or ineffective. The "low tech" approaches
of exploratory data analysis can, however, provide useful
tools for assessing and improving data quality.

This article first surveys some of the problems faced by
data collection systems in developing countries. Section III
introduces some exploratory data analysis techniques that are
well-suited to meeting these problems. Section III-B provides
some examples taken from two large data collection projects in
developing countries.

II. THE PROBLEM

Many developing countries have joined the trend toward
increasing use of large-scale data collection systems. Like
their counterparts in the developed world, developing country
policy and decision makers are demanding more data and information from their own universities, national research insti-
tutes, and international donor agencies. Much of the data is
collected in population surveys assessing agroeconomic, food,
and health levels. Usually both the decision makers and the
researchers ultimately responsible for the data collection and

analysis have received advanced degrees or significant training in developed countries. Often the institution operating
the data collection system owns a computer that will be used
for data entry, cleaning, and analysis -- usually located in
the capital city or some other urban center (where there is
electricity and its supply is reasonably constant.) Depending
on the make of the computer (often determined by the availability and quality of maintenance rather than the suitability
of the machine), various standard statistics packages may be
available.

However, at the primary (interviewer-respondent) and
secondary (supervisor-interviewer) levels, the challenges to
data quality can be much greater. We can group these challenges under two broad headings: logistics and personnel.

The two major logistic constraints are a frequent lack of
personal transportation and reliable electricity. In rural
agrarian areas, roads and transportation facilities may be
sparse at best. The interviewers' jobs are made more difficult and tiring. To decrease interviewer fatigue and maintain
a reasonable time schedule, a large number of interviewers are
often hired relative to the number that might be employed in a
developed country for a comparable sample size. The supervisor is similarly constrained and may not be able to adequately oversee interviewer teams in the field.

The major impact of lack of electricity is that it reduces the amount of time available for proofing and editing
survey forms as they are returned by the interviewers at the
end of the day. Transportation and mail services are often
slow and unreliable, so field survey directors hesitate to send
small packets of survey forms to the central processing center. In many cases a large number of survey forms will be
hand carried by the supervisor after a sample area has been
completed. This limits the ability of tertiary level analyses
to flag serious interviewer problems while they can still be
corrected.

The selection and training of field personnel can pose
special problems in developing countries. Many developing
countries have widely differing local languages as well as an
official national language. This necessitates hiring interviewers from among the better educated local people who can
both converse in the local language and read and write the
national language. In rural areas, where the majority of the
population is illiterate, "better educated" may mean a junior
high school or high school education at best.

Because the field supervisor will often have to spend long periods in isolated areas, staff members from the central institution who have lower seniority (and consequently less experience and training) are often assigned the job. They usually have had no direct responsibility for designing the questionnaire or the survey sampling scheme. They are also less likely to be aware of the ways in which the data are to be used.

III. EXPLORATORY DATA ANALYSIS

Exploratory data analysis (EDA) techniques were introduced by Tukey (1977) in his book by that name. Velleman and Hoaglin (1981) selected nine commonly used techniques and provided tutorial presentations, examples, and computer programs. EDA methods have several properties that recommend them as tools in improving the quality of data collected under the circumstances described in section II. First, they are designed to be computed by hand. Second, they are resistant to extreme data values -- usually with a large breakdown bound (Hampel, 1971) that provides a cushion of protection. Third, they emphasize the examination and display of residuals in ways that isolate outliers. Finally, they require no mathematics nor any arithmetic beyond the ability to order numbers, to add two numbers, and to divide by 2.

Exploratory methods can thus be used in several ways. First, field supervisors can use EDA display techniques to monitor data as it is collected. Extraordinary values can be identified early enough to permit confirmation or correction. Unexpected patterns can be investigated. (For example, a bimodal distribution in which one mode is solely due to one interviewer argues for careful checking of his work. Unexpected granularities in the data may indicate problems with the survey or with the interviewers.)

Second, EDA methods can be used in later data cleaning. Computer implementations of the methods are likely to be useful in this application because they will then check for data entry errors as well. The simplicity of EDA methods makes computer programs for many of the methods quite short and thus suitable for the smaller computers likely to be found in developing countries.

Finally, EDA can be used, as it is used in developed countries, as the first step in a more complex data analysis.

The general exploration of patterns in data is almost always a
good start for a data analysis.

A. *The Survey Setting*

Some of the examples in this paper use data from a large-
scale household dietary/socioeconomic survey carried out in a
rural island district of Indonesia as part of a project funded
by a USAID host-country grant to the government of Indonesia.
The survey design was a 13-round panel with 1700 households
studied from September 1980 until March 1982. Survey rounds
were separated by six-week intervals.

These households were sampled in clusters of 20 from 85
villages in the 9 subdistricts which make up the total district. Data collection was the overall responsibility of a
Central Research Institute located near Jakarta. To go from
the Center to the sample district involved a 1-1/2-hour trip
by jet and then either a 6-hour crossing by ferry or a 20-
minute flight, if one could make the required connection.

Supervisors were permanent staff of the Center and normally had the equivalent of a two-year associate degree. Several of the field supervisors were recent graduates while
others had been employed by the Center for 10 years or more.
During any survey round, two supervisors from the Center over-
saw field operations. The supervisors came from a pool of 8
people, and normally the same two supervisors would not work
consecutive survey rounds. This pool of supervisors was not
only responsible for the above survey but also for overseeing
another survey of similar magnitude and identical design in a
different region of Indonesia. During the life of these surveys, field supervisors spent a majority of their time working
in or shuttling among the two survey districts and the Center.

In both survey districts enumerators were hired locally
to save money and because the local languages were different
from each other and from the national language. Because the
Central Research Institute is under a government ministry, the
local government infrastructure was used for identification of
candidate enumerators. Local health centers in each of the
nine subdistricts were asked to submit names of candidates to
the district health officer. Thirty-two candidates were obtained.

An examination testing general knowledge of health and
nutrition was administered to these candidates by the district

health officer. A total of 16 candidates passed this exam.
From this group 12 enumerators were chosen by the head supervisor from the Center. Final selection was based on a written
exam testing knowledge in simple arithmetic and penmanship, an
individual interview, and assessment during three days of
field training. During the field training, enumerators were
observed on interview techniques, dedication, and their ability to relate to the respondents. No further formal training
was given to enumerators after the selection period. When
during the course of the survey an enumerator was replaced,
the new enumerator was given a brief orientation by the supervisors on duty at that survey round and then teamed with a
more experienced enumerator. No other training was provided.

Questionnaires, written in the national language, were
designed and printed at the Center. Several supervisors took
part in questionnaire design. Both the format and the content
of the survey forms were in large part determined by the perceived abilities of the local enumerators. For example, except for yes/no responses, coded responses were not used as it
was felt that local, inexperienced personnel could not use
them correctly. Instead, enumerators would record responses
as short-phrase answers. It was then the responsibility of
the data-entry personnel at the Center to classify these responses
into coded categories. Key punchers were thus required to
read each enumerator's response, assign it a known code, and
punch the code-number into the data file.

Supervisors were encouraged to make unannounced spot-
checks while enumerators were in the field. Some of the
supervisors did this sporadically. Some supervisors proofread
survey forms after each collection day. (Reasonably reliable
electricity was available at the district center where supervisors were billeted, and pocket calculators were available.)
Feedback to enumerators, when given, took place the following
morning when enumerators received their day's assignments and
alloted survey forms. Although never implemented in the
field, some EDA techniques were taught to supervisors several
months after the survey was underway. It was found that the
stem-and-leaf display was understood by the field supervisors
both in its construction and its uses.

Completed questionnaires were hand carried back to the
Center by returning supervisors at the end of each survey
round. One survey round usually required about 2-1/2 weeks to
complete, depending on the season of the year. Indonesia has
a single, well-defined monsoon season followed by a dry season
of equal length. During the wet season, which runs from

October through March, heavy rains fall daily and what little transportation there is becomes highly unreliable. Although there are some tarmac roads between major towns and a reasonable public transportation system, this is not the case among rural villages. Some of the enumerators used their personal motor scooters. In the rural areas, single-horse carts are a major means of transportation and can often be rented for the day. Supervisors were not supplied with their own vehicles during the survey.

B. *Exploratory Data Analysis*

Exploratory data analysis (EDA) methods are useful in three broad categories of application for monitoring data quality in large data collection systems in developing countries: (i) Monitoring data quality in the field, (ii) Intermediate analysis and displays, and (iii) Data exploration prior to a more traditional statistical analysis. Different EDA techniques are important in each of these applications, and different features of EDA methods are of key importance.

(i) Monitoring Data Quality in the Field. Data quality monitoring in the field is particularly valuable because it offers some chances to correct erroneous data by returning to the source, and because it can provide an important final step of education for field workers who may be recording some answers incorrectly or otherwise misinterpreting their instructions. Any method proposed for this application must be simple to use, require no calculations, be resistant to outliers, and be easy to teach to statistically unsophisticated field supervisors.

The EDA technique we recommend for this application is the stem-and-leaf display. Stem-and-leaf displays are becoming common in the literature of many fields of research. They provide all of the information provided by a histogram plus additional information about the distribution of final digits and outliers, while being much easier to produce than a histogram and easy to create sequentially as additional data arrive. If a field supervisor maintains a stem-and-leaf display for variables of key interest (or those he suspects may be least reliable), he will be able to compare new values, not just to arbitrary limits of plausibility, but to a reasonable estimate of the distribution of values already obtained. In this manner, observations that are unusual in any of a variety of ways can often be spotted easily.

In addition, unusual patterns (such as unexpected bimoda-
lities) can often be spotted. A strongly bimodal distribution
on an important variable often suggests that the population is
not homogeneous -- a conclusion that can affect the sampling
design if it is noticed early enough.

We refer readers to Velleman and Hoaglin (1981) for a
tutorial discussion of stem-and-leaf displays (and tutorial
discussions of each of the EDA methods used in this article);
we will not present detailed definitions of the methods, but
rather offer illustrative examples. Figure 1 exhibits the
amount of land owned by the families studied in one subdistrict of Indonesia. (The sample design called for half of the
households to own no land and for the others to own less than
50 *ares* (100 ares = 1 hectare = 10,000 square meters.)

```
        LEAF DIGIT UNIT =    1.0
        1 2 REPRESENTS 12.


(52)  +0*  0000000000000000000000000000000000000000000000000000
 48   +0.
 48    1*  00
 46    1.  555
 43    2*
 43    2.  55555555555
 32    3*  00000000
 24    3.  5
 23    4*  000000
 17    4.
 17    5*  000000000002
  5    5.
  5    6*  0
  4    6.
  4    7*  0

        HI  99, 99, 99
```

FIGURE 1.   Stem-and-leaf display of rice land owned.

Briefly, a stem-and-leaf display has three parts. The
middle column holds the *stems* -- here running from "0" to
"7". The right-hand part of the display holds the *leaves* --
these serve to form the histogram-style display of the distribution. The left-most column of numbers holds the *depths*,
which simply count the data values in from each edge of the

distribution. The stems and leaves together report the most
significant digits of the numbers being displayed. Thus, for
example, a leaf of 5 on the stem labeled "2" represents the
number 25. (Figure 1 includes a key that indicates where to
place the decimal point. In this case it says that a stem of
1 and a leaf of 2 would represent the number 12, so the decimal point follows the leaf for each number in the display.)

Clearly, the shape of the distribution depicted by a
stem-and-leaf display will provide the same information as a
histogram; we often produce histograms by representing each
data value with a mark of some kind on the appropriate line of
the plot. Here we have simply decided to make the marks informative by using digits of the numbers represented. This
additional information is often quite useful. For example, in
Figure 1, one leaf in particular stands out. All but one of
the leaves on the main body of the display are zeros or
fives. This is not an unusual granularity for data reported
in this way. (Although certainly the fields are not surveyed
accurately (or at all!) and their true dimensions are in no
way resricted to such 5 *are* jumps.) In this context a reported field size of 52 ares seems oddly precise and immediately suspect. Indeed, as Table 1 shows, this household does
not behave like a landowning household when we consider their
diet. We do not know the cause of this anomaly; perhaps the
correct value was 5 ares and a recording or keypunching error
was made.

*TABLE 1. Kcal Per Capita for Households with
Largest Land Ownership.*

Land owned (ares)	Kcal/capita (3 day recall)
99.	1144.00
70.	1144.00
52.	424.00
60.	869.00
99.	1292.00
99.	1846.00

One additional property of stem-and-leaf displays is
illustrated by Figure 1. They are usually constructed to display the main body of the data. Because the data values themselves are recorded as part of the display, it is easy to
record extreme values separately without sacrificing the

information conveyed or the usefulness of the display as a depiction of distribution shape. When we make stem-and-leaf
displays by hand, the decision to relegate extreme values to
stems labeled "LO" and "HI" can be made arbitrarily. Programs
for stem-and-leaf display contain a simple resistant scaling
algorithm that automates the decision. In this case the
"99's" represent values above 100; the coding scheme in the
data entry program permitted only two digits for this
variable.

Whenever a larger collection of numbers needs to be reduced to a summary based upon fewer numbers (either in the
field or later in the data analysis), a letter-value display
provides a convenient selection of summary values. Letter-
value displays present in simple tabular form the median,
fourths, eighths, and other selected fractiles out to the extremes. None of these values requires any more calculation
than averaging two adjacent numbers once a stem-and-leaf display has been constructed. Most can be found simply by counting in from the edges of that display (aided by the column of
"depths" on the stem-and-leaf display). Letter-value displays
usually also include a column labeled 'MID' holding the averages of the naturally paired fractiles and a column labeled
'SPREAD' holding the pairwise differences. The first provides
information about the center of the distribution and, in particular, indications of skewness. The second provides information about variability and can be used to characterize the
distribution itself (see Velleman and Hoaglin, Chapter 2).
Table 2 presents a letter-value display of kilocalories per
capita in one subdistrict over the entire study. We can immediately see the median (1086), the fourths (954 and 1272) and
so on up to the extremes (195 and 4522). The midpoints show a
consistent increase indicating skewness to the high end. The
spreads show a sudden jump at the extremes indicating a probable outlying value.

(ii) Simple Display and Analysis. In any large study it
is useful to monitor the data while the study is in progress.
Work in developing countries is often funded by a variety of
national and international agencies all of which expect
interim reports. Some EDA techniques are particularly well-
suited to interim monitoring and reporting. Among these are
letter-value displays, boxplots, coded tables, and suspended
rootograms. Each of these methods displays data in an informative and highly condensed way and each highlights the presence of outliers or unusual data values without permitting
them to destroy the display of the remainder of the data.

TABLE 2. *Letter-value Display kcal per Capita.*

Depth		Lower		Upper	Mid	Spread
N=	1290					
M	645.5		1086.0		1086.0	
F	323.0	954.0		1272.0	1113.0	318.0
E	162.0	715.0		1440.0	1077.5	725.0
D	81.5	636.0		1696.0	1166.0	1060.0
C	41.0	477.0		1908.0	1192.5	1431.0
B	21.0	369.0		2052.0	1210.5	1683.0
A	11.0	318.0		2333.0	1325.5	2015.0
Z	6.0	265.0		2544.0	1404.5	2279.0
Y	3.5	248.0		2641.0	1444.5	2393.0
X	2.0	198.0		2772.0	1485.0	2574.0
	1	195.0		4522.0	2358.5	4327.0

Boxplots are a simple and natural way to display data
partitioned into different categories on some other variable.
Technically, they offer a simple visual (and resistant) equivalent to a one-way Analysis of Variance. We have found that
even readers completely untrained in statistics will see
approximately the right things in a boxplot. Briefly, each
box in the display depicts the central 50% of the data. The
mark at the center of the box plots the median. The "whiskers"
emerging from the ends of the box extend either to the edges
of the data or as far as seems appropriate. Any points that
appear to be separated from the body of the data are plotted
individually as '*' for outliers and '0' for extreme outliers. (The specific algorithms used to identify these two
categories are specified by Tukey (1977) and by Velleman and
Hoaglin (1981).) The intervals indicated with pairs of parentheses are designed to be suitable as rough tests of the
equality of two of the medians at the 5% level.

Figure 2 offers an example. It plots staple food intake
(in Kilocalories per capita) in a survey round before the har-
vest (and thus a food stress period), according to the amount
of rice stocks reported to be on hand (four categories ranging
from "none" to "one week or more supply"). The fact that the
pattern is consistent with common sense -- households with
larger rice stocks are eating better--helps to confirm the
data. The pattern also provides a more complex (and more
powerful) background against which to search for anomalous
data. In particular those households appearing as outliers

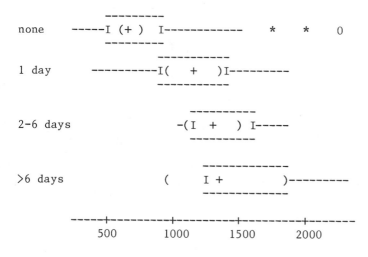

FIGURE 2. *Kcalories per capita by rice stocks.*

within their own categories (here households eating well despite low or nonexistant rice stocks) may deserve a second look.

Coded tables represent each number in a two-way table of numbers with one of seven coding symbols chosen to indicate the relative magnitudes of the numbers. By sweeping away the complexity of having many numbers to compare but leaving behind the general magnitudes and directions, coded tables often make patterns in the data easier to see. As with all EDA methods, they are resistant to the effects of outliers and will serve well to highlight extraordinary data values. Figure 3 includes a coded table.

Suspended rootograms provide a graphical and quantitative comparison of a distribution (e.g., in a histogram or stem-and-leaf display) to the Gaussian distribution. While one can learn to read the display easily, the theory behind this method is more complex than that behind the other EDA techniques discussed here. Readers are referred to Velleman and Hoaglin (1981) for details, examples, and computer programs.

(iii) Data Exploration Preparatory to Statistical Analyses. This is the "classical" application of exploratory data analysis. Data exploration is particularly important when the data are likely to have extraordinary or anomalous values interspersed within them, but is good practice in

almost all statistical analyses. Data exploration at this
stage will usually be performed on a computer. Fortunately,
these techniques are inexpensive computationally and will almost always be within the capabilities of the computers that
are available even when more sophisticated statistical techniques may not be. In addition to the techniques already discussed, we include under this heading three exploratory
methods that fit simple models to data: the resistant line,
non-linear data smoothing, and median polish. Following their
introduction by Tukey (1971), each of these methods has seen
additional statistical theory develop, so we now have a deeper
understanding of their performance as nonparametric statistical methods. The references given below point to some of
this work.

The resistant line is a nonparametric regression for y
against a single x. It retains all of its properties if x is
subject to error (rather than fixed and known exactly, as
classical least squares regression requires). Indeed, it is
resistant to the effects of errors in both y and x. (This
property is now known as having "bounded influence".) The
resistant line also carries with it a technique for assessing
nonlinearities in the data and for diagnosing simple transformations that might linearize the data. Johnstone and Velleman
(1982 and 1983) have derived the statistical properties of the
resistant line and determined its behavior in small samples.

Resistant non-linear data smoothing provides a collection
of techniques for dealing with time series or other sequenced
data. As with all EDA methods the techniques are resistant to
wild values (data spikes). Some theory has been provided by
Mallows (1980) and by Velleman (1980). Additional applications to the problem of assessing the need for transformations
to treat nonstationarity are discussed by Velleman (1982).

Median polish provides a resistant two-way additive decomposition of a table of responses. Briefly, it is an exploratory two-way analysis of variance. A median polish
decomposes a two-way table of values, $y(i,j)$, into the sum of
four quantities: a grand level, g, a row effect $r(i)$ for each
row, a column effect $c(j)$ for each column, and a residual
$e(i,j)$ for each cell:

$$y(i,j) = g + r(i) + c(j) + e(i,j) \qquad (*)$$

A median polish analysis is often especially useful for
stripping off the overall pattern of behavior so that underlying patterns and extraordinary values can be seen in the

residuals. Velleman and Hoaglin (1981) provide detailed descriptions, examples, and programs for the method.

Figure 3 illustrates a median polish with data from another socioeconomic survey performed in a rural province of the Philippines (Williamson, 1980). In the first table of Figure 3, the numbers in the original data table (not shown here) have been decomposed according to (*). The grand level, 14.34, is at the lower right. The right most column holds the row effects, the bottom row holds the column effects, and the body of the table holds the residuals. Following (*), we can reconstruct the original value of a cell (for example, the percentage of income derived from sale of livestock by those in the poorest income quartile) as the sum of four values at the corners of a square (for this example, 14.34 + 1.63 - 7.02 + 6.85 = 15.8%).

Because the main contribution of the median polish to this particular analysis is the removal of otherwise well-known patterns, the second table displays the residuals coded to represent their relative values. It is often easier to

Income Quartile	....*Sales of*:....					
	Wages	Livestock	Crops	Business	Misc.	
Poor ... 1	-37.03	6.85	26.67	-0.08	-4.13	1.63
2	-7.38	0.00	-1.18	7.08	1.62	0.08
3	7.38	-2.33	0.08	-4.66	0.58	-0.08
Rich ... 4	11.82	0.00	-0.08	0.08	-0.58	-2.11
	38.46	-7.02	6.86	0.0	-10.64	14.34

Coded Table of residuals

```
M  +  P  .  -
-  .  .  +  .
+  -  .  -  .
+  .  .  .  .
```

Key: Symbols in order from lowest to highest
            M = - . + # P

Where = is a "double minus", # is a "double plus", and M and P stand for MINUS and PLUS, respectively.

FIGURE 3.   Median polish analysis of household income (%) by source and income quartile

detect patterns in tables coded in this way than in tables of
numbers.

The marginal effects are not particularly interesting.
(The row effects have no interpretation at all because the
original table held row percentages. The column effects simply reflect the fact known to anyone acquainted with the data
that wages are the principal source of income.) The residuals, however, are somewhat more informative. Here we can see
that the profile for those in the lowest income quartile (1)
is actually quite different from that for other households.
In particular, these households receive far less income from
wages and more from sales, especially of crops. In this sample of poor and middle-class households, those with access to
wage-earning jobs tended to live in the provincial center.
The rural dwellers tended to be poorer and obtained the majority of their income from full-time labor in agriculture, usually on their own land.

IV. CONCLUSION

Field research in developing countries poses special
problems, many of which endanger the quality of the data
collected. Often it is also difficult to monitor data collection or check data automatically as it is collected. Exploratory Data Analysis provides a collection of tools that meet
many of these problems. EDA methods are resistant to the
effects of extraordinary observations. They are often easy to
compute by hand and can usually be taught to people who lack
college-level mathematics training. They provide graphical
displays that are easy to interpret and that are designed to
highlight extraordinary data points. Finally, EDA methods can
provide a valuable first step in standard statistical analyses. In addition to being computable by hand, EDA methods
are now readily available on a wide variety of computers in
several languages. They are generally inexpensive computationally, even for moderately large sets of data. Often they
can be placed on inexpensive microcomputers.

EDA methods have been used in teaching statistics for the
past ten years. Only more recently has their value to research been widely recognized. We expect to see their use in
applications such as those discussed here expand in the coming
years.

REFERENCES

Casley, D. J. and Lury, D. A. (1981). *Data Collection in Developing Countries*, Clarendon Press, Oxford.

Hampel, F. R. (1971). "A Qualitative Definition of Robustness," *Annals of Mathematical Statistics, 42*, 1887-1898.

Johnstone, I. and Velleman, P. F. (1982). "Tukey's Resistant Line and Related Methods: Asymptotics and Algorithms," *Proceedings of the Statistical Computing Section, 1981, American Statistical Association*, 218-223.

Johnstone, I. and Velleman, P. F. (1983). "The Resistant Line and Related Regression Methods," Technical Report 0483/026, Department of Economic and Social Statistics. Cornell University, Ithaca, N. Y.

Mallows, C. L. (1980). "Some Theory of Nonlinear Smoothers," *Annals of Statistics, 8*, 645-715.

Tukey, J. W. (1971). *Exploratory Data Analysis, Limited Preliminary Edition*, Ann Arbor, Michigan: University Microfilms.

Tukey, J. W. (1977). *Exploratory Data Analysis*, Addison-Wesley, New York.

Velleman, P. F. (1980). "Definition and Comparison of Nonlinear Data Smoothers," *Journal of American Statistical Association, 75*, 609-615.

Velleman, P. F. (1982). "Applied Nonlinear Smoothing," in Samuel Leinhardt (ed.), *Sociological Methodology, 1982*, Jossey-Bass, San Francisco.

Velleman, P. F. and Hoaglin, D. C. (1981). *Applications, Basics, and Computing of Exploratory Data Analysis*, Duxbury Press, Boston.

Williamson, D. F. (1980). "Utilization of MSG and its Potential as a Vehicle for Vitamin A Fortification in Two Provinces of the Phillippines," M. S. Thesis, Cornell University, Ithaca, N. Y.

APPLICATION OF PATTERN RECOGNITION
TECHNIQUES TO DATA ANALYSIS

R. C. Gonzalez

Electrical Engineering Department
The University of Tennessee
Knoxville, Tennessee

1. INTRODUCTION

The principal approaches to pattern recognition system design are briefly surveyed, with an emphasis on data analysis applications.

As used in this article, a *pattern* is a quantitative or qualitative description of an entity of interest (e.g., a signal derived from a sensor), while a *pattern class* is a set of patterns that share some common properties. The subject matter of pattern recognition deals with techniques for assigning patterns to their respective classes--automatically and with as little human intervention as possible.

Several major information transition processes take place between the time a pattern is input and a decision is made by the recognition system. These processes, which are summarized in block diagram form in Figure 1, extract from the input data the discriminatory information required for classification. The functions of the blocks shown in Figure 1 are briefly discussed as follows.

The sensor is simply the measurement device which transforms the input patterns into a form suitable for machine manipulation. Although some simple pattern recognition systems operate on the input data directly from the sensor, it is common practice to follow the sensor with a preprocessor and feature extractor. The preprocessor removes unnecessary or corrupting elements from the measured data, while the feature extractor extracts from the preprocessed data the features required for classification.

STATISTICAL METHODS
AND THE IMPROVEMENT OF DATA QUALITY

193

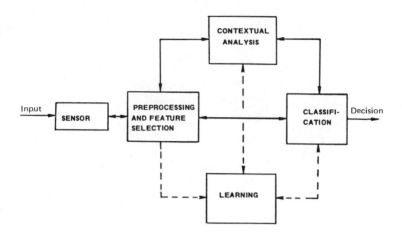

FIGURE 1.   Elements of a pattern recognition system.

The feature extraction process is often followed by contextual analysis in order to enhance the information content
present in a pattern.   Contextual analysis is used to detect
the occurrence of a certain sequence of important features.
In complex situations, such as the recognition of spoken
words, it is essential to take into account the context in
which the pattern (i.e., word) to be classified is being
used.   The results of the contextual analysis process are finally fed into the classification stage whose function is to
combine all the information extracted from the input pattern
and then arrive at a decision concerning the class membership
of that pattern.

In the above discussion it has been implicitly assumed
that the system "knows" the information processing operations
that must be performed on an input pattern in order to arrive
at a decision.   Although the general form of these operations
is specified by the system designer, each specific operation
is in most cases characterized by variable parameters which
must be adapted to a given pattern recognition problem.   The
adjustment of these parameters is usually carried out by uti-
lizing sample patterns in what is called a *learning* or *training* process (Tou and Gonzalez, 1974).

Machine learning techniques may be subdivided into two
principal categories: (1) *supervised* and (2) *unsupervised* (Tou
and Gonzalez, 1974).   In a supervised learning situation, the
system parameters are estimated by algorithms which utilize
training sample patterns whose class membership is specified
externally by the system designer.   In this manner, the unknown parameters are adjusted to fit a situation where the

pattern classes are specified and characterized by representative samples. Clearly, the ultimate success of this approach is dictated by the quality of the sample set used to train the pattern recognition system.

The unsupervised learning approach is used when there is little or no *a priori* knowledge about the pattern classes of a given problem. In essence, this approach attempts to extract the pattern classes present in a set of data in which the classification of the available sample patterns is not completely known. One of the tools most often used in unsupervised recognition is cluster analysis (Anderberg, 1973).

The learning process described above is shown as a dotted stage in Figure 1. This representation is adopted to indicate that learning may, but need not, be an integral part of the routine operation of a pattern recognition system. For example, a system that has been designed using a reasonably complete set of representative samples needs to be subjected to further learning only for updating purposes. On the other hand, a system that operates in a dynamic environment where the nature of the pattern classes changes rapidly may require continuous learning in order to perform satisfactorily (Gonzalez and Howington, 1977).

Approaches to pattern recognition system design may be divided into three principal categories: (1) the heuristic approach, (2) the decision-theoretic approach, and (3) the syntactic (structural) approach (Tou and Gonzalez, 1974; Gonzalez and Thomason, 1978). These approaches are discussed in the following sections.

II. HEURISTIC APPROACH

This approach deals with the development of models which attempt to duplicate in some sense the recognition processes employed by humans or other "intelligent" organisms. Since these processes are far from being fully understood, heuristic approaches to pattern recognition generally consist of a set of ad hoc procedures designed to perform specific recognition tasks. Consider, for example, the design of a pattern recognition system for classifying handwritten characters. The decision-performing logic of such a system can be based on the number, position, and spatial relationships of the strokes composing each character. This logic is clearly of a heuristic nature since the system designer must specify, based on

intuition and experience, how the components of a character
are evaluated to arrive at a decision.

Another example of the heuristic approach is found in
many automatic electrocardiogram interpretation systems. In
this case the problem is one of developing a system which
arrives at decisions by following as closely as possible the
process employed by a physician in interpreting an EKG. Thus,
the performance of such a system is almost entirely dependent
on how well it can imitate the physician's capability to
detect and interpret significant events in an EKG record.

III. DECISION-THEORETIC APPROACH

In the decision-theoretic approach, patterns are
represented in the form of column vectors, $\underline{x} = (x_1, x_2, \ldots, x_n)^T$,
where x_i is the ith measurement or feature extracted from a
given entity. For example the signal shown in Figure 2, if
sampled at discrete points $t_1, t_2, \ldots, t_n$, yields a pattern
vector simply by letting $x_i = f(t_i)$.

As a way of introduction to the decision-theoretic
approach, Figure 3 shows two pattern populations where each
point represents a two-dimensional pattern vector
$\underline{x} = (x_1, x_2)^T$. It is seen in this figure that the two classes
are easily separable by a straight line. Let $d(\underline{x}) = w_1 x_1 +
w_2 x_2 + w_3 = 0$ be the equation of a separating line where the
w's are parameters and x_1, x_2 are the general pattern
coordinate variables. It is clear from the figure that any
pattern $\underline{x}$ belonging to class ω_1 will yield a positive quantity
when substituted into $d(\underline{x})$. Similarly, $d(\underline{x})$ becomes negative
upon substitution of any pattern from class ω_2. Therefore,
$d(\underline{x})$ can be used as a *decision* (or *discriminant*) *function*
since, given a pattern $\underline{x}$ of unknown classification, we may say
that $\underline{x}$ belongs to class ω_1 if $d(\underline{x}) > 0$ or to ω_2 if $d(\underline{x}) < 0$.
If the pattern lies in the separating boundary, we obtain the
indeterminate condition $d(\underline{x}) = 0$.

When there are more than two classes, one approach is to
establish M decision functions $d_1(\underline{x})$, $d_2(\underline{x})$, ..., $d_M(\underline{x})$ with

the property that if a pattern $\underline{x}$ belongs to class ω_i, then

$$d_i(\underline{x}) > d_j(\underline{x}) \qquad j = 1,2,\ldots,M; \; j \neq i$$

where M is the number of classes. This equation specifies a decision rule in which each pattern to be classified is substituted into all decision functions. The pattern is then assigned to the class whose decision function yields the largest numerical value. Ties are resolved arbitrarily.

The above concepts need not be restricted to two-dimensional patterns and linear decision boundaries. In the n-dimensional case the decision functions may be expressed in the general form

$$d_k(\underline{x}) = \sum_{\ell=1}^{K} w_{k\ell} \; \phi_\ell(\underline{x}) \qquad k = 1,\,2,\ldots,\,M$$

where the $\{\phi_\ell(\underline{x})\}$ are real, single-valued functions of the pattern $\underline{x}$, and $\{w_{k\ell}\}$ are the coefficients of the decision function corresponding to class ω_k. This equation is quite general in the sense that it can represent a variety of very complex decision functions in n-dimensional space.

The usual approach in employing this formulation is to first specify the functions $\{\phi_\ell(\underline{x})\}$. The problem then becomes one of determining the coefficients $\{w_{k\ell}\}$ for each class. The decision-theoretic approach to pattern recognition deals with algorithms for estimating these parameters using sample patterns in a training process. Thus, if the pattern recognition system performs well during training with a well-chosen set of representative patterns, it may be expected to perform satisfactorily when confronted with "field" data during normal operation.

There exist numerous adaptive algorithms which can be used for training a pattern recognition system. These algorithms can be divided into (1) deterministic, and (2) statistical procedures (Tou and Gonzalez, 1974; Fukunaga, 1972). As evidenced by this breakdown, deterministic algorithms deal with the estimation of the decision function coefficients directly from patterns without resorting to statistical considerations, while statistical algorithms are based on the statistical properties of the various pattern

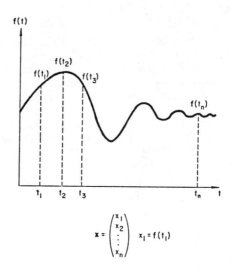

FIGURE 2.   *Example of how a pattern vector is generated.*

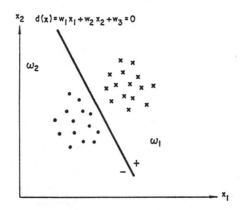

FIGURE 3.   *Two disjoint pattern populations.*

populations under consideration. One of the oldest approaches
to statistical pattern recognition is based on the Bayes decision rule, which is optimum in the sense that it minimizes the
average loss in classification. The principal drawback of
this formulation is that it requires detailed knowledge of the
probability density function of each class.   While this is a
manageable problem with one-dimensional patterns, density estimation techniques for multivariate data present significant
difficulties.

Although optimum techniques for deterministic classification are not nearly as well developed as statistical methods,
considerable progress has been made in recent years in the
formulation of algorithms for obtaining optimum (minimum-
error) decision functions without resorting to statistical
concepts (Gonzalez and Clark, 1981).

IV. SYNTACTIC APPROACH

The decision-theoretic approach discussed in the previous
section is ideally suited for applications where patterns can
be meaningfully represented in the form of numerical quantities. There are applications, however, where the structure of
a pattern plays a central role in the classification process.
In these situations the decision-theoretic approach suffers
from serious drawbacks because it lacks a suitable formalism
for handling pattern structures and their relationships. Scene
analysis is a good example where the decision-theoretic approach finds few applications since in this case the structure
and relationships of the various components of a scene are of
fundamental importance in establishing a meaningful recognition scheme.

The syntactic (the terms *linguistic, structural,* and
grammatical are also often used) approach to pattern recognition has been receiving increased attention during the past
few years because it possesses the structure-handling capability lacked by the decision-theoretic approach (Gonzalez and
Thomason, 1978).   Syntactic pattern recognition is based on
concepts from formal language theory, whose origin may be
traced to the middle 1950s with the development by Noam
Chomsky of mathematical models of grammars related to his work
in natural languages. One of the original goals of the work
of linguists working in this area was to develop mathematical
models capable of describing natural languages such as
English. The hope was that, if this could be done, it would

be a relatively simple matter to "teach" computers to interpret natural languages for the purposes of translation and
problem solving. Although it is generally agreed that these
expectations have been unrealized thus far, spinoffs of research in this area have had a significant impact on other
fields such as compiler design, computer languages, automata
theory and, more recently, pattern recognition.

    Basic to the syntactic pattern recognition approach is
the decomposition of patterns into subpatterns or primitives.
Figure 4(b) shows such a decomposition where the patterns
shown are expressed in terms of the primitives shown in Figure
4(a) to yield the string abcbabdbabcbabdb for the submedian
chromosome and the string ebabcbab for the telocentric chromosome.

    Suppose that we interpret each primitive as being a *word*
permissible in some grammar, where a *grammar* is simply a set
of rules of syntax for the generation of *sentences* from the
given words. These sentences certainly could consist of
strings of words such as the ones associated with the chromosome structures described above. It is further possible to
envision two grammars G_1 and G_2 whose rules allow the generation of sentences which correspond to submedian and telocentric chromosomes, respectively. Thus, the language $L(G_1)$
generated by G_1 would consist of sentences representing submedian chromosomes and the language $L(G_2)$ generated by G_2 of
sentences representing telocentric chromosomes.

    Once the two grammars G_1 and G_2 have been established,
the syntactic pattern recognition process is in principle
quite simple. Given a sentence representing an input pattern,
the problem is one of deciding over which language the input
sentence represents a valid sentence. Thus, if the sentence
belongs to $L(G_1)$, we say that the input is a submedian chromosome. If it belongs to $L(G_2)$ we say that it is a telocentric
chromosome. A unique decision cannot be made if the sentence
belongs to both languages. If the sentence is found to be
invalid over both $L(G_1)$ and $L(G_2)$, the input pattern is
assigned to a rejection class consisting of all invalid patterns.

    In the M-class case, the syntactic classification ap-
proach is the same as that described above, with the exception
that there are M grammars involved in the process. In this
case, a pattern is uniquely assigned to the ith class if it is
a sentence of only $L(G_i)$ and no other language. A unique

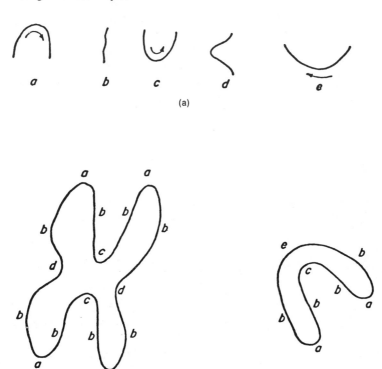

(a)

abcbabdbabcbabdb   ebabcbab

(b)

FIGURE 4.   (a) Pattern primitives, and (b) coded patterns.

decision cannot be made if the sentence belongs to more than
one language. And, as above, if a pattern is not a sentence
of any of the languages under consideration, it is assigned to
a rejection class.

A grammar is defined as the fourtuple

$$G = (N, \Sigma, P, S)$$

where

    N = set of nonterminals (variables),
    Σ = set of terminals (constants),
    P = set of productions or rewriting rules, and
    S = start symbol.

In pattern recognition, the set Σ contains the pattern primitives, and P is the set of rules which allow generation of the
pattern structures that form the language (i.e., pattern
class) L(G).

As an illustration of the syntactic approach, Figure 5
shows a typical normal human EKG. The smaller of the heart's
muscles, the *atria*, are stimulated first with a p pulse; the
subsequent stimulation of the larger muscles, the *ventricles*,
produces a larger r pulse followed by a t pulse as the ventricles repolarize after the pumping action. The regularity
of this class of normal waveforms may be described by a grammar of the form shown above with N = {S,A,B,C,D,E,H} and Σ =
{p,r,t,b} where p,r, and t are the waveforms just discussed

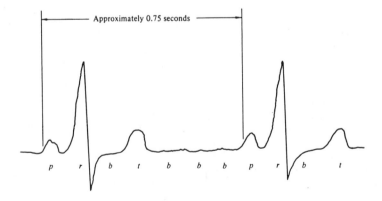

FIGURE 5. *Normal human EKG.*

and b represents units of quiescent time. The production
rules are

$$
\begin{array}{lll}
S \rightarrow pA & A \rightarrow rB & B \rightarrow bC \\
C \rightarrow tD & D \rightarrow b & D \rightarrow bE \\
E \rightarrow b & E \rightarrow bH & E \rightarrow pA \\
H \rightarrow b & H \rightarrow bS & H \rightarrow pA
\end{array}
$$

Starting with S and using these rules one can easily generate,
for instance, the string of symbols prbtbbbprbtbb, which corresponds to a waveform similar to the one shown in Figure 5.

In the actual recognition process, a pattern is coded
using the primitives and the objective is to determine the
class membership of the coded structure. One basic approach
to this problem is to generate an automaton for each grammar
(this is a straightforward procedure once a grammar is
known). Then, given a pattern, the recognition is accomplished by determining which automaton is capable of accepting
the given input (Gonzalez and Thomason, 1978). In other
words, an automaton corresponding to grammar G_i accepts a
given input pattern only if that pattern belongs to $L(G_i)$.

V. SUMMARY

In this article we have briefly reviewed and illustrated
the principal approaches to pattern recognition system design,
with an emphasis on data analysis.

Because of its broad range of applications, pattern recognition is an active area of work in a variety of fields, such
as defense, health care, and industrial automation.

The references provide an entry point to the literature on
pattern recognition theory and applications.

REFERENCES

Anderberg, M.R. (1973). *Cluster Analysis for Applications.*
     Academic Press, New York.
Fukunaga, K. (1972). *Introduction to Statistical Pattern
     Recognition.* Academic Press, New York.

Gonzalez, R.C. and Clark, D.C. (1981). "Optimal Solution of
    Linear Inequalities," *IEEE Trans. Pattern Anal. Mach.
    Intelligence*, Vol. PAMI-3, no. 6, 643-655.
Gonzalez, R.C. and Howington, L.C. (1977). "Machine
    Recognition of Abnormal Behavior in Nuclear Reactors,"
    IEEE Trans. Systems, Man and Cybernetics, Vol. SMC-7,
    no. 10, 717-728.
Gonzalez, R.C. and Thomason, M.G. (1978). *Syntactic Pattern
    Recognition: An Introduction*. Addison-Wesley, Reading,
    Massachusetts.
Tou, J.T. and Gonzalez, R.C. (1974). *Pattern Recognition
    Principles*. Addison-Wesley, Reading, Massachusetts.

CAN AUTOMATIC DATA EDITING BE JUSTIFIED?
ONE PERSON'S OPINION

Gunar Liepins

Energy Division
Oak Ridge National Laboratory
Oak Ridge, Tennessee

I. INTRODUCTION

Automatic Data Editing is the process whereby multivariate
data records are checked for consistency and, if found to be inconsistent, are analyzed to determine the most likely combination
of variables responsible for the inconsistency. Values are then
imputed to those suspect variables to render the resultant record
consistent. This procedure is done automatically, that is, on a
computer according to a pre-established code, and, most commonly,
the data so analyzed have been collected in response to a survey.

Three primary issues arise in the application of automatic
data editing: (1) Is the procedure based on sound theoretical
principles? (2) Is the procedure practical to implement? (3) Has
the procedure been justified in applications? This paper suggests that these questions cannot yet be unequivocally answered
in the affirmative; much additional research and empirical
follow-up are required. Directions for this additional work are
suggested.

II. THE GENERAL EDITING PROCEDURE

At present, although governmental agencies and private industry both mount massive data collection efforts, the collected
data are nonetheless often inconsistent and incomplete. Political issues aside, if the data warrant collection, they should be
accurate and complete relative to their intended purpose and subject to the practical limitations of time and funds. If the data
are to be published then, at the very least, they should be

STATISTICAL METHODS
AND THE IMPROVEMENT OF DATA QUALITY   205

accompanied by the following: (1) clear documentation of their
derivation, (2) guidelines of appropriate use, (3) statement of
limitations, and (4) documented audit trail for any data revisions.

The effort expended to ensure the accuracy and completeness
of the data should be commensurate first with the data's importance and second with the sensitivity of the analyses and policies based on the data to errors in the data. Unfortunately,
these criteria are rarely established, and the data custodian is
left with the sweeping tasks of characterizing data accuracy and
identifying and resolving inconsistencies - in short, editing the
data.

Data editing can be classified into one of two broad categories: automatic and judgmental. Automatic data editing is
based on a fixed set of rules and offers the advantage of explic-
itness and repeatability. Moreover, the term currently is identified with computerization. Automatic data editing's merit and
appropriateness can be debated (sometimes even analyzed mathema-
tically) in terms of its underlying assumptions. On the other
hand, judgmental editing, if carefully applied and based on in-
sightful experience, although not explicit or necessarily repeat-
able, may avoid the patently unrealistic results sometimes suggested by automatic methods. Thus, ideally it might be best to
blend the two: First edit the data automatically. Next, judg-
mentally review selected pairs (original record, modified record)
for reasonableness. Finally, whenever possible, it would be desirable to monitor the editing procedure through a comparison
with a sample of call-backs. A complete audit trail should always be kept.

III. AUTOMATIC DATA EDITING

As suggested in the previous paragraphs, automatic data editing is a three step process: (1) check the data records for
consistency, (2) analyze the inconsistent records to determine
the inconsistent variables, (3) impute consistent values to the
faulty variables. Do this automatically, that is, on a computer
according to a prescribed code.

Automatic data editing has broad potential application, and
is particularly suited to survey data such as an institutional
building's database consisting of energy use data and building
characteristics for about 15,000 buildings (Hirst, Carney, and

Knight, 1981). Although this is the best such data, every data record (string of variable values - window area, building orientation, square footage, etc.) has detectable internal inconsistencies (for example, window area reported greater than wall area) that cannot currently be resolved with any degree of certainty without a complete resurvey.

Generally, automatic data editing is an appropriate technique whenever (1) the database is subject to a substantial number of inconsistencies, (2) omission of the inconsistent records severely restricts the usefulness of the data (either because of suspected resultant biases due to the omissions or because of insufficient remaining data), and (3) manual follow-up of the inconsistencies with the respondents (call-backs) is either impossible or financially or temporally impractical. In such situations, the ultimate goal of automatic data editing is to reconstruct as many of the statistical properties of the true data as possible. Short of that, identification of the inconsistencies is useful per se to provide a rough indication of data reliability.

It is important to stress that data should not be capriciously revised, and that regardless of the revisions made, the original data should be retrievable. Finally, the application of automatic data editing raises three central issues: (1) Is the procedure theoretically sound? (2) Is the procedure practical to implement? (3) Has the procedure been tested and justified in application?

IV. JUSTIFIABILITY OF AUTOMATIC DATA EDITING

Although modest progress has been made in automatic data editing research, the broad interdisciplinary scope of very difficult and sometimes less (theoretically) attractive problems, the lack of a disciplinary identity, the need for coordination between theoretical and empirical studies, the difficulty and expense of empirical follow-up, and the meager funding of automatic data editing studies have slowed the progress of this research. Thus, by and large, "only selectively" is the best presently available answer to the three questions raised in the previous paragraph, as well as the question in the title of this paper; automatic data editing has not yet been broadly shown to be statistically sound.

In more detail, selected theoretical and applied studies
have been undertaken to establish the validity of automatic data
editing. These have introduced maximum likelihood, Bayesian, and
other distributional techniques,[a] (Chernick and Murthy, 1983;
Liepins and Pack, 1980, 1981; Naus, Johnson, and Montalvo, 1972;
and Rubin, 1976, 1978a, 1978b), have compared techniques actually
used with theoretically optimal techniques, and have investigated
diagnostic statistics (Greenberg, 1982 and Sande, 1976b).
Additional analyses have directly compared applied techniques,
and evaluated their efficacy by simulation (Bailar and Bailar,
1978; Cox and Folsom, 1978; Evans, Cooley, and Piserchia, 1979;
Freund and Hartley, 1967). A certain basis of experience with
automatic data editing methods has also been established,
especially at the U.S. Census Bureau and at Statistics Canada
(Ashraf and Macredie, 1978; Graves, 1976; Hill, 1978; Johnson,
Naus, and Chu, 1971; Liepins, et al, 1979; Mendelssohn, 1955;
Minton, 1969; Naus, 1975; Nordbotten, 1965; O'Reagan, 1969 and
1972; Pritzken, Ogus, and Hansen, 1965; Stuart, 1966; and
Szameitat and Zindler, 1965). Finally, research has been
directed at developing useful, efficient algorithms (Abadie,
1964; Bolour, 1979; Burger, 1956; Burkhard, 1973; Chernikova,
1964 and 1965; Duffin, 1974; Felligi and Holt, 1976; Friedman,
Bentley, and Finkel, 1977; Galperin, 1976; Garfinkel, 1979;
Geoffrion and Marsten, 1972; Greenberg, 1981; Hirsch and Dantzig,
1968; Kohler, 1967; Kruskal and Sankoff, 1982; Liepins, Garfinkel
and Kunnathur, 1982; Liepins, 1981a and 1981b; Matheiss and
Rubin, 1980; McKeown, 1973, 1975, 1981 and 1982; Rivest, 1974;
Rubin, 1972, 1975a, 1975b, and 1977; Sande, 1976a; and Walker,
1976. Nonetheless, in the opinion of this author, even these
efforts have not yet been sufficient to firmly establish
automatic data editing as a proven, broadly applicable,
well-understood, predictable, data analysis tool. Much
additional research is needed to fully understand its
consequences. For example, it would be useful and interesting to
have the following: 1. Estimates of what proportion of the
inconsistent data were correctly handled; 2. Estimates of the
discrepancy between the distribution of the (unknown) true data
and the revised data; and 3. Tests to guide the choice of
editing procedure to be used.

[a]The author openly acknowledges the incompleteness of the following references. These cited are intended only to introduce the
reader to the literature. Certainly, much equally good and
relevant work remains uncited.

Ideally, automatic data editing would begin with exploratory data analysis. This analysis would be directed at discovering as much as possible about the data and error structure. (Checks for duplicate records, for uniqueness of record identifier, for traceability from year to year, would also all be made.) Then, this knowledge of the error structure would guide the choice automatic data editing method to be employed. Next, estimates of the consequences of editing would be useful. Control, through a sample of call-backs would complete the process.

V. DIRECTIONS FOR FURTHER RESEARCH

Fundamental research should be directed toward a "theory of errors." Basic principles such as the maximal entropy principle and invariance under transformation groups should be investigated for the purpose of "allowing the data to speak for themselves," reducing the arbitrariness of present automatic data editing techniques, and guiding the choice of the techniques to be used (Ables, 1974; Dolby, 1977; Jaynes, 1957a, 1957b, 1968, 1977, 1979a and 1979b; Jeffreys, 1938; and Wickmann, 1963). It should not be surprising that such pure theoretical research might some-times suggest data analyses that are impractical in application. Hence, applied research is also needed. This research should be directed at reducing the fundamental theoretical results to effi-cient, practical, implementable algorithms that are able to rapidly process large data sets. Ideally, the compromise between theory and operational techniques could be understood and bounded. Finally, automatic data editing should be tested under controlled conditions. The techniques should be used with test survey data that are corrected by exhaustive call-backs. This would provide empirical evidence of the efficacy of the techniques. Such a research program in conjunction with publication of practical experiences in accessible open literature, would establish the theoretical underpinnings for automatic data editing and would provide empirical evidence of the success of the techniques employed.

REFERENCES

Abadie, J. (1964). "The Dual to Fourier's Method for Solving Linear Inequalities," *International Symposium on Mathematical Programming*, London.

Ables, J. G. (1974). "Maximum Entropy Spectral Analysis,"
    Astron. Astrophys. Suppl., 15, 383-393.
Ashraf, A. and Macredie, I. (1978). "Edit and Imputation in the
    Labor Force Survey," *Imputation and Editing of Faulty or
    Missing Survey Data,* 114-119, U.S. Department of Commerce.
Bailar, J. C. and Bailar, B. A. (1978). "Comparison of Two
    Procedures for Imputing Missing Survey Values," *Imputation
    and Editing of Faulty or Missing Data,* 65-75, U.S.
    Department of Commerce.
Bolour, A. (1979). "Optimality Properties of Multiple-Key
    Hashing Functions," *Journal of ACM, 26, #2,* 196-210.
Burger, E. (1956). "Uber Homogene Lineare Ungleichungssysteme,"
    Z. Angew. Math. Mech., Bd 36, Nr. 3/4, 135-139.
Burkhard, W. A. (1973). "Some Approaches to Best-Match File
    Searching," *Communications of ACM, 6, #4,* 231-236.
Chernick, M. R. and Murthy, V. K. (1983). "The Use of Influence
    Functions for Outlier Detection and Data Editing," *American
    Journal of Mathematical and Management Sciences,* to appear.
Chernikova, N. V. (1964). "Algorithm for Finding a General
    Formula for the Nonnegative Solutions of a System of Linear
    Equations," *USSR Comput. Math. Phys., 4, #4-6:* 151-158.
Chernikova, N. V. (1965). "Algorithm for Finding a General
    Formula for the Nonnegative Solutions of a System of Linear
    Inequalities," *USSR Comput. Math. Phys. 5, #1-3:* 228-233.
Cox, B. G. and Folsom, R. E. (1978). "An Empirical Investigation
    of Alternative Item Nonresponse Adjustments," *Imputation and
    Editing of Faulty or Missing Survey Data,* 51-55, U.S.
    Department of Commerce.
Dolby, J. L. (1977). "On the Notions of Ambiguity and Informa-
    tion Loss," *Information Processing and Management, 1,* 69-77.
Duffin, R. J. (1974). "On Fourier's Analysis of Linear
    Inequality Systems," *Mathematical Programming Study, 1,*
    71-95.
Evans, R. W., Cooley, P. C. and Piserchia, P. V. (1979). "A
    Test for Evaluating Missing Data Imputation Procedures,"
    *Proceedings of the Social Statistics Section of the American
    Statistical Association,* 469-474.
Felligi, I. P. and Holt, D. (1976). "A Systematic Approach to
    Automatic Edit and Imputation," *J. Am. Stat. Assoc. 71,
    #353:* 17-35.
Freund, R. J. and Hartley, H. O. (1967). "A Procedure for
    Automatic Data Editing," *J. Am. Stat. Assoc., 62, #318,*
    341-352.
Friedman, J. H., Bentley, J. L. and Finkel, R. A. (1977).
    "An Algorithm for Finding Best Matches in Logarithmic
    Expected Time," *ACM Trans. on Math Software, 3, #3:* 205-226.
Galperin, A. M. (1976). "The General Solution of a Finite System
    of Linear Inequalities," *Mathematics of Operations Research,
    1, #2,* 185-196.

Garfinkel, R. S. (1979). "An Algorithm for Optimal Imputation of
Erroneous Data," Working Paper No. 83, College of Business
Administration, University of Tennessee.

Geoffrion, A. M. and Marsten, R. E. (1972). "Integer Programming
Algorithms: A Framework and State-of-the-Art Survey,"
Management Science, 18, 465-491.

Graves, R. P. (1976). "CAN-EDIT, A Generalized Edit and
Imputation System in a Data Base Environment," A report to
the working party on Electronic Data Processing, Conference
of European Statisticians.

Greenberg, B. (1981). "Developing an Edit System for Industrial
Statistics," *Computer Science and Statistics: Proceedings
of the 13th Symposium on the Interface,* 13-16.

Greenberg, B. (1982). "Using an Edit System to Develop Editing
Specifications," *Proceedings of the Survey Sampling Research
Section, American Statistical Association,* 366-371.

Hill, Christopher J. (1978). "A Report on the Application of a
Systematic Method of Automatic Edit and Imputation to the
1976 Canadian Census," presented at the Annual Meeting of
the American Statistical Association, San Diego, California.

Hirsch, W. M. and Dantzig, G. B. (1968). "The Fixed Charge
Problem," *Naval Research Logistics Quarterly, 15,* 413-424.

Hirst, E. A., Carney, T., and Knight, P. (1981). "Energy Use of
Institutional Buildings Disaggregate Data and Data
Management Issues, ORNL/CON-73.

Jaynes, E. T. (1957a). "Information Theory and Statistical
Mechanics," *Physical Review, 106, #4,* 620-630.

Jaynes, E. T. (1957b). "Information Theory and Statistical
Mechanics," *Physical Review, 108, #2,* 171-190.

Jaynes, E. T. (1968). "Prior Probabilities," *IEEE Transactions
on Systems Science and Cybernetics, SSC-4, #3,* 227-248.

Jaynes, E. T. (1979a). "What is the Question," International
Meeting on Bayesian Statistics in Walencia, Spain.

Jaynes, E. T. (1979b). "Concentration of Distributions at
Entropy Maxima," presented at the *Nineteenth NBER-NSF
Seminar on Bayesian Statistics,* Montreal.

Jeffreys, H. (1938). "The Law of Error and the Combination of
Observations," *Philosophical Transactions of the Royal
Society, 237,* 231-271.

Johnson, T. G., Naus, J. I. and Chu, R. T. (1971). *Data
Validation Handbook,* GEOMET Report No. IF-69-1, GEOMET,
Inc.

Kohler, D. A. (1967). "Projections of Convex Polyhedral Sets,"
Doctoral Thesis Operations Research Center, ORC 67-29,
University of California, Berkeley.

Kruskal, J. B. and Sankoff, D. (eds.) (1982). *Time Warps,
String Edits, and Macromolecules: Theory and Practice
and Sequence Comparison,* To appear, (Bell Labs.).

Liepins, G. E., et al. (1979). "Data Analytic Tools in Support of Data Validation," unpublished report.

Liepins, G. E. (1980). "A Rigorous Systematic Approach to Automatic Data Editing and Its Statistical Basis," *Oak Ridge National Laboratory*/TM-7126.

Liepins, G. E. and Pack, D. J. (1980). "An Integrated Approach to Automatic Data Editing," *Proceedings of the American Statistical Association, Survey Research Section,* 777-781.

Liepins, G. E. and Pack, D. J. (1981). "Maximum Posterior Probability Error Localization," *Proceedings of the American Statistical Association, Survey Research Section,* 192-195.

Liepins, G. E. (1981a). "Algorithms for Error Localization of Discrete Data," ORNL/TM-8183.

Liepins, G. E. (1981b). "Fourier-Motzkin Elimination for Mixed Systems," ORNL/TM-8659.

Liepins, G. E., Garfinkel, R. S. and Kunnathur, A. S. (1982). "Error Localization for Erroneous Data: A Survey," *TIMS/Studies in the Management Sciences, 10,* 205-219.

Matheiss, T. J. and Rubin, D. S. (1980). "A Survey and Comparison of Methods for Finding All Vertices of Convex Polyhedral Sets," *Mathematics of Operations Research, 5, #2,* 167-185.

McKeown, P. G. (1973). "An Extreme Point Ranking Algorithm for Solving the Linear Fixed Charge Problem," Ph.D. Dissertation, The University of North Carolina.

McKeown, P. G. (1975). "A Vertex Ranking Algorithm for the Linear Fixed Charge Problem," *Operations Research, 23,* 1183-1191.

McKeown, P. G. (1981). "A Branch and Bound Approach to Solving Fixed Charge Problems," *Naval Research Logistics Quarterly, 28,* 607-617.

McKeown, P. G. (1982). "A Mathematical Programming Approach to Editing of Economic Survey Data," Unpublished paper, University of Georgia, Athens.

Mendelssohn, R. C. (1955). "Machine Methods in Employment Statistics," *Mon. Labor Rev., 78, #5,* 567-69.

Minton, G. (1969). "Inspection and Correction Error in Data Processing," *J. Am. Stat. Assoc., 64, #328,* 1257-75.

Naus, J. I., Johnson, T. G. and Montalvo, R. (1972). "A Probabilistic Model for Identifying Errors in Data Editing," *J. Am. Stat. Assoc., 67, #340,* 843-850.

Naus, J. I. (1975). *Data Quality Control and Editing Statistics: Text-Books and Monographs, 10,* Marcel Dekker, New York.

Nordbotten, S. (1965). "The Efficiency of Automatic Detection and Correction of Errors in Individual Observation as Compared with Other Means for Improving the Quality of Statistics," *International Statistical Review, 41,* 417-40.

O'Reagan, R. T. (1969). "Relative Costs of Computerized
   Error Inspection Plans," *J. Am. Stat. Assoc.*, *64*, *#328*,
   1245-55.
O'Reagan, R. T. (1972). "Practical Techniques for Computer
   Editing of Magnitude Data," U.S. Department of Commerce,
   Bureau of the Census.
Pritzker, L., Ogus, J. and Hansen, M. H. (1965). "Computer
   Editing Methods - Some Applications and Results,"
   International Statistical Review, *41*, 442-72.
Rivest, R. L. (1974). "Partial Match Retrieval Algorithms," *SIAM
   J. Comput.*, *5*, *#1*, 19-50.
Rubin, D. S. (1972). "Neighboring Vertices on Convex Polyhedral
   Sets," University of North Carolina paper.
Rubin, D. S. (1975a). "Vertex Generation and Cardinality
   Constrained Linear Programs," *Operations Research*, *23*,
   #3, 555-565.
Rubin, D. S. (1975b). "Vertex Generation and Linear
   Complementary Problems," University of North Carolina paper.
Rubin, D. S. (1977). "Vertex Generation Methods for Problems
   with Logical Constraints," *Ann. Discrete Math.*, *1*, 457-466.
Rubin, D. B. (1976). "Inference and Missing Data," *Biometrika*,
   63, 581-604.
Rubin, D. B. (1978a). "Bayesian Inference for Causal Effects:
   The Role of Randomization," *The Annals of Statistics*, *6*,
   #1, 34-58.
Rubin, D. B. (1978b). "Multiple Imputations in Sample Surveys, A
   Phenomonological Bayesian Approach to Nonresponse,"
   Imputation and Editing of Faulty or Missing Survey Data,
   1-18, U.S. Department of Commerce.
Sande, G. (1976a). "Searching for Numerically Matched Records,"
   Statistics Canada, unpublished paper.
Sande, G. (1976b). "Diagnostic Capabilities for a Numerical
   Edit Specification Analyzer," *Statistics Canada*, unpublished
   paper.
Stuart, W. J. (1966). "Computer Editing of Survey Data - Five
   Years of Experience in BLS Manpower", *J. Am. Stat. Assoc.*,
   61, 375-83.
Szameitat, K. and Zindler, H. J. (1965). "The Reduction of
   Errors in Statistics by Automatic Correction," *International
   Statistical Review*, *41*, 395-417.
Walker, W. E. (1976). "A Heuristic Adjacent Extreme Point
   Algorithm for the Fixed Charge Problem," *Management Science*,
   22, 587-596.
Wickmann, E. H. (1963). "Density Matrices Arising From
   Incomplete Measurements," *Journal of Mathematical Physics*,
   4, *#7*, 884-896.

MISSING DATA IN LARGE DATA SETS

Roderick J. A. Little[1]
Donald B. Rubin[2]

Datametrics Research, Inc.
Chevy Chase, Maryland

I. INTRODUCTION

Large data bases suffer from missing values for various
reasons, such as survey nonresponse or editing procedures
which eliminate unlikely values. Dealing properly with
missing data is not easy, yet it is necessary to make
decisions about how to handle missing values before any
analysis can proceed. In this article we discuss the
statistical issues that arise from missing data, using the
Current Population Survey (CPS) to illustrate ideas. Basic
problems are introduced via simple examples. A taxonomy of
methods is also presented. The explicit modelling approach is
discussed as a flexible but principled way to proceed in
practice. Finally, computational methods for the analysis of
incomplete data are briefly reviewed.

II. COMMON INCOMPLETE DATA PROBLEMS

We first consider problems where missing values are confined to a single outcome variable y, and interest concerns
the distribution of y, perhaps conditional on a set of one or

[1] *1982-83 American Statistical Association/National
Science Foundation Research Fellow at the U. S. Bureau
of the Census.*
[2] *Present address: The University of Chicago, Chicago,
Illinois.*

more predictor variables, x, that are recorded for all units
in the sample. Sometimes we have no information about the
missing values of y; at other times we may have partial information, for example, that they lie beyond a known censoring
point c.

A. *Mechanisms Leading to Missing Values*

Any analysis of incomplete data requires certain assumptions about the distribution of the missing values, and in
particular how the distributions of the missing and observed
values of a variable are related. The work of Rubin (1976a)
distinguishes three cases. If the process leading to missing
y values (and in particular, the probability that a particular
value of y is missing) does not depend on the values of x or
y, then the missing data are called *missing at random* and the
observed data are *observed at random*. If the process depends
on observed values of x and y but not on missing values of y,
the missing data are called missing at random, but the observed data are not observed at random. If the process depends on missing values of y, then the missing data are not
missing at random; in this case, particular care is required
in deriving inferences. Rubin (1976a) formalized these notions by defining a random variable m that indicates for each
unit whether y is observed or missing, and relating these conditions to properties of the conditional distribution of m
given x and y.

To illustrate these definitions, consider the problem of
missing income items in the March Income Supplement of the
Current Population Survey (CPS), conducted annually by the
U. S. Census Bureau. About 25 percent of the individuals have
incomplete or missing responses to one or more income questions in this important survey. If the missingness does not
depend on the income values, then the missing data are missing
at random and the observed data are observed at random; the
distribution of income is then the same in the respondent and
nonrespondent populations. This hypothesis seems unlikely,
and indeed the earnings data in Table 1, based on a match of
1980 CPS data to Internal Revenue Service (IRS) records, suggest that the probability of nonreporting is higher for those
with low and high earnings than for those with intermediate
earnings.

In practice, covariate information (x) is recorded for respondents and nonrespondents, such as geographical location
(x_1), urbanity (x_2), race (x_3), and educational level (x_4).
We can imagine tables such as Table 1 constructed for

individuals with shared values of these characteristics. If
the differential response rates in Table 1 are attributable to
differences in distribution of x between respondents and
nonrespondents, then the response rates in these adjusted
tables will be the same for all income levels. The missing
data would then be missing at random but the observed data
not observed at random since the missingness would depend on
observed values but not on missing values. If a residual
dependency exists, then the missing data are not missing at
random. Nearly all methods for handling missing values assume
that after adjustment for available covariate information the
missing data are missing at random. The success of these
methods depends crucially on the availability of useful covariates which render this assumption at least approximately
valid.

B. *Analysis of Variance*

The first incomplete data problem to receive systematic
attention in the statistics literature is that of *missing data
in designed experiments;* in the context of agricultural
trials, this problem is often called the missing plot problem
(Bartlett, 1937; Anderson, 1946). Designed experiments investigate the dependence of an outcome variable, such as yield of
a crop, on a set of factors, such as variety, type of fertilizer, and temperature. Usually an experimental design is
chosen that allows efficient estimation of important effects
as well as a simple analysis. The analysis is especially
simple when the design matrix is easily inverted, as with
complete or fractional replications of factorial designs. The
missing data problem arises when, at the conclusion of the experiment, the values of the outcome variable are missing for
some of the plots, perhaps because no values were possible, as
when particular plots were not amenable to seeding, or because
values were recorded and then lost. Standard analyses of the
resultant incomplete data assume the missing data are missing
at random; that is, the missingness can depend on the values of
the factors in the experimental design but not on the values
of the outcome variable itself. In practical situations the
plausibility of this assumption needs to be checked. The
analysis aims to exploit the "near-balance" of the resulting
data set to simplify computations. For example, one tactic is
to substitute estimates of the missing outcome values and then
to carry out the analysis assuming the data to be complete.
Questions needing attention then address the choice of appropriate values to substitute and the modification of subsequent
analyses to allow for such substitutions. For discussions of

this and other approaches, see Healy and Westmacott (1956), Wilkinson (1958), and Rubin (1972, 1976b).

TABLE I. *Proportion of White Men who are Non-Reporters by Earnings Interval*[a]

$ Earnings Interval	Wage, Self-Employment, and Farm Earnings	Wage & Salary Earnings
1 - 2999	19.8	18.7
3000 - 5999	19.2	17.3
6000 - 8999	18.1	16.4
9000 - 11999	17.4	14.9
12000 - 15999	16.6	14.2
16000 - 18999	15.3	14.0
19000 - 24999	16.9	15.5
25000 - 29999	18.2	17.1
30000. - 34999	18.5	16.1
35000 - 39999	20.5	19.3
40000 - 49999	27.0	23.5
50000 +	28.1	26.5

[a] Data are based on 1980 CPS, and earnings refer to 1979. Table from Lillard, Smith, and Welch (1982).

Missing plot techniques do not have much applicability to missing data in surveys such as CPS, since the type of balance which the methods exploit is usually not present, even if the data are complete. Unbalanced analysis of variance may be used, for example, in the comparison of income distributions between socioeconomic groups. Since the sample sizes in each group are not controlled by the sampler, the filled-in data will not yield easily inverted design matrices, as might occur in a designed experiment. Standard methods for unbalanced data can be applied to the completely recorded units, provided the missing at random assumption can be justified.

C. *Censored or Truncated Outcome Variable*

We have noted that standard analyses for missing plots assume that the missing data are missing at random, that is, the probability that a value is missing can depend on the

values of the factors but not on the missing outcome values.
This assumption is violated, for example, when the outcome
variable measures time to an event (such as death of an experimental animal, failure of a light bulb), and the times for
some units are not recorded because the experiment was termi-
nated before the event had occurred; the resulting data are
censored. In such cases the analysis must include the information that the units with missing data are censored, since if
these units are simply discarded, the resulting estimates can
be badly biased.

The analysis of censored samples from the Poisson, binomial and negative binomial distributions is considered by
Hartley (1958). Other distributions, including the normal,
log-normal, exponential, gamma, Weibull, extreme value, and
logistic are covered most extensively in the life testing
literature (for reviews, see Mann, Schafer and Singpurwalla,
1974; Tsokos and Shimi, 1977). Nonparametric estimation of a
distribution subject to censoring is carried out by life table
methods, formal properties of which are discussed by Kaplan
and Meier (1958). Much of this work can be extended to handle
covariate information (Glasser, 1969; Cox, 1972; Aitkin and
Clayton, 1980; Laird and Oliver, 1981). The EM algorithm,
discussed here in Section IV, is a useful computational device
for such problems.

Censored data occur in the public-use tape of the 1973
CPS data, since amounts above $50,000 are recoded to $50,000.
Clearly, omitting such cases from an analysis, or even treat-
ing such incomes as $50,000, would lead to biased estimates.
Greenlees, Reece, and Zieschang (1982) deal with the censored
values by maximum likelihood methods in the context of normal
linear regressions of log (wage and salary) on covariates.
Likelihood-based methods like this are outlined in Section
III-B below.

This form of censoring is a particular case of grouped
data, where values are known to lie within a particular interval (here, 50,000 to infinity). The analysis of grouped data
has considerable literature; see, for example, Hartley (1958),
Kulldorff (1961) and Blight (1970). Hasselblad, Stead, and
Galke (1980) provide an example of maximum likelihood estimation for a regression of blood lead values on race, year, and
age, where the levels are grouped into seven intervals. The
results differ substantially from the results of the crude
procedure where individuals are assigned the midpoint value of
the intervals in which they fall and these values are used in
the regression.

Another variant of censored data occurs when the number
of censored values is unknown. The resulting data are called
truncated, since they can be regarded as a sample from a truncated distribution. A considerable literature exists for this
form of data (Hartley, 1958; Dempster, Laird, and Rubin, 1977;
Blumenthal, Dahiya, and Gross, 1978).

D. Sample Survey Data

Rubin (1978) introduces the terms *ignorable* and *nonignorable* to describe response mechanisms which lead to missing
data which are missing at random, or not missing at random,
respectively. For large data sets, nonresponse bias associated with nonignorable missing data mechanisms is frequently a
more important problem than increased variance from the reduced sample size. The missing data mechanisms in Section
II-C are nonignorable, but known, in the sense that censoring
and grouping points are known. A common and more intractable
problem occurs when the missing data mechanism is nonignorable
and at best partially known.

Nonreporting of CPS income is a good example of a potentially nonignorable response mechanism which is not fully
understood. Unless particularly good covariate information
(like the matched IRS income) is available for analysis, the
missing income values are unlikely to be missing at random;
that is, the distributions of income among respondents and
nonrespondents are likely to differ in some unknown way, even
after taking into account covariates. A particularly trouble-
some feature of nonresponse for some components of income,
such as social security benefits, arises from the fact that
some in the population are nonrecipients and hence have zero
values of the variable. Often nonresponse and nonrecipiency
are to some degree confounded so that the probability of nonresponse is higher for nonrecipients than recipients. The
bias resulting from this problem is often difficult to deal
with by analysis, and hence data collection systems should be
designed to collect information on recipiency (amount positive) vs. nonrecipiency (amount zero) and on amount for
recipients.

Editing provides another example of a nonignorable missing data mechanism. Values which fail range or structure
checks are often deleted from the data file. Deletions caused
by coding or punching errors can sometimes be treated as missing at random, but other deleted values may be caused by
flawed response correlated with the correct value or may be

genuine exceptional values. Most of the extensive literature
on outliers treats the deleted values as missing at random,
although the assumption may not be justifiable.

The effect of survey nonresponse is minimized by (a)
designing data collection methods to minimize the level of
nonresponse, (b) interviewing a subsample of nonrespondents,
and (c) collecting auxiliary information to allow the reduction of nonresponse bias through analysis. Models for nonrandomly missing data, as developed by Nelson (1976), Heckman
(1976) and Rubin (1977), can also be applied here. Estimates
derived from these models, however, are sensitive to aspects of
the model that cannot be tested with the available data
(Rubin, 1978; Little, 1982; Greenlees, Reece, and Zieschang,
1982; Lillard, Smith and Welch, 1982). A thorough discussion
of survey nonresponse is given in the work of the National
Academy of Sciences Panel on Incomplete Data (National Academy
of Sciences, 1983).

E. *Multivariate Incomplete Data*

The incomplete data structures discussed so far are
univariate, in the sense that the missing values are confined
to a single outcome variable. We now turn to incomplete data
structures that are essentially *multivariate* in nature.

Many multivariate statistical analyses, including least
squares regression, factor analysis, and discriminant analysis
are based on an initial reduction of the data to the sample
mean vector and covariance matrix of the variables. The question of how to estimate these moments with missing values in
one or more of the variables is, therefore, an important one.
Early literature was concerned with small numbers of variables
(two or three) and simple patterns of missing data (Anderson,
1957; Afifi and Elashoff, 1966). Subsequently, more extensive
data sets with general patterns of missing data were addressed
(Buck, 1960; Trawinski and Bargmann, 1964; Orchard and
Woodbury, 1972; Rubin, 1974; Beale and Little, 1975; Little
1976).

The reduction to first and second moments is generally
not appropriate when the variables are categorical. In this
case, the data can be expressed in the form of a multiway contingency table. Most of the work on incomplete contingency
tables has concerned maximum likelihood estimation assuming a
Poisson or multinomial distribution for the cell counts. Bivariate categorical data form a two-way contingency table; if

222   Roderick J. A. Little and Donald B. Rubin

some observations are available on a single variable only,
then they can be displayed as a supplemental margin. The
analysis of data with supplemental margins is discussed by
Hocking and Oxspring (1974) and Chen and Fienberg (1974).
Extensions to log-linear models for higher way tables with
supplemental margins are discussed in Fuchs (1982).

   Most missing data problems in survey data are multivariate in nature. In the CPS income example, for instance,
individual income is made up of four broad income types: wages
and salary, self-employment income, retirement income, and
other sources. Nonreporters report some of these income components but not others, and the components which are missing
vary across nonreporters. Thus missing income is a multivariate
problem. Multivariate missing data methods have been applied
only very little to such problems, although considerable gains
are possible by exploiting the covariance structure between
the missing variables. We discuss a method for achieving this
in Section IV.

   Essentially, all of the methods for handling multivariate
missing data in the literature rely on the assumption that the
missing data are missing at random. Many of the methods in
common use also rely on the assumption that the observed data
are observed at random. Together these assumptions imply that
the process that creates missing data does not depend on any
values, missing or observed, usually an unrealistic assumption.

III. METHODS FOR HANDLING INCOMPLETE DATA

A. *A Broad Taxonomy of Methods*

   Methods for handling incomplete data generally belong to
one or more or the following categories:

   (i) *Deleting partially observed cases.* A common method
is to discard units with data missing in some variables and
analyze only the units with complete data (for example, Nie et
al., 1975). This is not a commonly used option for CPS public
use tapes, because the Census Bureau imputes the missing
values. However since flags are included to indicate missing
values, this method could be used with these tapes.

   (ii) *Weighting procedures.* Randomization inferences
from sample survey data without nonresponse are commonly based

on *design weights*, which are inversely proportional to the
probability of selection. For example, let y_i be the value of
a variable y for unit i in the population. Then, the population mean is often estimated by

$$\sum \pi_i^{-1} y_i \,/\, \sum \pi_i^{-1} \,, \tag{1}$$

where the sums are over sampled units, π_i is the probability
of selection for unit i, and π_i^{-1} is the design weight for unit
i.

     Weighting procedures modify the weights to allow for non-
response. The estimator (1) is replaced by

$$\sum (\pi_i p_i)^{-1} y_i \,/\, \sum (\pi_i p_i)^{-1} \,, \tag{2}$$

where the sums are now over sampled units which respond, and
p_i is an estimate of the probability of response for unit i.
Usually the probability of response is estimated by the proportion of responding units in a subclass of the sample,
called a *weighting class* or an *adjustment cell*. Weighting is
related to mean imputation; for example, if the design weights
are constant in subclasses of the sample, then imputing the
subclass mean for missing units in each subclass and weighting
responding units by the proportion responding in each subclass
lead to the same estimates of population means, although not
the same estimates of sampling variance unless adjustments are
made to the data with means imputed. A recent discussion of
weighting with extensions to two-way classifications is provided by Scheuren (1983).

     Since design weights are defined for units, weighting
methods are commonly applied to handle *unit nonresponse*, where
all the survey items for some units are missing because of
noncontact or refusal. The only information available to form
weighting classes is from survey design variables. The design
weights for the CPS, for example, include unit nonresponse
adjustments calculated within each weighting class consisting
of a group of similar primary sampling units (psu's) (Bureau
of the Census, 1978). The implied missing at random assumption is questionable since respondents and nonrespondents
probably have different characteristics within each weighting
class. Satisfactory methods for correcting for bias from unit
nonresponse require some information about nonrespondents,
either from previous surveys or from reinterviews.

   (iii) *Imputation Methods.* The missing values are filled
in and the resulting completed data are analyzed by standard
complete-data methods. For valid inferences to result, modi-
fications to the standard analyses are required to allow for
the differing status of the real and imputed values. In distinguishing imputation methods, it is useful to decompose a
missing value y_i in the form

$$y_i = \mu_i + e_i \, ,$$

where μ_i is the mean of y_i in some subgroup of the population,
defined by covariate information known for the nonrespondent
(for example, an adjustment cell), and $e_i = y_i - \mu_i$ is a
residual. Certain imputation methods substitute estimates
$\hat{\mu}_i$ of μ_i for y_i. For example *mean* imputation substitutes the
mean of the responding units in the relevant subgroup of the
population. More generally, *regression* imputation substitutes
the predicted value $\hat{\mu}_i$ from the regression of y_i on known
covariates, with regression coefficients calculated from the
responding units.

   These methods yield good estimates of aggregate linear
quantities from the filled-in sample, but do not preserve the
distributions of the imputed items in the sample. For example, mean imputation yields the same imputed value for all
missing values in a particular subclass. These imputed values
distort the distribution of the imputed variable in the subclass. An unfavorable consequence occurs when values of y are
grouped into intervals for cross-tabulation, because all the
imputed values in the subclass appear in one of the intervals
thus formed.

   Because of these drawbacks, many practical imputation
schemes impute values of the form $\hat{\mu}_i + \hat{e}_i$, where a residual $\hat{e}_i$
has been attached to the predicted mean. The simplest version
of this procedure is *hot deck* imputation, where values of responding units are substituted for missing values. The hot
deck analog of mean imputation divides the population into
adjustment cells which include nonrespondents and respondents,
and then imputes for a missing value in a cell a randomly selected respondent value in the subclass. Theoretical properties of this method have been discussed by Ernst (1980), Ford

(1983), and Herzog and Rubin (1983). The CPS uses a modified
version of this method to impute missing income values.

(iv) *Model-based procedures.* A broad class of procedures
is generated by defining a model for the incomplete data and
basing inferences on the likelihood under that model, with
parameters estimated by procedures such as maximum likelihood.
Advantages of this approach are: flexibility; the avoidance
of adhocery, in that model assumptions underlying the resulting methods can be displayed and evaluated; and the availability of large sample estimates of variance based on second
derivatives of the log-likelihood, which take into account
incompleteness in the data. Disadvantages are that computational demands can be large, particularly for complex
patterns of missing data, and that little is known about the
small sample properties of many of the large sample approximations.

B. *The Modelling Approach to Incomplete Data*

Any procedure that attempts to handle incomplete data
must, either implicitly or explicitly, model the process that
creates missing data. We prefer the explicit approach since
assumptions are then clearly stated.

Explicit model-based procedures are not used to handle
missing data in the CPS, but such procedures are often used in
analyzing the data, for example, in regression analyses based
on the general linear model, or in contingency table analyses
based on loglinear models. The CPS hot deck is based on an
implicit model positing that the distributions of donor and
receptor incomes are the same, conditional on the covariates
used to define adjustment cells. Unlike regression imputation, where interactions between the covariates are usually
omitted, the CPS hot deck implicitly includes all interactions
between covariates in the systematic component μ_i. This lack
of parsimony is reflected in the fact that some covariates
retained in regression imputation are dropped in the hot deck
scheme when no donors can be found which match a missing
unit. The possibility of combining the two methods, by adding
a hot deck residual r_i to a systematic component μ_i from a
regression, has been suggested by Scheuren (see Schieber,
1978), and could improve on the existing CPS method.

The parametric form of the modelling argument can be
expressed as follows (Rubin, 1976a). Let y_p denote data that

are present and y_m data that are missing. Suppose that
$y = (y_p, y_m)$ has a distribution $f(y_p, y_m | \theta)$ indexed by an unknown parameter θ. If the missing data are missing at random,
the likelihood of θ given data y_p is proportional to the
density of y_p, obtained by integrating $f(y_p, y_m | \theta)$ over y_m:

$$L(\theta | y_p) \propto \int f(y_p, y_m | \theta) dy_m . \qquad (3)$$

Likelihood inferences are based on $L(\theta | y_p)$. Occasionally in
the literature, the missing values y_m are treated as fixed
parameters, rather than integrated out of the distribution
$f(y_p, y_m | \theta)$, and joint estimates of θ and y_m are obtained by
maximizing $f(y_p, y_m | \theta)$ with respect to θ and y_m (e.g., Press
and Scott (1976), present a procedure which is essentially
equivalent to this). This approach is not recommended since
it can produce badly biased estimates which are not even consistent unless the fraction of missing data tends to zero as
the sample size increases. Also, the model relating the missing and observed values of y is not fully exploited, and if
the amount of missing data is substantial, the treatment of y_m
as a set of parameters contradicts the general statistical
principle of parsimony. For further discussion, see Little
and Rubin (1983).

An important generalization of (3) is to include in the
model the distribution of a vector of variables m indicating
whether a value is observed or missing. The full distribution
can be specified as

$$f(m, y_p, y_m | \theta, \phi) = f(y_p, y_m | \theta) f(m | y_p, y_m, \phi) , \qquad (4)$$

where θ is the parameter of interest and ϕ relates to the
mechanism leading to missing data. The extended formulation
is necessary for nonrandomly missing data such as arise in
censoring problems.

To illustrate (3) and (4), suppose the hypothetical complete data $y = (y_1, \ldots, y_n)$ is a random sample of size n from
the exponential distribution with mean θ. Then

$$f(y_p, y_m | \theta) = \theta^{-n} \exp(-t_n / \theta) ,$$

where $t_n = \sum_{i=1}^{n} y_i$ is the total of the n sampled observations.

If $r < n$ observations are present and the remaining $n-r$ are missing, then the likelihood ignoring the response mechanism is proportional to the density

$$f(y_p \mid \theta) = \theta^{-r} \exp(-t_r / \theta) , \qquad (5)$$

regarded as a function of θ, where t_r is the total of the recorded observations.

Let $m = (m_1, \ldots, m_n)$ where $m_i = 1$ or 0 as y_i is recorded or missing, respectively, $r = \Sigma m_i$. We consider two models for the distribution of m given y. First, suppose observations are independently recorded or missing with probability ϕ and $1-\phi$, respectively. Then

$$f(m \mid y, \phi) = \phi^r (1-\phi)^{n-r} ,$$

and

$$f(y_p, m \mid \theta, \phi) = \phi^r (1-\phi)^{n-r} \theta^{-r} \exp(-t_r / \theta). \qquad (6)$$

The likelihoods based on (5) and (6) differ by a factor $\phi^r (1-\phi)^{n-r}$, which does not depend on θ, provided that θ and ϕ are distinct; that is, their joint parameter space factorizes into a θ-space and a ϕ-space. Hence we can base inferences on (5), ignoring the response mechanism.

Suppose instead that the sample is censored, in that only values less than a known censoring point c are observed. Then

$$f(m \mid y, \phi) = \prod_{i=1}^{n} f(m_i \mid y_i) ,$$

$$f(m_i \mid y_i) = \begin{cases} 1 & \text{if } m_i = 1 \text{ and } y_i < c \text{ or } m_i = 0 \text{ and } y_i > c ; \\ 0 & \text{otherwise} . \end{cases}$$

The full likelihood is then proportional to

$$f(y_p,m \mid \theta) = \prod_{i:m_i=1} f(y_i \mid \theta)f(m_i \mid y_i < c) \prod_{i:m_i=0} pr(y_i > c \mid \theta)$$

$$= \theta^{-r}\exp(-t_r/ \theta) \exp\left[-(n-r)c/ \theta\right] . \qquad (7)$$

In this case the response mechanism is not ignorable, and the likelihoods based on (5) and (7) differ by a factor involving θ. In particular, the maximum likelihood estimate of θ based on (5) is t_r/r, the mean of the recorded observations, which is less than the maximum likelihood estimate of θ based on (7), namely $\left[t_r+(n-r)c\right]/r$. The latter estimate has the simple interpretation as the total time at risk for the uncensored and censored observations divided by the number of failures (r).

C. *Special Data Patterns: Factoring the Likelihood*

For certain special patterns of multivariate missing data, maximum likelihood estimation can be simplified by factoring the joint distribution in a way that simplifies the likelihood. Suppose for example the data have the *monotone* (or *nested*) pattern in Figure 1, where y_j represents a set of variables observed for the same set of observations and y_j is more observed than y_{j+1}, $j=1,...,J-1$. The joint distribution of $y_1,...,y_J$ can be factored in the form

$$f(y_1,...,y_J \mid \theta) = f_1(y_1 \mid \theta_1)f_2(y_2 \mid y_1,\theta_2) \cdots$$

$$\cdots f_J(y_J \mid y_1,...,y_{J-1},\theta_J) ,$$

where f_j denotes the conditional distribution of y_j given $y_1,...,y_{j-1}$, indexed by the parameters θ. If the parameters $\theta_1,...,\theta_J$ are distinct, then the likelihood of the data factors into distinct complete-data components, leading to simple maximum likelihood estimators for θ (Anderson, 1957; Rubin, 1974).

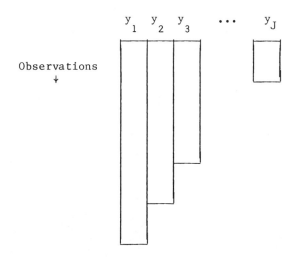

*FIGURE 1.   Schematic representation of a monotone (or nested)
              data pattern.*

        A numerical illustration of this method is given in an
analysis by Marini, Olsen, and Rubin (1980) of panel study
data. The data pattern, given in Table II does not have a
nested pattern, but a nested pattern can be achieved by discarding those data superscripted by the letter b in the
table.[1] The resulting pattern is nested as in Figure 1, with
J=4, y_1=W, y_2=X, y_3=Y and y_4=Z. Assuming normality, ML estimates of the mean and covariance matrix of (W,X,Y,Z) can be
found by the following procedure:

    1) Calculate the mean vector and covariance matrix for
        the W variables, from all the observations.
    2) Calculate the multivariate linear regression of X on
        W, from observations with W and X recorded.
    3) Calculate the multivariate linear regression of Y on
        W and X, from observations with W, X, and Y recorded.
    4) Calculate the multivariate linear regression of Z on
        W, X and Y, from observations with W, X, Y, and Z
        recorded.

[1]*The data are discarded for estimating the parameters of the
model. If the model is used to supply imputations, all
observed values can be retained in the imputed data set.*

ML estimates of the means and covariance matrix of (W,X,Y,Z)
can be obtained as functions of the parameter estimates in 1)
to 4). The computational details, involving the powerful
Sweep operator, are omitted (See Rubin, 1976c.) Results are
displayed in Table III.

The first column gives a description of the variables
W,X,Y and Z. The next two columns give ML estimates of the
means (μ_{ML}) and the standard deviations (σ_{ML}) of each
variable. The rest of the table compares estimates of two
alternative methods of estimation. Estimates (μ_p, σ_p) from the
Pairwise Deletion method are the sample means and standard
deviations using all the observations available for each variable. (The term "pairwise deletion" refers to the fact that
correlations are estimated using all observations where the
values of both variables involved in the covariance are
present.) The two columns after the estimates indicate the
magnitude of differences between the ML and P methods, measured in percent standard deviations. Estimates from Pairwise
Deletion are quite close to the ML estimates, indicating some
virtue for the former method in this example. However, the
method is not recommended for measures of association, such as
covariances or regression coefficients (Marini, Olsen and
Rubin, 1980; Haitovsky, 1968).

The last four columns of the table present and compare
estimates based only on the 1594 complete observations. Estimates of means from this procedure can differ markedly from
the ML estimates. For example, the estimate for grade point
average is .35 of a standard deviation higher than the ML
estimate, indicating the fact that students lost to follow-up
appear to have lower scores than average. The results indicate the ability of the ML estimates to reduce the effects of
this type of nonresponse bias.

IV. GENERAL DATA PATTERNS: THE EM ALGORITHM

The *expectation-maximization (EM) algorithm* (Dempster,
Laird, and Rubin, 1977) is an iterative method of maximum
likelihood estimation that applies to any pattern of missing
data. Let $\ell(\theta|y_p, y_m) = \ln f(y_p, y_m|\theta)$ denote the loglikelihood
of parameters θ based on the hypothetical complete data
(y_p, y_m). Let $\theta^{(i)}$ denote an estimate of θ after iteration i

TABLE II. *Patterns of Missing Data Across Subsets of Observations*[d]

Pattern	Adolescent Variables (W)	Variables Measured for All Follow-Up Respondents (X)	Variables Measured Only for Initial Follow-Up Respondents (Y)	Parent Variables (Z)	Number of Cases	Percentage of Cases
A	1[a]	1	1	1	1,594	36.6
B	1	1[b]	1[b]	0	648	14.9
C	1	1	0	1[c]	722	16.6
D	1	1[b]	0	0	469	10.8
E	1	0	0	1[c]	499	11.5
F	1	0	0	0	470	9.6
					4,352	100.0

[a] 1 = observed, 0 = missing.

[b] Observations falling outside nested pattern 2 (W more observed than Z; Z more observed than X; X more observed than Y).

[c] Observations falling outside nested pattern 1 (W more observed than X; X more observed than Y; Y more observed than Z).

[d] Taken from Marini, Olsen, and Rubin (1980).

TABLE III. *Maximum Likelihood Estimates of Means and Standard Deviations Obtained for the Total Original Sample and Comparisons with Two Alternative Sets of Estimates*

Variable	Maximum Likelihood Estimates for Total Sample (n=4352)		Estimates Based on Pairwise Deletion (n=4152)				Estimates Based on Data for Pattern A Only (n=1594)			
	Mean	s.d.	Mean	s.d.	$\frac{(\mu_P-\mu_{ML})\times100}{\sigma_{ML}}$	$\frac{(\sigma_P-\sigma_{ML})\times100}{\sigma_{ML}}$	Mean	s.d.	$\frac{(\mu_A-\mu_{ML})\times100}{\sigma_{ML}}$	$\frac{(\sigma_A-\sigma_{ML})\times100}{\sigma_{ML}}$
Variables Measured During Adolescence (W)										
Father's education	11.702	3.528	11.702	3.528	0.0	0.0	12.050	3.449	9.9	-1.6
Mother's education	11.508	2.947	11.508	2.947	0.0	0.0	11.864	2.865	12.1	-2.4
Father's occupation	6.115	2.904	6.115	2.904	0.0	0.0	6.407	2.868	10.1	-1.2
Intelligence	106.625	12.910	106.625	12.910	0.0	0.0	109.036	11.174	18.7	-13.4
College preparatory curriculum	0.411	0.492	0.411	0.492	0.0	0.0	0.528	0.499	13.4	1.4
Time spent on homework	1.589	0.814	1.589	0.814	0.0	0.0	1.633	0.795	5.4	-2.3
Grade point average	2.324	0.773	2.324	0.773	0.0	0.0	2.594	0.701	34.9	-9.3
College plans	0.488	0.500	0.488	0.500	0.0	0.0	0.595	0.491	21.4	-1.8
Friends' college plans	0.512	0.369	0.512	0.369	0.0	0.0	0.572	0.354	16.3	-4.1
Participation in extra-curricular activities	0.413	0.492	0.413	0.492	0.0	0.0	0.492	0.500	15.8	1.4
Membership in top leading crowd	0.088	0.283	0.088	0.283	0.0	0.0	0.131	0.338	8.6	19.4
Membership in inter-mediate leading crowd	0.170	0.376	0.170	0.376	0.0	0.0	0.198	0.399	5.6	4.1
Cooking/drinking	0.570	1.032	0.570	1.032	0.0	0.0	0.483	0.835	-8.4	-9.4
Dating frequency at time of survey	4.030	4.802	4.030	4.802	0.0	0.0	3.701	4.523	-6.8	-5.8
Liking for self	2.366	0.525	2.366	0.525	0.0	0.0	2.364	0.515	-0.4	-1.9
Grade in school	2.432	1.048	2.432	1.048	0.0	0.0	2.496	1.064	6.1	1.5

TABLE III (continued)

Variables measured for All Follow-Up Respondents (X)										
Educational attainment	13.625	2.295	13.274	2.262	6.5	-1.4	14.196	2.204	24.9	-4.0
Occupational prestige	44.405	13.008	45.085	12.893	5.2	-0.9	47.056	12.745	20.4	-2.0
Marital status	0.940	0.238	0.940	0.238	0.0	0.0	0.940	0.237	0.0	-0.4
Number of children	1.991	1.306	1.973	1.304	-1.4	-0.2	1.928	1.242	-4.8	-4.9
Age	30.629	1.221	30.655	1.225	2.1	0.3	30.726	1.152	7.9	-5.4
Father's occupational prestige	43.998	14.821	44.258	14.786	1.8	-0.2	44.782	14.333	5.3	-3.2
Variables Measured Only for Initial Questionnaire Respondents to the Follow-Up (Y)										
Personal esteem	3.128	0.377	3.148	0.378	5.2	0.3	3.148	0.373	5.3	-1.1
Dating frequency during last two years of high school	4.374	3.408	4.202	3.261	-5.1	-1.4	4.213	3.352	-4.7	-1.6
Number of siblings	2.219	1.748	2.099	1.744	-6.9	-0.2	2.055	1.660	-9.4	-5.0
Variables Measured on Parents' Questionnaire (Z)										
Family income	4.092	1.530	4.075	1.538	-1.1	0.5	4.215	1.570	8.0	2.6
Parental encouragement to go to college	0.714	0.434	0.706	0.455	-1.6	4.8	0.754	0.431	8.0	-0.7
Number of children in family of origin	3.039	1.539	3.067	1.671	1.8	8.6	2.975	1.551	-4.2	0.8

of the algorithm. Iteration $(i + 1)$ consists of an
E-step and an M-step. The E-step consists of taking the ex-
pectation of $\ell(\theta|y_p, y_m)$ over the conditional distribution of
y_m given y_p, evaluated at $\theta = \theta^{(i)}$. That is, the averaged
loglikelihood

$$\ell*(\theta|y_p, \theta^{(i)}) = \int \ell(\theta|y_p, y_m) f(y_m|y_p, \theta^{(i)}) dy_m$$

is formed.

The M-step consists in finding $\theta^{(i+1)}$, the value of θ
which maximizes $\ell*$. This new estimate, $\theta^{(i+1)}$, then replaces
$\theta^{(i)}$ at the next iteration. Each step of EM increases the
loglikelihood of θ given y_p, $\ell(\theta|y_p)$. Under quite general
conditions, the algorithm converges to a maximum value of the
loglikelihood $\ell(\theta|y_p)$. In particular, if a unique finite
maximum likelihood estimate of θ exists, the algorithm finds
it.

An important case occurs when the complete data belong to
a regular exponential family. In this case, the E-step reduces to estimating the sufficient statistics corresponding to
the natural parameters of the distribution. The M-step corresponds to maximum likelihood estimation for the hypothetical
complete data, with the partly missing sufficient statistics
replaced by the estimated sufficient statistics from the
E-step.

The EM algorithm was first introduced for particular
problems (e.g, Hartley, 1958, for counted data and Blight,
1970, for grouped or censored data). The regular exponential
family case was presented by Sundberg (1974). Orchard and
Woodbury (1972) discussed the algorithm more generally, using
the term "missing information principle" to describe the link
with the complete-data loglikelihood. Dempster, Laird and
Rubin (1977) introduced the term EM, developed convergence
properties, and provided a large body of examples. Recent
applications include missing data in discriminant analysis
(Little, 1978) and regression with grouped or censored data
(Hasselblad, Stead, and Galke, 1980).

The EM algorithm converges reliably, but it has slow convergence properties if the amount of information in the missing data is relatively large. Also, unlike methods like

Newton-Raphson that need to calculate and invert an information matrix at each iteration, EM does not automatically provide asymptotic standard errors for the maximum likelihood
estimates as output from the calculations. Its popularity
derives from its link with maximum likelihood for complete
data and its consequent, usually simple, computational form.
The M-step often corresponds to a standard method of analysis
for complete data and thus can be carried out with existing
technology. The E-step often corresponds to imputing values
for the missing data y_m, or more generally, for the sufficient
statistics that are functions of y_m and y_p, and as such relates maximum likelihood procedures to imputation methods.

*A. Example: Estimating a Mean and Covariance Matrix from
Incomplete Data*

     Many multivariate statistical analyses, including mul-
tiple linear regression, principle component analysis, factor
analysis, discriminant analysis, and canonical correlation
analysis are based on the initial summary of the data matrix
into the sample mean and covariance matrix of the variables.
Thus the efficient estimation of these quantities for an arbitrary pattern of missing values is a particularly important
problem. In this section we discuss ML estimation of the mean
and covariance matrix from an incomplete multivariate normal
sample, assuming the data are missing at random. Although the
assumption of multivariate normality may appear restrictive,
the methods discussed here can provide consistent estimates
under weaker assumptions about the underlying distribution.
Furthermore, the normality can be relaxed somewhat when we
consider linear regression.

     Suppose that we measure K variables $(y_1, y_2,\ldots,y_K)$ which
have a K-variate normal distribution with mean
$\mu =(\mu_1,\ldots,\mu_k)^t$ and covariance matrix $\Sigma =(\sigma_{jk})$. We write
$y = (y_p,y_m)$, where y represents a random sample of size n on
$(y_1,\ldots,y_K)$, y_p represents the set of present values and y_m
the missing data. We write

$$y_p = (y_{p1},y_{p2},\ldots,y_{pn})$$

where y_{pi} represents the set of variables observed for observation i, i=1,$\ldots$,n.

To derive the EM algorithm, we note that the hypothetical complete data y belong to the regular exponential family with sufficient statistics

$$\sum_{i=1}^{n} y_{ij}, \quad j=1,\ldots,K \quad \text{and} \quad \sum_{i=1}^{n} y_{ij}y_{ik}, \quad j,k=1,\ldots,K \ .$$

At the tth iteration, let $\theta^{(t)} = \left(\mu^{(t)}, \Sigma^{(t)}\right)$ denote current estimates of the parameters. The E-step of the algorithm consists in calculating

$$E\left(\sum_{i=1}^{n} y_{ij}\middle| y_p, \theta^{(t)}\right) = \sum_{i=1}^{n} y_{ij}^{(t)}, \quad j=1,\ldots,K$$

$$E\left(\sum_{i=1}^{n} y_{ij}y_{ik}\middle| y_p, \theta^{(t)}\right) = \sum_{i=1}^{n} (y_{ij}^{(t)}y_{ik}^{(t)} + c_{jk}^{(t)}), \quad j,k=1,\ldots,K,$$

where

$$y_{ij}^{(t)} = \begin{cases} y_{ij}, & \text{if } y_{ij} \text{ is present,} \\[2ex] E(y_{ij}|y_{pi},\theta^{(t)}), & \text{if } y_{ij} \text{ is missing,} \end{cases}$$

and

$$c_{jk}^{(t)} = \begin{cases} 0, & \text{if } y_{ij} \text{ or } y_{ik} \text{ is present;} \\[2ex] \text{cov}(y_{ij},y_{ik}|y_{pi},\theta^{(t)}), & \text{if } y_{ij} \text{ and } y_{ik} \text{ are missing.} \end{cases}$$

Missing values y_{ij} are thus replaced by the conditional mean of y_{ij} given the set of values y_{pi} observed for that observation. These values, and the non-zero conditional covariances $c_{jk}^{(t)}$, are easily found from the current parameter estimates by sweeping the augmented covariance matrix so that the variables y_{pi} are predictors in the regression equation and the remaining variables are outcome variables.

The M-step of the EM algorithm is straightforward. The new estimates $\theta^{(t+1)}$ of the parameters are estimated from the estimated complete data sufficient statistics. That is

$$\mu_j^{(t+1)} = n^{-1} \sum_{i=1}^{n} y_{ij}^{(t)}, \quad j=1,\ldots,K;$$

$$\sigma_{jk}^{(t+1)} = n^{-1} E(\sum_{i=1}^{n} y_{ij}y_{ik} | y_p) - \mu_j^{(t+1)}\mu_k^{(t+1)}$$

$$= n^{-1} \sum_{i=1}^{n} [(y_{ij}^{(t)} - \mu_j^{(t+1)})(y_{ik}^{(t)} - \mu_k^{(t+1)}) + c_{jk}^{(t)}],$$

$$j,k=1,\ldots,K.$$

Beale and Little (1975) suggest replacing the factor n^{-1} in the estimate of σ_{jk} by $(n-1)^{-1}$, which parallels the correction for degrees of freedom in the complete data case. Theory for what factor is most appropriate does not currently exist.

It remains to suggest initial values of the parameters. A good choice is to use the sample mean and variance of each variable over all observations with that variable observed and the identity matrix for the correlations.

The link between ML estimation and an efficient form of imputation for the missing values is clear from the EM algorithm. The E-step imputes the best linear predictors for the missing values, using current estimates of the parameters. It also calculates the adjustments c_{jk} to the estimated covariance matrix needed to allow for imputation of the missing values.

The EM algorithm for multivariate normal data can be viewed as an iterative version of Buck's (1960) method for imputing missing values (Beale and Little, 1975). It was first described by Orchard and Woodbury (1972). Earlier, the Newton-Raphson algorithm for this problem had been described by Trawinski and Bargmann (1964); the iterating equations for this algorithm are presented in an elegant form by Hartley and Hocking (1971). An important difference between the Newton-Raphson algorithm and the EM algorithm is that the former algorithm requires inversion of the information matrix of μ and Σ at each iteration. These quantities finally supply

estimates of the asymptotic covariance matrix of the ML estimates, which are not directly obtained from the EM algorithm.
However, the inversion of the information matrix of Σ at each
iteration is not attractive, because it is a large matrix if
the number of variables is large. For the K variable case,
the information matrix of Σ has dimension $1/2$ K(K+1), and
when K=30 it has over 100,000 elements!

B. *Two versions of the EM Algorithm and a Combined Version*

    Two versions of the EM algorithm can be defined. The
first stores the raw data (Beale and Little, 1975). The
second stores the cross products for each pattern of missing
data (Dempster, Laird, and Rubin, 1977). The version that
takes less storage is to be preferred. Obviously, we can mix
the two versions, storing raw data for those patterns with few
units and storing sufficient statistics for those patterns
with many units.

V. MULTIPLE IMPUTATION

    Methods like the EM algorithm are computationally feas-
ible, but require special programs and some degree of statistical expertise to implement. Subject matter researchers
using public-use tapes have a natural preference for a clean
imputed data set which can be analyzed by standard statistical
methods, without having to worry about missing data problems.
They would like to be able to regard imputation as an editing
process which can be largely ignored by data users. Unfortunately, it is clear that even if imputed values are supplied
from a satisfactory model of the missing data process, inferences which treat a single imputed data set as if no data had
been imputed are always likely to be incorrect. The method of
multiple imputation, advocated by Rubin (1978), allows valid
inferences to be derived by applying standard statistical
methodology to imputed data.

    The basic idea of the method is to supply $J > 1$ imputed
values $\{y_{ij}, \; j=1,\ldots,J\}$ for each missing value y_i in the data
set, where the imputed values are drawn from a distribution.
For example, in a simple case the distribution might be the
values from a set of observed units which are matched to the
missing unit using available data. More generally, the imputed values take the form $\mu_i + e_{ij}$, where μ_i is a predicted

mean from a regression model, common to all imputations, and e_{ij} is chosen from a distribution of residuals.

The analyst can use a multiply imputed data set to guarantee valid inferences, as follows. First, inferences are derived by standard complete-data methods using the first imputed value y_{i1} for each missing value y_i. In particular, suppose

$$\hat{\theta}_1 \pm 2s_1$$

is a 95 percent interval for a quantity θ estimated by θ_1, with estimated standard error s_1. The process is then repeated J-1 times, so that in analysis j the jth imputed value y_{ij} is substituted for missing value y_i, yielding estimates $\hat{\theta}_j$ and s_j. The best estimate of θ from these J analyses is the mean,

$$\bar{\theta} = \sum_{j=1}^{J} \hat{\theta}_j / J \ .$$

Furthermore, the variance of the estimates $\hat{\theta}_j$ reflects the uncertainty added by imputation. An approximately valid estimate of variance is

$$s^2 = \sum_{j=1}^{J} s_j^2 / J + \frac{1}{J-1} \sum_{j=1}^{J} (\hat{\theta}_j - \bar{\theta})^2 \ .$$

The estimated interval $\bar{\theta} \pm 2s$ is a valid 95 percent interval for θ. An appealing aspect of this argument is that it applies to any quantity θ, linear or nonlinear in the data. The accuracy of the method increases with the number of imputations J, but Rubin shows that a small value of J (say 3) is sufficient to provide nearly efficient estimates and satisfactory estimates of precision, at least in simple cases.

VI.   CONCLUSION

A principled approach to the problem of missing data in large data bases requires a plausible model for the missing data mechanism and estimation procedures which remove or

minimize biases introduced by the incompleteness of the data.
We have outlined some of the more recently developed methods
with these objectives in mind. Although methods such as the
EM algorithm and multiple imputation are powerful tools which
have wide application, many problems remain. For example,
nonnormal likelihoods occur more commonly with incomplete data
than with complete data, and much remains to be learned about
the appropriateness of many incomplete data methds when
applied to real data.

REFERENCES

Afifi, A. A. and Elashoff, R. M. (1966). "Missing Observations
    in Multivariate Statistics I: Review of the Literature,"
    J. Am. Statist. Assoc., *61*, 595-604.
Aitkin, M. and Clayton, D. (1980)."The Fitting of Exponen-
    tial Weibull and Extreme Value Distributions to Complex
    Censored Survival Data Using GLIM," *Applied Statistics*,
    156-163.
Anderson, R. L (1946). "Missing Plot Techniques," *Biometrics*,
    20, 41-47.
Anderson, T. W. (1957). "Maximum Likelihood Estimates for a
    Multivariate Normal Distribution When Some Observations
    Are Missing," *J. Am. Statist. Assoc.*, *51*, 200-203.
Beale, E. M. L. and Little, R. J. A. (1975). "Missing Values
    in Multivariate Analysis," *J. Roy. Statist. Soc. B*, *37*,
    129-146.
Blight, B. J. N. (1970). "Estimation from a Censored Sample
    for the Exponential Family," *Biometrika*, *57*, 389-395.
Blumenthal, S., Dahiya, R. C. and Gross, A. S. (1978).
    "Estimating the Complete Sample Size from an Incomplete
    Poisson Sample," *J. Am. Statist. Assoc.*, *73*, 182-187.
Buck, S. F. (1960). "A Method of Estimation of Missing Values
    in Multivariate Data, Suitable for use with an Electronic
    Computer," *J. Roy. Statist. Soc.*, *B*, *22*, 302-306.
Chen, T. and Fienberg, S. E. (1974). "Two Dimensional Contin-
    gency Tables with Both Completely and Partially Classified
    Data," *Biometrics*, *30*, 629-641.
Cox, D. R. (1972). "Regression Models and Life Tables (with
    discussion)," *J. Roy. Statist. Soc.*, *B*, *34*, 187-220.
Darroch, J. N. and Ratcliff, D. (1972). "Generalized Iterative
    Scaling for Log-linear Models," *Ann. Math. Statist.*, *43*,
    1370-1480.

Dempster, A. P., Laird, N. M. and Rubin, D. B. (1977).
    "Maximum Likelihood from Incomplete Data via the EM
    Algorithm (with discussion)," *J. Roy. Statist. Soc. B, 39,*
    1, 1-38.
Ford, B. N. (1983). "An Overview of Hot Deck Procedures," In
    Incomplete Data in Sample Surveys, Vol. 2, (W. G. Madow,
    I. Olkin, and D. B. Rubin, eds.), Academic Press, New York.
Fuchs, C. (1982). "Maximum Likelihood Estimation and Model
    Selection in Contingency Tables with Missing Data," *J.
    Am. Statist. Assoc., 77,* 270-278.
Glasser, M. (1967). "Exponential Survival with Covariance,"
    J. Am. Statist. Assoc., 62, 561-568.
Greenlees, W. S., Reece, J. S. and Zieschang, K. D. (1982).
    "Imputation of Missing Values when the Probability of
    Response Depends upon the Variable Being Imputed." *J.
    Am. Statist. Assoc., 77,* 251-261.
Hartley, H. O. (1958). "Maximum Likelihood Estimation from
    Incomplete Data," *Biometrics, 27,* 783-808.
Hasselblad, V., Stead, A. G. and Galke, W. (1980). "Applica-
    tion of Regression Analysis to Grouped Blood Lead Data,"
    J. Am. Statist. Assoc., 75, 771-779.
Healy, M. and Westmacott, M. (1956). "Missing Values in
    Experiments Analysed on Automatic Computers,"
    Appl. Statist., 5, 203-206.
Heckman, J. D. (1976). "The Common Structure of Statistical
    Models of Truncation, Sample Selection and Limited
    Dependent Variables and a Simple Estimator for Such
    Models," *Annals of Economic and Social Measurement, 5,*
    475-492.
Herzog, T. N. and Rubin, D. B. (1983). "Using Multiple Impu-
    tations to Handle Nonresponse in Sample Surveys", In *In-
    complete Data in Sample Surveys, Vol. 2,*(W. G. Madow,
    I. Olkin, and D. B. Rubin, eds.), Academic Press, New York.
Hocking, R. R. and Oxspring, H. H. (1974). "The Analysis of
    Partially Categorized Contingency Data," *Biometrics, 30,*
    469-483.
Kaplan, E. L. and Meier, P. (1958). "Nonparametric Estimation
    from Incomplete Observations," *J. Roy. Statist. Assoc.,
    53,* 475-481.
Kulldorff, G. (1961). *Contributions to the Theory of
    Estimation From Grouped and Partially Grouped Samples.*
    Almquist and Wiksell, Stockholm and Wiley, New York.
Laird, N. and Oliver, D. (1981). "Covariance Analysis of
    Survival Data Using Log-linear Analysis Techniques," *J.
    Am. Statist. Assoc., 76.,* 231-240.

Lillard, L., Smith, J. P. and Welch, F. (1982). "What Do We Really Know about Wages: The Importance of Non-reporting and Census Imputation," *Rand Corporation*, 1700 Main Street, Santa Monica, CA 90406.

Little, R. J. A. (1976). "Inference About Means from Incomplete Multivariate Data," *Biometrika, 63*, 593–604.

Little, R. J. A. (1978). "Consistent Methods for Discriminant Analysis with Incomplete Data," *J. Am. Statist. Assoc. 73*, 319–322.

Little, R. J. A. (1982). "Models for Nonresponse in Sample Surveys," *J. Am. Statist. Assoc., 77*, 237–250.

Little, R. J. A. and Rubin, D. B. (1983). "On Jointly Estimating Parameters and Missing Data by Maximizing the Complete Data Loglikelihood," *The American Statistician, 37*.

Mann, N. R., Schafer, R. E. and Singpurwalla, N. D. (1974). *Methods for Statistical Analysis of Reliability and Life Data*, John Wiley & Sons, New York.

Marini, M. M., Olsen, A. R., and Rubin, D. B. (1980), "Maximum Likelihood Estimation in Panel Studies with Missing Data," in *Sociological Methodology 1980*, Jossey-Bass, San Francisco.

National Academy of Sciences (1983). *Incomplete Data in Sample Surveys, Vols. I–III*, W. G. Madow, H. Nisselson, I. Olkin, and D. B. Rubin, eds., Academic Press, New York.

Nelson, F. D. (1977). "Censored Regression Models with Unobserved, Stochastic Censoring Thresholds," *Journal of Econometrics, 6*, 581–592.

Nie, N. H., Hill, C. H., Jenkins, J. G., Steinbrenner, K. and Bent, D. H. (1975). *SPSS, Second Edition*, McGraw Hill, New York.

Orchard, T. and Woodbury, M. A. (1972). "A Missing Information Principle: Theory and Applications." *Proc. 6th Berkeley Symposium on Math. Statist. and Prob., 1*, 697–715.

Press, S. J. and Scott, A. J. (1976). "Missing Variables in Bayesian Regression II," *J. Am. Statist. Assoc., 71*, 366–369.

Rubin, D. B. (1972). "A Noniterative Algorithm for Least Squares Estimation of Missing Values in Any Analysis of Variance Design," *Appl. Statist., 21*, 136–141.

Rubin, D. B. (1974). "Characterizing the Estimation of Parameters in Incomplete Data Problems," *J. Am. Statist. Assoc., 69*, 467–474.

Rubin, D. B. (1976a). "Inference and Missing Data," *Biometrika, 63*, 581–592.

Rubin, D. B. (1976b). "Noniterative Least Squares Estimates, Standard Errors, and F-tests for any Analysis of Variance Design with Missing Data," *J. Roy. Statist. Soc. B, 38, 3,* 270-274.

Rubin, D. B. (1976c). "Comparing Regressions When Some Predictor Variables are Missing," *Technometrics, 18,* 201-206.

Rubin, D. B. (1977). "Formalizing Subjective Notions about the Effect of Nonrespondents in Sample Surveys," *J. Am. Statist. Assoc., 72,* 535-543.

Rubin, D. B. (1978). "Multiple Imputations in Sample Surveys - A Phenomenological Bayesian Approach to Nonresponse" (with discussion and reply), *Proceedings of the Survey Research Methods Section, American Statistical Association,* 20-28.

Rubin, D. B. (1980). *Handling Nonresponse in Sample Surveys by Multiple Imputations.* U. S. Department of Commerce, Bureau of the Census Mongraph.

Scheuren, F. (1983). "Weighting Adjustment for Unit Nonresponse." In *Incomplete Data in Sample Surveys, Vol. 2,* (W. G. Madow, I. Olkin, and D. B. Rubin, eds.), Academic Press, New York.

Schieber, S. J. (1978). "A Comparison of Three Alternative Techniques for Allocating Unreported Social Security Income on the Survey of Low-Income Aged and Disabled," *Proceedings of the Survey Research Methods Section of the American Statistical Association,* 212-218.

Sundberg, R. (1974). "Maximum Likelihood Theory for Incomplete Data from an Exponential Family," *Scand. J. Statist., 1,* 49-58.

Trawinski, I. M. and Bargmann, R. W. (1964). "Maximum Likelihood Estimates with Incomplete Multivariate Data," *Ann. Math. Statist., 35,* 647-657.

Tsokos, C. P. and Shimi, I. N. (1977). *The Theory and Applications of Reliability,* Academic Press, New York.

Wilkinson, G. N. (1958). "The Analysis of Variance and Derivation of Standard Errors for Incomplete Data." *Biometrics, 14,* 360-384.

REDUCING THE COST OF STUDYING SURVEY MEASUREMENT ERROR:
IS A LABORATORY APPROACH THE ANSWER?

Judith T. Lessler
Richard A. Kulka

Research Triangle Institute
Research Triangle Park, North Carolina

I. INTRODUCTION

Several years ago Horvitz (1978) recommended that a Survey Design Information System be established which would collect and disseminate information about the quantitative impact of various sources of error on the total error of survey estimates. From time to time various people have commented on the feasibility and usefulness of such a system. Major objections to proceeding to establish such a system have been (1) that little information on the impact of nonsampling errors is available and (2) that for such a system to operate effectively one needs a total error model which integrates the information on the impact of the various sources of error.

This paper argues first that one of the reasons for the paucity of information on the impact of nonsampling errors is that our current survey error models imply that field experiments are needed to quantify the impact of errors and second that a Survey Design Information System should not be dependent upon either the development of complex total error models or upon models that require field experiments to quantify. Rather a Survey Design Information System should employ a variety of approaches for quantifying the effects of errors including:

(1) The development of models and methods for quantifying the impact of an error source that can be applied in laboratory type settings, thus avoiding the cost of complex field experiments. Information gathered in the laboratory would be used as a supplement to field studies.

STATISTICAL METHODS
AND THE IMPROVEMENT OF DATA QUALITY
245

(2) The development of simpler "design-effect type" models that reflect the combined effect of multiple sources of measurement errors (and other types of non-sampling errors) in a particular survey relative to a more optimum survey design. These models would be used when designing surveys under modest budgets for which modeling the total error is too expensive.

(3) The adoption of an integrated approach to the study of survey measurement methods that uses consecutively: laboratory tests, pilot tests, and finally full field tests.

A Survey Design Information System that gathered information from such a variety of methods would accumulate knowledge more quickly than one that relied exclusively on the information coming from field experiments and that required the development of complex total error models before implementation. Such a system could be implemented immediately. The argument is based upon the results of a recently completed review of methods that have been used for the study of survey errors. During this review, four major sources of error were identified: (1) frame errors, (2) sampling errors, (3) nonresponse errors, and (4) measurement errors. The status of total error models that assess the combined impact of various sources of error was examined. A few partial models were found which treated a maximum of three of the four major categories of error listed above. In addition, Bill Kalsbeek (Lessler, Kalsbeek, and Folsom, in press) outlined the components that would be needed for a total error model, and a major conclusion that was reached is that the task of quantifying a total error model using field experiments would be extraordinarily complex and expensive. Other methods that would be less costly are needed. In the remainder of the paper, the potential usefulness of laboratory studies is illustrated by focusing upon measurement errors.

It is a well known fact that repeated measurements on the same material will not yield the same results. Presumably this failure to achieve consistency in repeated measurements is due to errors in the measurements. One of the major concerns of survey researchers during the past thirty years has been to understand the nature of this measurement variability in surveys. This search for understanding involves the development of mathematical models for the impact of errors in measurement on the survey results and the development of experimental procedures for quantifying the components of these mathematical models.

II. MEASUREMENT ERROR MODELS

There are two major approaches that have been taken by survey
researchers for modeling the impact of measurement error. One
approach, by far the most common, assumes that the measurements are random variables. The other approach argues that
measurements should not be modeled as random variables because
to do so is to define quantities that are in principle unmeasurable.

   Survey measurements take place in a milieu that is composed of many factors. Some of these factors we have controlled to a high degree such as the design of the sample and
the questionnaire; others we have controlled to a lesser
degree such as interviewer actions which have been prescribed
by the training and field protocols. Others we have little
control over such as the mood of the respondent, the political
climate at the time of the interview, and the respondent's
reaction to the characteristics of the interviewer such as his
age, race, sex, or social class. Hansen, Hurwitz, and Bershad
(1961) have called this whole complex of factors the *general
conditions* of the survey. Hansen, Hurwitz, and Madow (1953)
call the conditions that are subject to the control of the
researcher the *essential survey conditions;* these are a subset
of the general conditions. It is assumed that the uncontroll-
able factors in the survey milieu induce or cause the measurements to behave like random variables.

   Not everyone has accepted the concept of response variability, however. Zarkovich (1966) provides an extensive
discussion of the concept and then rejects its practical usefulness because he believes that quantities that are in principle unmeasurable are defined.

   The *response variability approach* has been the most
widely accepted approach. It is typified by the Hansen,
Hurwitz, and Bershad model and its extensions by various
people at the US Census Bureau. This model first appeared in
1951 in a paper by Hansen, Hurwitz, Marks, and Mauldin and has
evolved in several ways. However, the basis of the theory is
still explained in terms of the general conditions of the survey inducing the measurements to behave as random variables
(Bailey, Moore, and Bailar (1978) and recent US Census
publications).

   One consequence of the theory that the general conditions
of the survey induce the measurements to behave as random

variables is the inherent implication that experiments to measure the components of error must be conducted in the field or
under similar conditions. Such *field experiments* are very
expensive, however, and are rarely done. Thus, this emphasis
on field studies has prevented the rapid accumulation of
knowledge in the area of data collection methods. For survey
measurement methods to advance, we need to move toward a more
laboratory approach to the study of how errors can enter a
survey. In section III, we consider an example of an early
laboratory type experiment.

III. THE PEARSON LABORATORY EXPERIMENT

Pearson (1902) was interested in measuring the *personal
equation* for astronomers. This was of interest because
astronomers were involved in measuring the distance traveled
by stars during the night and errors of judgment could enter
these measurements. The theory that Pearson started with was
as follows.

The *personal equation* for a human measurer is the average
over a large series of judgments or measurements of the
errors that an observer makes in his measurement of a fixed
quantity; i.e., using Pearson's terminology, if ξ is the
actual value of some physical quantity, x_1 its value according
to the judgment of an observer, then the mean value of $x_1 - \xi$
over a large series of judgments, p_{01}, is the personal equation of the observer. Briefly the theory or model for measurement error was as follows.

Let ξ = true value of the quantity being measured;
     x_j = value obtained by the j-th observer.

Then for every observer,

$$E\{x_j - \xi\} = p_{0j},$$ the personal equation of the j-th
                          observer;
and
$$V\{x_j - \xi\} = \sigma_{0j}^2,$$ the variability of the j-th observer's
                          judgment.

It was assumed that the x_j are independently normally
distributed. The goodness of the observer is then measured by
two characteristics:

"(1) the smallness of his personal equation, P_{0j} and

(2) the smallness of the variability of his judgment, σ^2_{0j}."

Now, in most natural measurement situations ξ is not known so that it was only possible to measure $x_j - x_{j'}$, the relative error of judgment of two observers.

However, Pearson noted that if we had three observers we could determine σ^2_{0j} for each of them because:

$$V(x_j - x_{j'}) = V(x_j) + V(x_{j'}) - 2\ Cov(x_j, x_{j'}).$$

Since the $Cov(x_j, x_{j'})$ is zero, then with 3 observers we can measure each stability as follows.

Let $V(x_j - x_{j'}) = \sigma^2_{jj'}$.
Then for three observers, we have

$$\sigma^2_{12} = \sigma^2_{01} + \sigma^2_{02}\ ;$$

$$\sigma^2_{13} = \sigma^2_{01} + \sigma^2_{03}\ ;$$

$$\sigma^2_{23} = \sigma^2_{02} + \sigma^2_{03}\ .$$

These give the following as estimates for the variability in judgments:

$$\sigma^2_{01} = \frac{\sigma^2_{12} + \sigma^2_{13} - \sigma^2_{23}}{2}\ ;$$

$$\sigma^2_{02} = \frac{\sigma^2_{12} + \sigma^2_{23} - \sigma^2_{13}}{2}\ ;$$

$$\sigma^2_{03} = \frac{\sigma^2_{13} + \sigma^2_{23} - \sigma^2_{12}}{2}\ .$$

Based upon this theoretical development, Pearson designed two experiments to measure the variability in judgments. These experiments were not conducted during the actual measurements of star paths, but were rather laboratory experiments that were designed to be prototypes of the process that

went on during the actual measurement process. Pearson built
a machine that caused a bright light to transverse a distance
and a bell to sound at a certain point in the path. Three
observers were to mark the distance traveled at the time the
bell sounded. Five hundred trials of the experiment were
done. The second experiment consisted of having the observers
each bisect five hundred line segments.

In each of these experiments, Pearson was able to measure
the true values as well as the measured values, allowing him
to calculate the absolute and relative personal equations of
his three observers.

Much to Pearson's surprise, he found that there was a
positive correlation between the errors of judgment made by
the 3 observers. Table 1 shows some of Pearson's results.
Pearson was not able to explain this correlation since the
judgments were made independently and spoke of "some particular source of mental or physical likeness which leads to this
correlation in judgments."

*TABLE I. Results from the Bright Series of Experiments
Conducted by Karl Pearson. Extracted from Table II,
Pearson (1902).*

	x_1	x_2	x_3	$x_2 - x_3$	$x_3 - x_1$	$x_1 - x_2$
Mean	0.06724	−1.14906	−0.48563	−0.66343	−0.55287	+1.21630
Standard deviation	1.19495	1.17546	1.18599	1.74616	2.01091	1.66454

Thus, Pearson was able to discover in the context of
a laboratory experiment that errors of measurement may be correlated from one individual to the other...a result that has
been verified time and time again during the last three quar-
ters of a century. We believe that the time has come for us
to begin to systematically design laboratory experiments that
investigate the nature of measurement in surveys.

IV. CONSIDERATIONS FOR THE LABORATORY EXPERIMENT APPROACH

In contemplating the potential desirability of adopting a
laboratory experimental approach to the study of survey error,
it is important to distinguish among (1) *assessing* or

quantifying measurement errors, which has constituted perhaps the majority of survey methodology activity until the last decade or so; (2) procedures developed to adjust or *correct* for such errors (e.g., imputation and other statistical adjustments); and (3) a focus on *reducing* such errors through the systematic testing of alternative survey approaches. In general, survey statisticians have tended to emphasize the former two approaches at the expense of the latter, which are epitomized by the pioneering research of survey methodologists such as Charles Cannell (e.g., Cannell, Marquis, and Laurent, 1977; Cannell, Oksenberg, and Converse, 1977; Cannell, Miller, and Oksenberg, 1981), Seymour Sudman, and Norman Bradburn (e.g., Sudman, 1980; Bradburn, Sudman, and Associates, 1979; Sudman and Bradburn, 1982). Interestingly, however, Sudman and Bradburn's (1974) classic review of response error of almost a decade ago is an admirable example of the descriptive or assessment approach to measurement error, while their more recent works (Sudman, 1980; Bradburn et al., 1979; Sudman and Bradburn, 1982) typify a more experimental and prescriptive treatment of survey error.

Although it is possible to conceive of the use of experimental paradigms in support of each of these three basic approaches to survey error, studies directed at testing various alternatives for reducing measurement error are perhaps those most amenable to a laboratory approach. For example, studies of coder variability and systematic coding bias are probably better studied first by the systematic manipulation of factors in protocols to be coded. Using this approach, more factors can be manipulated simultaneously than could ever occur naturally together in an ongoing survey. Similarly, the use of a laboratory approach which permits the simultaneous manipulation of factors associated with question wording, order, and context may provide the only efficient means of unraveling the complex web of questionnaire effects on survey responses (Schuman and Presser, 1981) and ultimately to control or reduce the influence of such factors. In contrast, quantifying the amount of error in a particular survey implies the use of field experiments, although even these efforts could be improved or supplemented by a greater emphasis on laboratory studies and the adaptation of classic experimental approaches (Rossi and Nock, 1982).

In advocating such an approach, however, *we do not deny the ultimate need for a full-scale field experiment for the systematic treatment of most variables related to measurement error*. Rather, we suggest that the decision to take this step in research on survey measurement error may often be

premature, generally made at a considerable cost and with a
potential loss of information. Perhaps the most compelling
logic in support of this point of view is offered by the stag-
gering array of factors generally regarded as having a significant influence on the quality of measurements in contrast
with inevitable limitations on the number and variety of such
factors which can be examined in the context of ongoing surveys or large-scale field experiments. The following is a
partial (though sobering) list of the sources of errors in
measurement noted in various papers reviewed in connection
with our recent taxonomy project (Lessler, et al., in press).

Errors that arise during planning

    a. Data specification being inadequate and inconsistent
with respect to the objectives of the census or survey
(Murthy, 1967).

    b. Failure to preceive what information would be useful
(Deming, 1960).

Choice of methods

    a. Poor question design (US Census, 1977).

    b. Measurement with inadequate or ambiguous schedules and
definitions (Murphy, 1967).

    c. Biased measurement procedures and biased tools such as
questionnaires (Zarkovich, 1966).

    d. Using the wrong test instrument (Deming, 1960).

    e. Incomplete or wrong identification particulars of units
or faulty methods of enumeration (Murthy, 1967).

    f. Form of question: dichotomous, multiple choice, open,
or free answer; improper wording of questions, which
allows misinterpretations; use of problem words, concept
words, and abbreviations; using loaded or leading
questions; order of questions (Payne, 1951; Zarkovich,
1966).

    g. Conditions of the survey including: length of
question, order of questions, question structure,
question content, and question wording (Moser and
Kalton, 1972; Belson, 1981).

h. The interview task (Kahn and Cannell, 1957; Cannell and
    Kahn, 1968; Sudman and Bradburn, 1974; Dijkstra and Van
    der Zouwen, 1982) including

Task structure

(1) type of question, i.e., open-ended or closed;
(2) supplementary devices such as aided-recall
     techniques, diaries, records, cards, etc.;
(3) questions for which the respondent must admit
     ignorance in order to answer truthfully;
(4) questions which evoke a tendency to acquiesce.

Saliency of the requested information

(1) nature of the recall task including the recency,
     importance, complexity and associated effect of
     the event to be remembered and
(2) clarity of the attitude to the respondent.

Personnel

Interviewers (Boyd and Westfall, 1965, 1970; Freeman and
Butler, 1976; Collins, 1980).

a. Interview effects. When an interviewer is used, his
    understanding or misunderstanding of the survey
    can have important effects on the results of the
    data collected. This is especially true for questions
    that are subject to problems in definitions and
    interpretation (US Census, 1977).

b. Lack of trained and experienced investigators (Hauck
    and Steinkamp, 1964; Murthy, 1967).

c. Extra roll characteristics of the interviewer such as
    age, race, sex, educational level, social class, and
    religious, ethnic or political affiliation (Hyman et
    al., 1954; Sudman and Bradburn, 1974).

d. Characteristics of interviewers. This includes
    personal characteristics such as age, sex, education,
    and social type. Also, includes temperament and
    personality type. Opinions of interviewers.
    Interviewer expectations. This includes, attitude-
    structure expectations and answers to early questions
    which raise expectations in the interviewer concerning
    answers in later parts of the interview (Singer and

Kohnke-Aguirre, 1979; Bradburn et al., 1979). Role
expectations. Interviewers expect the old to be different from the young, etc. Probability expectations.
A certain distribution of opinions or characteristics
is expected among the responents (Hyman et al., 1954;
Moser and Kalton, 1972).

Instructions: Prescribed Conditions of Data Collection

a. Poor choice of respondent. Different responses often
    occur from the head of the household rather than a
    subordinate family member (U.S. Census, 1977).

b. Lack of adequate inspection and supervision of
    primary staff (Hauck and Steinkamp, 1964; Murthy,
    1967).

c. Biased instructions (Zarkovich, 1966).

d. Interviewer role demands. This includes the degree
    to which the researcher attempts to structure the
    interviewer behavior. The range is from exactly
    prescribed behavior to instructions which allow the
    interviewer to get the information in the way he deems
    best for a particular situation (Sudman and Bradburn,
    1974; Bradburn et al., 1979; Dijkstra and Van der
    Zouwen, 1982).

e. Interviewer instructions, designated respondents,
    place of interview, interest in survey, and sponsorship
    (Moser and Kalton, 1972).

Errors that Arise During Data Collection

Record Surveys

a. Terms used in documents may vary in meaning from
    document to document (Moser and Kalton, 1972).

b. Looking up the wrong price or computing it incorrectly
    (Deming, 1960).

Direct Observations

a. Lack of representativeness of the observed behavior;
    problems with assessing the relative frequency of
    behaviors; observer bias; the observer may alter

the normal process and produce a control effect
(Moser and Kalton, 1972).

b. Errors in counting and weighing (Deming, 1960).

Questionnaire Approach: Self-administered

a. Interaction of the question wording with the degree of
    literacy of the respondent; lack of control over who
    completes the questionnaire; the absence of an
    opportunity for probing (Moser and Kalton, 1972).

b. Difficulties involved in the actual data collection
    arising from recall error and other types of errors
    on the part of the respondent (Murthy, 1967).

c. Errors due to wrong entries on the part of the
    respondents (Murthy, 1967).

d. Lack of information on the part of the respondent
    (Cannell et al., 1981).

e. Memory problems. As time passes decay of memory
    occurs. Also telescoping errors can occur whereby
    events that have occurred over a longer period of
    time are reported as having occurred in a shorter,
    specified period (Sudman and Bradburn, 1974).

f. Lack of motivation to respond carefully (Cannell and
    Henson, 1974).

g. Deliberate misrepresentation (Gove, 1982).

    Reasons why this could occur are

    (1) Concern over the possibility that the
         information is not kept secret.
    (2) Desire of the respondent to put himself in a
         favorable light in the eyes of the interviewer
         (prestige bias).

h. Non-deliberate misrepresentation.

i. Recording information incorrectly (US Census, 1977).

j. Understanding of concepts by respondents, ignorance of
    the answer, desires to maintain prestige, recall
    problems and accidental errors in recording

information (Hansen, Hurwitz, and Madow, 1953; Cochran, 1977; Jessen, 1978).

k. Knowledge of the respondent (Cannell and Kahn, 1968).

l. Interjection by the respondent of his own ideas about the meaning and aims of the survey.

m. Social background of the respondent.

n. Tendency by the respondent to round off.

o. Emotional background-fear of the survey, emotional reactions to stereotypes, etc.

p. Prestige errors.

q. Memory problems affected by length of reference period, structure of reference period (open, closed, etc.), recall period, and problems with locating events in time, termed *end effects* (Zarkovich, 1966).

r. Errors Arising from the Respondents. This includes lack of knowledge, memory problems, misunderstandings, conscious or unconscious misstatements (Moser and Kalton, 1972).

Questionnaire Approach: Interview

a. The interaction between the interviewer and the respondent; the interviewer may record responses incorrectly and introduce biases in the results when interpreting verbal answers of the respondents. Probing, cheating (Cannell and Kahn, 1968; Hyman et al., 1954; Moser and Kalton, 1972).

b. Wrong entries on the part of investigators (Murthy, 1967).

c. Failure to ask some questions. Asking questions not on the questionnaire (Deming, 1960).

d. Understanding of concepts by the interviewers, biases of interviewers (Hansen, Hurwitz and Madow, 1953; Cochran, 1977; Jessen, 1978).

e. Interviewer role behavior. This involves the degree to

which an interviewer actually follows the prescribed behavior (Dijkstra and Van der Zouwen, 1982).

f. Respondent role behavior, the motivation to respond well (Sudman and Bradburn, 1974; Cannell, Oksenberg, and Converse, 1977).

g. Interviewer effects. When an interviewer is used, his understanding or misunderstanding of the survey can have important effects on the results of the data collected. This is especially true for questions that are subject to problems in definition and interpretation.

h. Conditioning effect. In continuing surveys, very often the respondent can get conditioned towards giving certain responses to the interviewer's questions. Also, as the survey continues, he also might get tired of responding and the quality of his responses deteriorates (Census, 1978).

Plus the respondent problems (a-r) listed above.

Errors that Arise During the Processing, Tabulation, and Analysis (Sonquist and Dunkelberg, 1977).

a. Tabulation errors. Errors associated with inadequate scrutiny of the basic data; errors in data processing operations such as coding, punching, verification, tabulation, etc.; and errors committed during presentation and printing of tabulated results, graphs, etc. (Murthy, 1967).

b. Processing errors: editing, coding, punching, and tabulation (Zarkovich, 1966).

c. Ineffective rules for coding. Ineffective tabulations. Failure to recognize secular changes that take place in the universe before the results are written up and recommendations made. Bias arising from bad curve fitting, wrong weighting; incorrect adjustment. Unwarranted deductions from the results. Mistakes in calculation and in transcription (Deming, 1960).

It is obviously impossible to ever study such a broad array of error sources in the context of a field experiment. This is especially so because in many cases, as was noted by Brooks and Bailar (1978) in their error profile of the Current

Population Survey, it is not so much the single source of error that we are interested in but rather the *interaction* of various error sources. Attempting to study the effect of this broad variety of sources and their interactions in an ongoing survey is tantamount to aeronautical engineers building a 747 to test the effect of a new shape of wing tip. Clearly the effect of wing tip shape must eventually be examined in an actual flying machine, but many designs can be tested and rejected in laboratory prototypes long before a 747-type machine is actually built.

A field experiment can never manipulate the full range of variables likely to influence survey response; nor can it take full advantage of the added control permitted by the laboratory and associated technology currently available.

At least two general points emerge from this line of thought. First the laboratory context offers the potential for much greater control over different factors presumably operative in the survey interview than the survey itself. Second, it is also possible to co-manipulate numbers and types of relevant factors that would be virtually impossible to study in a field experiment unless the sample were enormous or unless the combinations of factors studied were restricted in some way (e.g., through the use of fractional factorial designs), presumably based on a well-developed theory of survey measurement. It is important to note, however, that no such theory currently exists, and the development of an adequate conceptual model for this purpose may well require a systematic program of laboratory experimentation to isolate these critical combinations for subsequent testing in the field.

In social research, the typical tradeoff for the greater precision and control offered by the laboratory is a lack of realism for the participants and reduced generalizability to other contexts and circumstances (McGrath, 1982). Although realism and generalizability are clearly at issue with regard to the strategy we propose here, it is important to recall that the survey interview itself, although a distinct form of social interaction, is nevertheless a "staged" or artificial social interaction, and, as a result, studying its key features and components via laboratory experimentation is perhaps somewhat more legitimate and revealing than similar research involving more "natural" forms of social interaction (forms which in spite of these limitations have been subjected to laboratory experimentation for decades).

An additional limitation with regard to the state-of-the

art in research on survey error is that in many (if not most) field experiments we do not know what is the "correct" response, and we are only partially cognizant of the survey context. For example, in comparisons of various survey procedures or modes for which no validity criteria external to survey are available, we are forced to rely on certain assumptions about the nature of response and measurement, such as "higher reporting is better reporting" (Waksberg and Neter, 1964; Kovar and Wright, 1973; Cannell, Oksenberg, and Converse, 1977; Woltman et al., 1980), or withhold judgment until additional research is conducted. As a result, interpretation of such results is often fraught with necessary equivocations even where resources committed to the research are considerable. Under such circumstances, to more efficiently determine and assess the nature of key factors that may be manipulated to reduce response error, would it not seem preferable to "stack the cards" more in our favor through the use of a laboratory approach?

Let us now turn to a few examples of how more emphasis on laboratory type studies holds promise for improving our knowledge of survey measurement error. First, consider the fact that a large number of surveys depend heavily on respondent recall of key information as a basis for meeting their major objectives. Yet it is well known that respondents have difficulty remembering such information and especially perhaps, in placing events in time. Particularly salient events tend to be remembered as occurring in the more recent past than less important events, and relatively unimportant events will often not be reported at all during the survey, although if questions are designed properly and respondents sufficiently motivated, they will more likely remember these events (Cannell and Henson, 1974).

In order to prevent the telescoping of events into the more recent time periods, at least three major national surveys currently conduct an initial interview purely as a bounding interview with the data not being used in estimation. This is, of course, an extraordinarily expensive procedure, and most one-time surveys could never afford to use it. In spite of a wholesale shift to such "bounding" interviews by the government, however, there has been little research conducted on how one might avoid this extreme measure. Despite some evidence, for example, suggesting that memory tends to be organized with regard to either consensual or individual *landmark* events, there has been little research on how this and other approaches might be used to reduce telescoping without the use of a bounding interview.

The time appears ripe for combining new developments in computer technology and knowledge of cognitive behavior, biophysical correlates of psychological phenomena, and the effect of role expectations and task structure on task performance to study the nature of survey measurement and error. For example, the areas of experimental, social, and general psychology have great potential relevance to the motivational aspects of survey participation and response. Cannell's work on the use of instructions, commitment, and especially feedback (reinforcement) are derived from some of the most basic experiments in psychology on the influence of commitment and verbal reinforcement on behavior.

In addition to attending to such classic paradigms, however, several contemporary areas of research are also worthy of careful examination. For instance, recent experimentation in social psychology has paid a great deal of attention to what have been called the "demand characteristics" of the experiment (Page, 1972 and 1981), the mechanisms by which these may influence subject behavior independent of the experimental manipulation(s), and the paradigms developed to explore these influences have some obvious relevance to the survey interview, in which we seek to manipulate such "demand characteristics" to achieve accurate reporting of information. Lacking a complete understanding of how these mechanisms operate, however, we are somewhat at their mercy. For example, some have argued that the higher reporting of health characteristics observed using the procedures developed by Cannell and his colleagues (Cannell et al., 1977, 1981) may merely reflect the demand characteristics associated with their experimental strategy rather than better reporting of health variables. To properly evaluate the "higher reporting is better reporting" hypothesis, either a carefully designed field experiment using two-directional record checks (Marquis, 1978) or (better) an experiment in which what is to be recalled and reported is precisely known as required to elucidate these various alternatives.

The use of traditional experimental outcomes such as reaction times, physiological measures, etc. may also be used to evaluate the effectiveness of alternative survey strategies or procedures for reducing survey error. For example, reaction time or response latency has long been used in marketing research as a measure of level of certainty (La Barbera and MacLachlan, 1979) and in cognitive research to determine how information is stored for retrieval.

Consider a hypothetical experiment that might be done

using the telephone. Apparently some people can or are willing to give good information over the phone while others are
not. One indication of whether the respondent is giving good
information might be the latency time between the question and
the answer. One could imagine that respondents who had long
latency times were having difficulty answering the questions;
conversely, those who answer very quickly might also be giving
poor quality answers because they were not taking adequate
time to consider their responses. If the relationship between
latency time and the quality of the response were known from a
laboratory experiment, response latency could be measured for
the first few questions in a telephone survey. Those respondents with latency times within a certain range could be identified and routed to a different questionnaire. Alternately,
one might wish to request a personal interview with these respondents, to switch to a form of the questionnaire that asked
only the key questions, that contained more prompting, or
whatever alternative had been found to increase the quality of
response for this group of respondents.

While studies of telephone versus personal interviewing
would ultimately require a field test of some sort, laboratory
studies of mediated versus direct communication (Williams,
1977), where different formats and approaches are tried, might
be a more fruitful approach to improving the telephone approach, at least in its initial stages.

Similarly, using interview coding procedures such as
those developed by Cannell et al., (1975) could we not learn
more about the efficacy of various training techniques on interviewer behaviors, such as adequate probing, asking questions appropriately, etc., through a standardized simulation
of the interview, prior to full-scale field tests of such procedures?

As a final example, consider recent methodological research on the use of the randomized response technique for
reducing response bias arising from respondent concerns about
revealing sensitive information (Horvitz, Greenberg, and
Abernathy, 1975; Tracy and Fox, 1981). While considerable
progress has been made in the development of statistical
theory underlying this approach, and its efficacy has been
validated in a variety of field applications, the technique
depends heavily for its success on the respondents' understanding and trust or confidence in the method, or more accurately, the particular design implemented, of which there are
many competing devices and strategies. In future evaluations
of these various competitors, it will be necessary to

carefully and systematically weigh the need for providing sufficiently adequate protection to respondents against desires
for efficiency in estimation, a requirement especially well-
suited for preliminary experimentation in the laboratory,
after which the most promising candidates would be subjected
to full-scale field experimentation.

V. SUMMARY

     In summary we suggest that a Survey Design Information
System should not wait for a grand total error model that integrates information on many (all) types of survey errors.
Rather we need simpler mathematical models that can serve as
surrogates for complex models. In addition for developing new
survey methods, we need to follow a scenario in which many
different approaches are tested in laboratory settings...the
selection of more promising approaches for verification and
testing in settings that closer approximate an actual survey,
such as a special research panel located in a particular community...and finally, full field testing and verification of
the methods that survive the first two steps. Finally, we
need to develop laboratory models (mathematical and experimental) that can be used to quantify the error in survey data in
order to control the cost of error studies.

REFERENCES

Bailey, L., Moore, T. F. and Bailar B. (1978). "An Interviewer
     Variance Study for the Eight Impact Cities of the National
     Crime Survey Cities Sample," *Journal of the American Sta-
     tistical Association, 73,* 16-23.
Belson, W. A. (1981). *The Design and Understanding of Survey
     Questions,* Gower Publishing Co. Ltd, London.
Boyd, H. W. and Westfall, R. (1965). "Interviewer Bias
     Revisited," *Journal of Marketing Research, 2,* 58-63.
Boyd, H. W. and Westfall, R. (1970). "Interviewer Bias Once
     More Revisited," *Journal of Marketing Research, 7,* 249-
     253.
Bradburn, N. M., Sudman, S., and Associates (1979). *Improving
     Interview Method and Questionnaire Design,* Jossey-Bass,
     San Francisco.

Brooks, C. A. and Bailar, B. A. (1978). "Statistical Policy
     Working Paper 3, An Error Profile: Employment as Measured
     by the Current Population Survey," U. S. Department of
     Commerce, Office of Federal Statistical Policy and
     Standards.
Cannell, C. F., Groves, R. M. and Miller, P. V. (1981). "The
     Effects of Mode of Data Collection on Health Survey Data,"
     *Proceedings of the Section on Social Statistics, American
     Statistical Association,* 1-6.
Cannell, C. F. and Henson, R. (1974). "Incentives, Motives,
     and Response Bias," *Annals of Economic and Social Measure-
     ment, 3,* 307-317.
Cannell, C. F., Miller, P. V., and Oksenberg, L. (1981).
     "Research on Interviewing Techniques," In S. Leinhardt
     (Ed.), *Sociological Methodology,* Jossey Bass, San
     Francisco.
Cannell, C. F., Oksenberg, L., and Converse, J. M. (1977).
     "Striving for Response Accuracy: Experiments in New
     Interviewing Techniques," *Journal of Marketing Research,
     14,* 306-315.
Cannell, C. F., Marquis, K. H., and Laurent, A. (1977). "A
     Summary of Studies of Interviewing Methodology," *Vital and
     Health Statistics, Series 2, No. 26,* i-65.
Cannell, C. F., Lawson, S. A., and Hauser, D. L. (1975). *A
     Technique for Evaluating Interviewer Performance.* Survey
     Research Center, Ann Arbor, Michigan.
Cannell, C. F. and Kahn, R. L. (1968) "Interviewing," In G.
     Lindzey and E. Aronson (Eds). *The Handbook of Social
     Psychology (Vol. 2),* Addison-Wesley, Reading, MA.
Cochran, W. G. (1977). *Sampling Techniques, 3rd ed.,* John
     Wiley and Sons, Inc., New York.
Collins, M. (1980). "Interviewer Variability: A Review of the
     Problem," *Journal of the Market Research Society, 22,* 77-
     95.
Deming, W. E. (1960). *Sample Design in Business Research,* John
     Wiley & Sons, Inc., New York.
Dijkstra, W. and Van der Zouwen, J. (1982). *Response Behaviors
     In the Survey Interview,* Academic Press, London.
Freeman, J., and Butler, E. W. (1976). "Some Sources of Inter-
     viewer Variance in Surveys," *Public Opinion Quarterly, 40,*
     79-92.
Gove, W. R. (1982). "Systematic Response Bias and Characteris-
     tics of the Respondent," in W. Dijkstra and J. Van der
     Zouwen (Eds.), *Response Behaviour in the Survey Interview,*
     Academic Press, London.
Hansen, M. H., Hurwitz, W. N., and Bershad, M. A. (1961).
     "Measurement Errors in Censuses and Surveys," *Bull.
     International Statistical Institute, 38,* 359-374.

Hansen, M. H., Hurwitz, W. N., Marks, E. S., and Mauldin,
    W. P. (1951). "Response Errors in Surveys," *Journal of the
    American Statistical Association, 46,* 147–190.
Hansen, M. H., Hurwitz, W. N. and Madow, W. G. (1953). *Sample
    Survey Methods and Theory, Volume II,* John Wiley and Sons,
    Inc., New York.
Hauck, M. and Steinkamp, S. (1964). *Survey Reliability and
    Interviewer Competence,* Bureau of Economic and Business
    Research, University of Illinois, Urbana.
Horvitz, D. G., Greenberg, B. G., and Abernathy, J. R.
    (1975). "The Randomized Response Technique," In H. W.
    Sinaike, and L. A. Broedling (Eds.), *Perspectives on
    Attitude Assessment: Surveys and Their Alternatives,*
    Smithsonian Institution, Washington, D. C.
Horvitz, D. G. (1978). "Some Design Issues in Sample Surveys,"
    In N. K. Namboodiri (Ed.), *Survey Sampling and Measure-
    ment,* Academic Press, New York.
Hyman, H. H., Cobb, W. J., Feldman, J. J., Hart, C. W., and
    Stember, C. H. (1954). *Interviewing in Social Research,*
    University of Chicago Press, Chicago.
Jessen, J. (1978). *Statistical Survey Techniques,* John Wiley
    & Sons, Inc., New York.
Kahn, R. L. and Cannell, C. F. (1957). *The Dynamics of Inter-
    viewing,* John Wiley & Sons, Inc., New York.
Kovar, M. G. and Wright, R. A. (1973). "An Experiment with
    Alternative Respondent Rules in the National Health Inter-
    view Survey," *Proceedings of the Social Statistics
    Section, American Statistical Association,* 311–316.
La Barbera, P. A. and MacLachlan, J. M. (1979). "Response
    Latency in Telephone Interviews," *Journal of Advertising
    Research, 19,* 49–55.
Lessler, J. T., Kalsbeek, W. D., Folsom, R. E. (In Press).
    Errors in Surveys, John Wiley and Sons, Inc., New York.
Marquis, K. H. (1978). "Inferring Health Interview Response
    Bias from Imperfect Record Checks," *Proceedings of the
    Section on Survey Research Methods, American Statistical
    Association,* 265–270.
McGrath, J. E. (1982). "Dilemmatics: The Study of Research
    Choices and Dilemmas," in J. E. McGrath, J. Martin, and
    R. A. Kulka (Eds.) *Judgment Calls in Research,* SAGE
    Publications, Beverly Hills.
Moser, C. A. and Kalton, G. (1972). *Survey Methods in Social
    Investigation, Second Edition,* Basic Books, Inc., New
    York.
Murthy, M. (1967). *Sampling Theory and Methods,* Statistical
    Publishing Society, Calcutta.

Page, M. M. (1972). "Demand Characteristics and the Verbal Operant Conditioning Experiment," *Journal of Personality and Social Psychology, 23,* 372-378.

Page, M. M. (1981). "Demand Compliance in Laboratory Experiments," In J. T. Tederschi (Ed.), *Impression Management Theory and Social Psychological Research.* Academic Press, New York.

Payne, S. L. (1951). *The Art of Asking Questions,* Princeton University Press, Princeton.

Pearson, K. (1902). "On the Mathematical Theory of Errors of Measurement," *Philosophical Transactions Royal Society of London, Series A, 198,* 235-299.

Rossi, P. H. and Nock, S. L. (Eds.) (1982). *Measuring Social Judgments: The Factorial Survey Approach,* SAGE Publications, Beverly Hills.

Schuman, H. and Presser, S. (1981). *Questions and Answers in Attitude Surveys: Experiment on Question Form, Wording, and Context,* Academic Press, New York.

Singer, E. and Kohnke-Aguirre, L. (1979). "Interviewer Expectation Effects: A Replication in Psychological Research," *Journal of Personality and Social Psychology, 32,* 368-380.

Sonquist, J. A. and Dunkelberg, W. C. (1977) *Survey and Opinion Research: Procedures for Processing and Analysis.* Prentice-Hall, Englewood Cliffs, N.J.

Sudman, S. and Bradburn, N. M. (1982). *Asking Questions: A Practical Guide to Questionnaire Design,* Jossey-Bass, San Francisco.

Sudman, S. (1980). "Reducing Response Errors in Surveys," *The Statistician, 29:*237-273.

Sudman, S. and Bradburn, N. (1974). *Response Effects in Surveys,* Aldine Publishing Company, Chicago.

Tracy, P. E. and Fox, J. A. (1981). "The Validity of Randomized Response for Sensitive Measurements," *American Sociological Review, 46,* 187-200.

Waksberg, J. and Neter, J. (1964). "A Study of Response Errors in Expenditures Data from Household Surveys," *Journal of the American Statistical Association, 59,* 18-55.

Williams, E. (1977). "Experimental Comparison of Face-to-Face and Mediated Communication: A Review," *Psychological Bulletin, 84,* 963-976.

Woltman, H. F., Turner, A. G., and Bushery, J. M. (1980). "A Comparison of Three Mixed-mode Interviewing Procedures in the National Crime Survey." *Journal of the American Statistical Association, 75,* 534-543.

Zarkovich, S. S. (1966). *Quality of Statistical Data,* Food and Agriculture Organization of the United Nations, Rome.

THE IMPLICATION OF SAMPLE DESIGN ON SURVEY DATA ANALYSIS

Rick L. Williams
Ralph E. Folsom
Lisa Morrissey LaVange

Research Triangle Institute
Research Triangle Park, North Carolina

I. INTRODUCTION

Data are usually collected so that insight may be gained concerning the population from which the data were obtained. To this end, some form of statistical inference is often used to generalize the results beyond the observed study data to the population of interest, the target population. The likelihood that a researcher's extrapolation of results will be valid is directly tied to the methods used to collect and analyze the data. The thrust of this paper is the contention that valid statistical inference requires an analysis strategy that is sensitive to important features of the data collection design. Specifically, the paper explores sample design implications on the analysis of survey data.

The next section of this paper presents three general classes of data collection systems. Section III explores the effects of stratification, multi-stage clustering, and unequal probability selection on Wald statistics that assume a multinomial (simple random) sampling model. Explicit forms are obtained for the effects of unequal weighting, stratification and clustering on the asymptotic distribution of the multinomial Wald statistic. It is shown that assuming a simple random sample may or may not reject the null hypothesis too often depending upon the relative magnitudes of the different effects of the design. The final section presents examples of the analyses of two recent surveys conducted by Research Triangle Institute (RTI). These studies illustrate the potential problems of ignoring the sample design when analyzing sample survey data.

Copyright © 1983 by Academic Press, Inc.
All rights of reproduction in any form reserved.
ISBN 0-12-765480-1

II. TYPES OF DATA COLLECTION SYSTEMS

Koch, et al.(1980) have suggested classifying sampling processes and, hence, data collection systems into three categories:

1. *Historical data* from all units in a study population
   having a natural or fortuitious definition.

2. *Experimental data* involving the random allocation of
   units in a study population to different treatments.

3. *Sample survey data* involving the random selection of
   units from a larger study population.

Historical data arise from designs which do not employ an
explicit probability randomization process in the selection of
units for study. Examples of such data are

-   registries of automobile accidents, cancer deaths,
    births;

-   administrative records of Medicaid claims, hospital
    admissions files;

-   manufacturing records of production, numbers and types
    of defects, inventory;

-   personnel records;

-   sales data.

Since historical data are derived from self-selecting units
in a natural or fortuitious grouping, inference is initially limited to the particular units under study. Extrapolation of the
results to a larger population is usually dependent upon unverifiable assumptions. While inference to a larger population may
be appropriate, the conclusions drawn will always be open to
criticism for this reason.

Data obtained through the random allocation of all the members of a study population to treatment groups is usually referred to as *experimental data*. Examples of experimental data a-
bound in the literature of most fields of research. As is the
case for historical data, inferences from experimental data are,
in the strictest sense, limited to those units under study. However, with experimental data the researcher enjoys the privilege
of selecting which units enter the study and controlling many of

the conditions under which they are studied. Thus, the researcher may select units from all the extremes of the target population to which inference is desired. In this way, the assumptions
necessary for inference to a larger target population may be
studied and placed on a firmer foundation. The conclusions drawn
about the larger target population are still based on assumptions
which are open to criticism since the units under study are usually those conveniently obtained at the judgment of the researcher. However as Deming (1975) notes

> ...much of man's knowledge in science has been
> learned through use of judgement-samples in an-
> alytic studies. Rothamsted and other experi-
> mental stations are places of convenience. So
> is a hospital, or a clinic, and the groups of
> patients therein that we may study.

Sample survey data are characterized by the random selection
of units from the target population with prespecified selection
probabilities. Examples of sample surveys are

- National Health Interview Survey of the National Center
  for Health Statistics,

- acceptance sampling of a large lot of material for
  defects or value,

- quality control samples, and

- opinion polls.

By constructing the data collection design so that each unit in
the target population has a known nonzero probability of being
selected into the study group, it is possible to make statistical
inferences to the target population that are relatively free of
unverifiable assumptions.

A probability sample can be combined with the other two
classes of data collection systems. For example, if a historical
database were too large to be economically analyzed directly, a
sample could be drawn from it and analyzed. Using sampling techniques, rigorous statistical inferences could then be made about
the historical database as a whole. Further judgmental extrapo-
lations to the target population could then be entertained.
Likewise, in an experimental situation, a probability sample of
experimental units could be drawn from the target population and
the treatments then assigned at random to the sample of experimental units. In this way conclusions about the effects of the

treatments in the target population can be validly drawn without
any additional assumption concerning the representativeness of
the study units for the target population.

III. SAMPLE DESIGN EFFECTS ON FINITE POPULATION INFERENCE

     The effect of sample design on the analysis of survey data
has been the subject of considerable debate in recent years.
Most of the arguments on one side or the other of this debate
tend to have parallels in the ongoing controversies regarding the
effects of design randomization on the analysis of experimental
data. While such arguments concerning theoretical foundations
often stimulate creative research, it would be unfortunate if
many students and practitioners view such arguments as license to
ignore traditional sample design issues when it comes to making
statistical inference about relationships in survey data. One
way to dispel such a notion is to develop analytic expressions
that explicitly display the effects of sample design features on
the distribution of classical test statistics. Rao and Scott
(1979) took this tack in their development of a simple design
effect type adjustment for the chi-square goodness-of-fit test
and for applications of the large sample Wald statistic to more
general hypotheses.

     Rao and Scott considered the asymptotic distribution of Wald
statistics with estimated variance-covariance matrices based on a
multinomial sampling model (the with-replacement simple random
sampling case) when the actual sample design might involve multi-
-stage, stratified, unequal probability selections. To illustrate these results, let the (R-1) element column vector $\underset{\sim}{P}$
denote the population distribution with respect to a categorical
survey outcome variable with R response levels. The sample de-
sign based estimate of $\underset{\sim}{P}$ will be denoted by $\underset{\sim}{p}$. For a sample
size of m, the (R-1) by (R-1) variance-covariance matrix estima-
tor for $\underset{\sim}{p}$ based on the multinomial (M) sampling model
has the form

$$v_M = [\mathrm{Diag}(\underset{\sim}{p}) - \underset{\sim}{p}\,\underset{\sim}{p}^T]/m = S_M/m \qquad (3.1)$$

with $\mathrm{Diag}(\underset{\sim}{p})$ depicting a diagonal matrix with the elements of $\underset{\sim}{p}$
on the diagonal and the superscript T indicating matrix transpo-
sition. The Wald statistic for testing the hypothesis

$$H_0 : \quad \underset{\sim}{P} = \underset{\sim 0}{P}$$

assuming the multinomial sampling model is

$$\chi_M^2 \equiv m \; (\underset{\sim}{p} - \underset{\sim 0}{P})^T \; S_M^{-1} \; (\underset{\sim}{p} - \underset{\sim 0}{P}). \qquad (3.2)$$

Assuming that p is asymptotically multivariate normal with mean vector $\underset{\sim 0}{P}$ and design based variance-covariance matrix V_D, then χ_M^2 is distributed asymptotically as the weighted sum of $(R-1)$ squared normal variates with mean zero and variance one, say Z_a^2 $(a = 1, \ldots, R-1)$, with weights λ_a that depict the eigenvalues of the generalized design effect matrix

$$\Lambda = V_M^{-1} \; V_D \qquad (3.3)$$

where V_M is the population version of v_M with the hypothesized distribution $\underset{\sim 0}{P}$ replacing the sample based estimate. With these definitions, the asymptotic distribution of χ_M^2 can be depicted by

$$\chi_M^2 \sim \sum_{a=1}^{R-1} \lambda_a \; Z_a^2 . \qquad (3.4)$$

To illustrate the effect of specific sample design features, Rao and Scott considered the balanced two-stage design with n primary sampling unit (psu) selections and $\overline{m}$ second-stage units drawn from each psu. When the psu's are drawn with probabilities strictly proportional to size M(k) and with-replacement, the single draw selection probability for psu(k) is

$$\phi(k) = M(k)/M(+)$$

where

$$M(+) = \sum_{k=1}^{N} M(k)$$

is the aggregate size measure over the N primary frame units. When M(k) denotes the number of population members belonging to psu(k), M(+) is the total population size.

For each of the n with-replacement primary sampling unit
selections, $\overline{m}$ second stage units (ssu's) are drawn with equal
probabilities and with-replacement. If $x(ij)$ denotes a column
vector of $(R-1)$ response indicator variables for the j-th ssu
selection from the i-th sample psu, then the unbiased two-stage
sample estimator for $\underset{\sim}{P}$ is

$$
\begin{aligned}
\underset{\sim}{p} &= \sum_{i=1}^{n} \sum_{j=1}^{\overline{m}} x(ij)/n\overline{m} \\
&= \sum_{i=1}^{n} \underset{\sim}{p}(i)/n .
\end{aligned}
\tag{3.5}
$$

For the balanced equal-probability sample design outlined above,
the variance-covariance matrix for $\underset{\sim}{p}$ has the form

$$
V_D = \Sigma_M [I + (\overline{m}-1)\Delta]/n\overline{m}
\tag{3.6}
$$

where $\Sigma_M/n\overline{m}$ is the variance-covariance matrix of $\underset{\sim}{p}$ for the
multinomial model and Δ is an $(R-1)$ by $(R-1)$ matrix analogue of
the intra-cluster correlation coefficient. Specifically,

$$
\begin{aligned}
\Delta &\equiv (\Sigma_M^{-1})(\sum_{k=1}^{N} \phi(k)[\underset{\sim}{P}(k)-\underset{\sim}{P}][\underset{\sim}{P}(k)-\underset{\sim}{P}]^T) \\
&= (\Sigma_M^{-1})(\Sigma_B)
\end{aligned}
\tag{3.7}
$$

with $\underset{\sim}{P}(k)$ denoting the response distribution for the $M(k)$ population members residing in psu(k). Recall that the $\phi(k)$ single
draw probabilities depict the relative size measures $[M(k)/M(+)]$.

For the balanced two-stage cluster sample design described
above, the generalized design effect matrix can now be represented in the form

$$
\Lambda = V_M^{-1} V_D = [I + (\overline{m}-1) \Delta].
\tag{3.8}
$$

Taking note of the form of Λ in equation (3.8), the eigenvalue
weights in the asymptotic chi-square representation of χ_M^2 can

now be written as

$$\lambda_a = [1 + (\overline{m}-1)\delta_a]$$

with δ_a denoting the a-th largest eigenvalue of Δ, the intra-cluster correlation matrix. With this representation for the design effect eigenvalues, the multinomial Wald statistic is distributed asymptotically under H_0 as

$$\chi_M^2 \sim \sum_{a=1}^{R-1} [1 + (\overline{m}-1)\delta_a] \ z_a^2. \qquad (3.9)$$

Noting that the multinomial variance-covariance component matrix Σ_M is the sum of the between psu variance-covariance component matrix Σ_B defined in equation (3.7) and the within psu variance-covariance component matrix

$$\Sigma_W = \sum_{k=1}^{N} \phi(k)\{ \text{Diag}[\underset{\sim}{P}(k)] - \underset{\sim}{P}(k)\underset{\sim}{P}(k)^T \},$$

it is clear that for any row vector C of R-1 contrast coefficients

$$(C \ \Sigma_M C^T) = (C\Sigma_B C^T) + (C\Sigma_W C^T)$$

and therefore for all C

$$0 \le (C\Sigma_B C^T)/(C\Sigma_M C^T) \le 1. \qquad (3.10)$$

The inequalities in (3.10) guarantee that the eigenvalues of $\Delta = \Sigma_M^{-1}\Sigma_B$ will all lie on the zero-one interval; that is,

$$0 \le \delta_a \le 1 \qquad (3.11)$$

for a = 1, ..., R - 1. These inequalities show that the multinomial model Wald statistic χ_M^2 in equation (3.9) is generally bigger than a central chi-square variate with (R-1) degrees of freedom. The fact that the test based on χ_M^2 will reject too frequently follows immediately from (3.9) and (3.11), noting that

$$\chi^2_M = \sum_{a=1}^{R-1} z^2_a + (\overline{m}-1) \sum_{a=1}^{R-1} \delta_a z^2_a$$

$$\geq \sum_{a=1}^{R-1} z^2_a .$$

Thus,

$$\chi^2_M \geq \chi^2(R-1)$$

where $\chi^2(R-1)$ denotes a central chi-square variate with $(R-1)$ degrees of freedom.

An asymptotically valid Wald statistic for testing H_0 when the balanced two-stage design is employed, uses the unbiased variance-covariance matrix estimator

$$\hat{V}_D = S_D/n \qquad\qquad (3.12)$$

where

$$S_D = \sum_{i=1}^{n} [\underset{\sim}{p}(i)-\underset{\sim}{p}][\underset{\sim}{p}(i)-\underset{\sim}{p}]^T/(n-1).$$

The with-replacement selection of psu's renders the psu level vectors $\underset{\sim}{p}(i)$ independent and identically distributed with mean vector $\underset{\sim}{P}$ and variance-covariance matrix

$$\Sigma_D = \Sigma_M[I + (\overline{m}-1)\Delta]/\overline{m}.$$

For fixed $\overline{m}$, the distribution of the design based Wald statistic

$$\chi^2_D = n(\underset{\sim}{p}-\underset{\sim}{P}_0) \; S_D^{-1} \; (\underset{\sim}{p}-\underset{\sim}{P}_0)^T, \qquad\qquad (3.13)$$

under H_0 tends to a central chi-square distribution with $(R-1)$ degrees of freedom as the number of psu selections n increases. Alternately, if one fixes the number of primary selections n and lets the number of second-stage draws per psu $(\overline{m})$ tend to infinity, then we would expect χ^2_D to converge in distri-

bution to Hotelling's T^2 under suitable regularity conditions.
In this case, the transformed statistic

$$F_D = [(n-R+1)/(n-1)(R-1)]\chi_D^2 \qquad (3.14)$$

will tend to Snedecor's F with (R-1) numerator and (n-R+1) denom-
inator degrees of freedom.

The key result leading to the enlightening representation
of χ_M^2 in equation (3.9) is the design effect partitioning for
the variance-covariance matrix presented in equation (3.6).
Folsom, et al (1981) have extended this result to display the effects of stratification and without-replacement unequal probability selections at each stage of a balanced multi-stage design.
The effect of unequal weighting resulting from imperfect size
measures and disproportionate stratum allocations is also explicitly displayed. For a without-replacement analogue of a balanced two-stage design, the Horvitz-Thompson combined ratio
estimator for $\underset{\sim}{P}$ has the form

$$\underset{\sim}{p} = \sum_{i=1}^{n} \sum_{j=1}^{\overline{m}} w(ij)\underset{\sim}{x}(ij)/w(\text{++})$$

where w(++) depicts the sample sum of the inverse selection probability weights

$$w(ij) = \left\{ [n\phi(i)] \; [\overline{m}/M(i)] \right\}^{-1}.$$

Letting the effect of stratification at the primary stage be reflected implicitly through its impact on the proportional to size
inclusion probabilities $\pi(i) = n\phi(i)$ and the joint inclusion
probabilities $\pi(ii')$, the Taylor series variance-covariance matrix approximation for $\underset{\sim}{p}$ has the form

$$V_D = \Sigma_B[I+(n-1)R_B]/n + \Sigma_W[I+(\overline{m}-1)R_W]/n\overline{m} \; . \qquad (3.15)$$

With $\theta(k)$ denoting the true relative-size of psu(k), namely
$\theta(k) = M(k)/M(+)$, the between and within psu component matrices
are defined by

$$\Sigma_B = \sum_{k=1}^{N} [\theta(k)^2/\phi(k)][\underset{\sim}{P}(k)-\underset{\sim}{P}][\underset{\sim}{P}(k)-\underset{\sim}{P}]^T$$

and

$$\Sigma_W = \sum_{k=1}^{N} [\theta(k)^2/\phi(k)]\{Diag[\underset{\sim}{P}(k)]-\underset{\sim}{P}(k)\underset{\sim}{P}(k)^T\}. \qquad (3.16)$$

Note, that when the relative size measures $\phi(k)$ used to specify the psu inclusion probabilities are equivalent to the actual relative sizes, then the Σ_B and Σ_W matrices defined in (3.16) are equivalent to the previous with-replacement components. The R_W matrix is analogous to the negative cross-correlation between sampling units induced by without-replacement selections. This matrix is defined by

$$R_W = -\Sigma_W^{-1} (\sum_{k=1}^{N} [\theta(k)^2/\phi(k)]\Sigma_M(k)/[M(k)-1])$$

where $\Sigma_M(k)$ denotes the multinomial component matrix for $\underset{\sim}{p}(k)$. This multinomial component matrix is defined explicitly by the expression in curly brackets of equation (3.16).

The R_B matrix reflects both the negative cross-correlation effects of without-replacement primary unit selection and the effects of primary stratification. For a primary design with L strata and $n(h) = 2$ without-replacement primary selections per stratum, one can parameterize R_B in terms of a stratification effect matrix Γ_S^2 and an average without-replacement selection effect matrix $\overline{R}_B$. Letting $\phi(h) = n(h)/n$ depict the primary unit allocation fraction for stratum h, Γ_S^2 is defined in terms of the following between stratum component matrix

$$\Sigma_S = \sum_{h=1}^{L} [\theta(h)^2/\phi(h)][\underset{\sim}{P}(h)-\underset{\sim}{P}][\underset{\sim}{P}(h)-\underset{\sim}{P}]^T \qquad (3.17)$$

where $\theta(h)=M(h)/M(+)$ denotes the actual relative size of stratum h in terms of population members. The stratification effect matrix is then defined by

$$\Gamma_S^2 = \Sigma_B^{-1} \Sigma_S.$$

The average between psu cross-correlation effect matrix $\overline{R}_B$ resulting from paired without replacement selections within primary strata is defined in terms of within stratum covariance and cross-covariance matrices $\Sigma_B(h)$ and $\Sigma R_B(h)$. The within stratum covariance component matrix is defined by

$$\Sigma_B(h) = \sum_{k=1}^{N(h)} [\theta(k|h)^2/\phi(k|h)][\underset{\sim}{P}(hk)-\underset{\sim}{P}(h)][\underset{\sim}{P}(hk)-\underset{\sim}{P}(h)]^T \tag{3.18}$$

where $\theta(k|h) = M(hk)/M(h+)$ is the actual size of psu(hk) relative to the stratum h total population size $M(h+)$. The sampling relative size measure $\phi(k|h)$ conditional on stratum h membership is defined in terms of approximate psu sizes $S(hk)$ such that $\phi(k|h)=S(hk)/S(h+)$. The global psu relative size measure $\phi(hk)$ involved in the previous component definitions has the form $\phi(h)\phi(k|h)$ for a stratified primary sample with $\phi(h) = n(h)/n$ depicting the stratum h allocation fraction.

For the paired selection design $\phi(h) = 2/n$ for all h. The cross-covariance matrices $\Sigma R_B(h)$ are defined in terms of scaled joint inclusion probabilities that take the form

$$\phi(k\ell|h) = \pi(k\ell|h)/n(h)[n(h)-1],$$

where $\pi(k\ell|h)$ denotes the probability that psu's (hk) and (hℓ) will both be selected from stratum h. For the paired selection design $\phi(k\ell|h) = \pi(k\ell|h)/2$. In terms of these double draw probabilities

$$\Sigma R_B(h) = \sum_{k=1}^{N(h)} \sum_{\ell \neq k} \Big[\phi(k\ell|h)[\theta(k|h)\theta(\ell|h)/\phi(k|h)\phi(\ell|h)] \tag{3.19}$$

$$[\underset{\sim}{P}(hk)-\underset{\sim}{P}(h)][\underset{\sim}{P}(h\ell)-\underset{\sim}{P}(h)]^T \Big].$$

The average cross-correlation matrix $\overline{R}_B$ can now be defined as a generalized combined ratio across strata; namely,

$$\overline{R}_B = \{ \sum_{h=1}^{L} [\Sigma_B(h)/\phi(h)] \}^{-1} \{ \sum_{h=1}^{L} [\Sigma R_B(h)/\phi(h)] \} . \tag{3.20}$$

With these definitions, the original cross-correlation matrix R_B used in equation (3.15) can be partitioned into its separate stratification and with-replacement selection effects as follows:

$$R_B = [-\Gamma_S^2 + (I-\Gamma_S^2)\overline{R}_B]/(n-1) . \tag{3.21}$$

The result in equation (3.21) allows one to recast the design variance matrix V_D from equation (3.15) in the design effect form

$$V_D = \Sigma_T [I + \overline{m} \, \xi + (\overline{m}-1)\zeta]/n\overline{m} \tag{3.22}$$

where

$$\Sigma_T \equiv \Sigma_B + \Sigma_W$$

$$\xi = \Delta[-\Gamma_S^2 + (I-\Gamma_S^2)\overline{R}_B],$$

and

$$\zeta = \Delta + (I-\Delta)R_W .$$

The Δ matrix in the ξ and ζ defining equations is the fraction of total variation Σ_T that is accounted for by the between psu co-variance component matrix Σ_B; that is,

$$\Delta = \Sigma_T^{-1} \Sigma_B.$$

A matrix W reflecting the effect of unequal weighting is now defined. This design feature can have both positive and nega-tive effects on the precision of $\underset{\sim}{p}$. Planned disproportionate allocations of primary units to strata can reduce the variance while unplanned weight variations within strata due to imprecise size measures typically inflate the variance. The matrix W is defined in terms of the universe level weighted distribution vec-tors

$$P = [\sum_{k=1}^{N} \sum_{\ell=1}^{M(k)} w(k\ell) \underset{\sim}{X}(k\ell)/ \sum_{k=1}^{N} \sum_{\ell=1}^{M(k)} w(k\ell)],$$

the universe mean of the $w(k\ell)$ inverse selection probability weights, say $\bar{w}$, and the global sampling fraction $f = [n\bar{m}/M(+)]$. In terms of these parameters, one can show that

$$W = \Sigma_M^{-1}\ \Sigma_T \tag{3.23}$$

$$= [f\bar{w}][\Sigma_M^{-1}\ \{\text{Diag}[P] - (P)\underset{\sim}{P}^T - \underset{\sim}{P}(P^T) + \underset{\sim\sim}{PP}^T\}]\ .$$

Since one can show that f^{-1} is equivalent to the universe level harmonic mean of the $w(k\ell)$ weights by noting that

$$w(k\ell)^{-1} = n\bar{m}\ \phi(k)/M(k)$$

and that the relative size measures $\phi(k)$ sum to unity, one observes that the bracketed scalar multiple $[f\bar{w}]$ in equation (3.23) always exceeds one. This result follows from the fact that the arithmetic mean of positive quantities always exceeds the associated harmonic mean. To examine the bracketed matrix in equation (3.23), consider a dichotomous response distribution with $R = 2$. In this case, the bracketed matrix in equation (3.23) reduces to the scalar quantity

$$Q = \{[P/P] - [(1-P)/(1-P)] - 1\}\ . \tag{3.24}$$

This component of the unequal weighting factor will reflect any gains due to optimum specification of the selection probabilities. Note that Q is less than one when $P \le .5$ if $P < P$. The weighted proportion of population members with $x = 1$ is smaller than P when population members with $x = 1$ have a higher probability of selection on average than members with $x = 0$.

Exploiting the partitioning of the design covariance matrix V_D displayed in equation (3.22), Folsom, et al (1981) arrived at the following representation for the distribution of the multinomial goodness-of-fit Wald statistic

$$\chi_M^2 \sim \sum_{a=1}^{(R-1)} w_a [1 + \bar{m}\ \xi_a + (\bar{m}-1)\zeta_a]\ z_a^2. \tag{3.25}$$

The effects w_a, ξ_a and ζ_a are defined in terms of the matrix of eigenvectors for the generalized design effect matrix

$$\Lambda \equiv W[I + \bar{m}\ \xi + (\bar{m}-1)\zeta]\ . \tag{3.26}$$

The matrix of column eigenvectors E of Λ lead to the following singular value decomposition of Λ

$$E^{-1} \Lambda E = A$$

where A is an $(R-1)$ by $(R-1)$ diagonal matrix with diagonal elements λ_a, the eigenvalues of Λ. The form of Λ in equation (3.26) leads to the identity

$$\lambda_a = (E^a \ \underset{\sim}{W} E_a) + \overline{m}(E^a \ \underset{\sim}{W} \xi E_a) + (\overline{m}-1)(E^a \ \underset{\sim}{W} \zeta E_a)$$

$$\equiv w_a + \overline{m} w_a \ \xi_a + (\overline{m}-1) w_a \zeta_a$$

with $E_{\underset{\sim}{a}}$ denoting the a-th column of E and E^a the a-th row of E^{-1}.

Recalling the representation of ξ in equation (3.22), one observes that ξ_a combines the variance reducing effects of primary stratification $(-\Gamma_S^2)$ and without replacement selection at the primary stage $(\overline{R}_B)$. The ζ_a component combines the variance inflating effect of clustering (Δ) and the variance reducing effect of without replacement selection at the second stage (R_W). This analysis suggests that the multinomial chi-square statistic can be conservative for sample designs where the deleterious effects of clustering and accidental unequal weighting are overcome by the beneficial effects of stratification and without-replacement selections. Folsom, et al (1981) obtained analogous results for simultaneously testing vector valued nonlinear hypotheses of the form

$$H_0 : \quad \underset{\sim}{G}(\underset{\sim}{p}_1, \underset{\sim}{p}_2, \ldots, \underset{\sim}{p}_D) = \Phi \tag{3.27}$$

where the $\underset{\sim}{p}_d$ represent subpopulation d specific estimates of the response distribution for a particular questionnaire item and Φ is the g element null vector. The Wald statistic for simultaneously testing such hypotheses based on the D independent multinomials model has the form of (3.25) with the sum containing g elements; namely, one for each independent hypothesis specified by (3.27). General hypotheses for D by R contingency tables such as those symbolized by (3.27) are asymptotically equivalent to linear contrasts of the form

$$C(t) = \sum_{d=1}^{D} \sum_{r=1}^{R-1} h_t(dr)P(dr).$$

Using an ANOVA factorial effect analogy, the clustering effect for a single sample proportion is related to the main effect of psu's, while the clustering effect for a contrast is analogous to a psu by contrast interaction. It is not therefore so surprising to observe that multinomial based chi-square statistics for general hypotheses like (3.27) are often smaller than an asymptotically valid design based test statistic. When the sample design incorporates effective stratification at the second and subsequent stages so that the negative R_W cross-correlation effects are magnified, the likelihood that the multinomial Wald statistic χ_M^2 will be conservative is increased.

IV. EXAMPLES OF SURVEY DATA ANALYSIS AND EFFECTS OF DESIGN

A. *Introduction*

Most large national surveys employ a complex stratified multi-stage probability sample. Such sample designs allow economical data collection. However, they complicate data analysis since most standard statistical procedures implicitly assume simple random sampling from an infinite population. As discussed in the previous sections, classical analysis methods which ignore the sample design may lead to erroneous inferences from sample survey data. Several other authors, such as Shah, Holt, and Folsom (1977) and Fellegi (1980), have also examined the consequences of ignoring the sample design when analyzing survey data.

The challenge to researchers is to properly account for the sample design when analyzing survey data. Articles by Koch, Freeman, and Freeman (1975), and Freeman, Freeman, and Brock (1977) have advocated a weighted least squares approach. This is an extension of the methodology developed by Grizzle, Starmer and Koch (1969) for categorical data analysis. This style of analysis requires two steps. First, for analyzing differences between subpopulations, estimates of the parameter of interest are calculated for the various subpopulations along with the corresponding variance-covariance matrix. Second, weighted least squares is applied to evaluate relevant hypotheses concerning subpopulation effects. During the first stage of the analysis, the parameters and their variance-covariance matrix are estimated in accordance with the sample design. The secondary analysis can then proceed in a more classical vein using weighted least squares or standard multivariate techniques.

Unfortunately, most researchers are ill-equipped to carry out the first step of the proceeding analysis strategy since virtually all traditional software available to them ignores the design structure inherent in sample survey data. Methods to alleviate this problem for tests of goodness-of-fit and independence in a two way table have been proposed by Rao and Scott (1981) and Fellegi (1980). Under their proposals, classical test statistics for these two problems are scaled by an average sample design effect.

The remainder of section IV presents example analyses for two major surveys conducted by RTI. Inferential statistics assuming a simple random sample are compared with the asymptotically correct sample design based statistics for both surveys.

B. *National Assessment of Educational Progress*

Survey Background

The National Assessment of Educational Progress (NAEP) is a continuing survey of the knowledge, skill, understanding and attitudes of young Americans, ages 9, 13, or 17. Each year from 75,000 to 100,000 persons are assessed in one or more learning areas. NAEP employs a three-stage unequal probability stratified design. The first-stage stratification variables include geographic region, size and type of community, and socioeconomic status. The stages of the design are geographic units, schools, and finally students. Each selected student is administered one or more packages of exercises (also called items) in a particular subject area.

Theoretical Background

The methodology used in this section is analogous to the development in section III. The specific results required in this section are summarized here. Consider the vector $\underset{\sim}{P} = (p_1, p_2, \ldots, p_d)'$ where p_i is the proportion of students responding correctly to a particular exercise for student subgroup i. Let $\underset{\sim}{p}$ be an estimate of P calculated from the sample and assume that $\underset{\sim}{p}$ is asymptotically multivariate normal with variance-covariance matrix V. Classical analysis methods, which assume simple random sampling, lead to the dispersion matrix $S = \text{Diag}\{p_i(1-p_i)/n_i\}$. In this setting, the hypothesis for testing subgroup differences or contrasts may be stated as:

$$H_0: \underset{\sim}{CP} = \phi \quad \text{vs.} \quad H_A: \underset{\sim}{CP} \neq \phi$$

where C is a matrix of d linearly independent contrasts and ϕ is the (d × 1) null vector. The usual test statistic ignoring the sample design is

$$\chi_M^2 = (\hat{C\underset{\sim}{P}})^T[CSC^T]^{-1}(\hat{C\underset{\sim}{P}}).$$

On the other hand, the appropriate test of this hypothesis accounting for the sample design is based on the Wald statistic

$$\chi_w^2 = (\hat{C\underset{\sim}{P}})^T[CVC^T]^{-1}(\hat{C\underset{\sim}{P}}),$$

which is asymptotically distributed as a chi-square with d degrees of freedom under H_0.

   A result similar to that shown by Rao and Scott (1981) is that under the null hypothesis $H_0: CP = \phi$,

$$\chi_M^2 = \sum_{i=1}^{d} \lambda_i Z_i^2$$

where $Z_1, \ldots, Z_d$ are asymptotically independent $N(0,1)$ random variables and $\lambda_1 \geq \lambda_2 \geq \cdots \geq \lambda_d$ are the eigenvalues of $\Lambda = [CSC^T]^{-1}[CVC^T]$. Rao and Scott refer to these eigenvalues as "generalized design effects." Following Rao and Scott's suggestion for tests of independence, χ_M^2 can be scaled by $\bar{\lambda} = (\Sigma\lambda_i)/d$ to bring the test more nearly into line with the Wald statistic χ_w^2. Notice that this adjustment factor is dependent on the exact contrast being considered and requires full knowledge of the matrices S and V. Rao and Scott indicate that the average eigenvalue of $S^{-1}V$ may provide an adequate adjustment for a general contrast. In the cases that will be addressed in this paper, S is a diagonal matrix and the average eigenvalue of $S^{-1}V$ is also the average of the subgroup design effects.

Empirical Investigation

Initially, five NAEP exercises per age class were selected for analysis from the Year 09 Mathematics Assessment. Each item was recorded one for correct and zero for incorrect. An additional score was defined for each student as the proportion of the items analyzed on a package that the student answered correctly. This score was analyzed within each age class to form three mean scores for analysis.

Four domain or subgroup defining variables were also selected. These were, with their corresponding levels:

Sex	*Race*
Male	White
Female	Other
Type of Community (TOC)	*Parental Education (PARED)*
Extreme Rural	Not High School Graduate
Metro	High School Graduate
Other	Post High School

The ultimate goal of this study was to compare sample design based analyses of NAEP data with those assuming a simple random sample. This approach proceeds by first estimating a vector of domain statistics and its corresponding covariance matrix. Various hypotheses concerning this vector can then be evaluated using weighted least squares and large sample Wald statistics. Two vectors of domain means were formed for each of the 15 item scores and the three mean scores. The first vector contained 12 elements corresponding to the complete cross-classification of Race, Sex, and Parents Education (PARED). The second vector was derived from the cross-classification of Sex, Type of Community (TOC), and PARED and was of length 18. For the 15 item scores, these vectors consisted of simple proportion correct p-values. Two covariance matrices were then estimated for each vector. One was based upon the actual sample design and the other assumed a simple random sample of students. The covariance matrices were estimated using a Taylor series linearization approach.

At this point several exercises were excluded from the study because their estimated covariance matrices were singular. For the Race*Sex*PARED cross-classification only one item was excluded. However, for the Sex*TOC*PARED cross-classification it was necessary to exclude five items.

A linear model was then fitted, via weighted least squares, to each of the remaining domain mean vectors. For the

Race*Sex*PARED domain cross-classification vectors the model contained the main effects of Race and Sex, a linear effect of PARED
and the four possible two- and three-way interactions among these
three effects. The Sex*TOC*PARED domain classification model had
the same form except that TOC was substituted for Race. These
models were fitted two ways -- one weighted with the design based
covariance matrix and the other weighted with the simple random
sampling covariance matrix. The lack of fit of each model and
the significance of each effect in the model was then assessed.
These tests are labeled one through eight in Tables I and II.

In addition, nine other hypotheses were considered and are
labeled 9 through 17 in Tables I and II. These hypotheses were
tested via direct contrasts of the domain means. The tests labeled "average" (numbers 10, 11, 12 and 13) average the effect
over the combined levels of the other two variables. On the other hand, the "nested" tests (numbers 14, 15, 16 and 17) test for
all the indicated simple effects being simultaneously null over
the combined levels of the other two variables.

Two test statistics were entertained for each hypothesis.
The first test was a Wald statistic chi-square based upon the actual NAEP sample design. A second Wald-like statistic was also
calculated assuming a simple random sample of students and will
be referred to as the simple random sampling chi-square. These
two test statistics were calculated for each hypothesis for 14
NAEP items and three mean scores for the Race*Sex*PARED cross-
classification, as well as for 10 NAEP items plus three mean
scores for the Sex*TOC*PARED cross-classification.

The design effects (DEFFs) for each domain p-value and mean
score used in the analyses are summarized in Tables III, IV, and
V. Each table presents the minimum, median, maximum, and
mean DEFFs for a particular NAEP item or mean score across the
levels of the indicated domain defining cross-classification
(i.e., Race*Sex*PARED or Sex*TOC*PARED). The design effects reported in these three tables are consistent with previous NAEP
experience and tend to average around 1.4. Also, as discussed a-
bove, the mean DEFF's given in the last column of each table are
the exact quantities proposed by Rao and Scott (1981) and Fellegi
(1980) for adjusting simple random sampling (SRS) based Wald statistic chi-squares to reflect the effects of the sample design.
These are the adjustment factors used in the subsequent discussion.

As was noted earlier, two different methods of analyses or
hypothesis testing often used by researchers were considered.
The first fitted a linear model to the estimated domain statistics. Relevant hypotheses were then tested via contrasts of the

TABLE I.   *Hypothesis Tests for the Race*Sex*PARED Cross-Classification*

Test Number	d.f.	Description
Linear Model Tests		
1	4	Lack of fit
2	1	Race
3	1	Sex
4	1	PARED linear
5	1	Race*Sex
6	1	Race*PARED linear
7	1	Sex*PARED linear
8	1	Race*Sex*PARED linear
Contrast Tests		
9	11	All cells equal
10	1	Average Race effect
11	1	Average Sex effect
12	2	Average PARED effect
13	1	Average PARED linear effect
14	6	Nested Race effect
15	6	Nested Sex effect
16	8	Nested PARED effect
17	4	Nested PARED linear effect

TABLE II.   *Hypothesis Tests for the Sex*TOC*PARED Cross-Classification*

Test Number	d.f.	Description
Linear Model Tests		
1	6	Lack of fit
2	1	Race
3	2	TOC
4	1	PARED linear
5	2	Sex*TOC
6	1	Sex*PARED linear
7	2	TOC*PARED linear
8	2	Sex*TOC*PARED linear
Contrast Tests		
9	17	All cells equal
10	1	Average Sex effect
11	2	Average TOC effect
12	2	Average PARED effect
13	1	Average PARED linear effect
14	9	Nested Sex effect
15	12	Nested TOC effect
16	12	Nested PARED effect
17	6	Nested PARED linear effect

TABLE III. *NAEP Item Design Effects for the Race*Sex*PARED Cross-Classification*

NAEP Item	Minimum DEFF	Median DEFF	Maximum DEFF	Mean DEFF
N0222A	.79	1.23	3.08	1.48
N0227A	.80	1.36	1.94	1.40
N0305C	.62	1.39	1.93	1.35
N0323A	.59	1.27	1.67	1.14
T0105A	.91	1.50	2.84	1.63
T0110A	.56	1.26	2.38	1.43
T0203A	.99	1.72	2.29	1.66
T0223A	.69	1.13	2.32	1.28
T0224A	1.00	1.31	2.82	1.47
S0108A	.63	.94	1.99	1.11
S0117A	.61	1.17	2.44	1.23
S0121A	.39	1.09	3.71	1.37
S0206A	.72	1.25	3.44	1.40
S0225A	.59	.84	1.83	.99
Average	.71	1.25	2.48	1.35

TABLE IV. *NAEP Item Design Effects for the Sex*TOC*PARED Cross-Classification*

NAEP Item	Minimum DEFF	Median DEFF	Maximum DEFF	Mean DEFF
N0222A	.21	1.17	2.49	1.25
N0305C	.37	1.53	2.21	1.35
T0105A	.49	1.40	4.32	1.61
T0110A	.64	1.28	3.02	1.31
T0203A	.27	1.36	4.46	1.62
T0223A	.68	1.14	2.10	1.25
S0108A	.44	1.03	2.01	1.14
S0117A	.35	1.11	2.14	1.14
S0206A	.48	1.53	4.17	1.66
S0225A	.47	.93	2.37	1.04
Average	.44	1.25	2.93	1.34

TABLE V. Mean Scores Design Effects

Model/Age	Minimum DEFF	Median DEFF	Maximum DEFF	Mean DEFF
RACE*SEX*PARED				
9-year-olds	.57	1.45	3.32	1.50
13-year-olds	.78	1.31	2.33	1.46
17-year-olds	.49	1.09	2.57	1.16
Average	.61	1.28	2.74	1.37
SEX*TOC*PARED				
9-year-olds	.80	1.52	3.47	1.66
13-year-olds	.59	1.50	3.57	1.66
17-year-olds	.75	1.30	2.61	1.45
Average	.71	1.44	3.32	1.59

estimated linear model parameters. The parameters were estimated weighting inversely proportional to the SRS covariance matrix of the domain statistics to obtain the SRS test statistics. Another set of parameter estimates was obtained by weighting by the inverse of the design based covariance matrix and the asymptotically correct test statistics were calculated. The second method of analysis evaluated hypotheses via direct contrasts of the domain statistics. Again this was first accomplished using the SRS covariance matrix to obtain the SRS test statistics and was then repeated using the design based covariance matrix to obtain the asymptotically correct tests. Results in the rest of this section will be presented separately for these two modes of analysis (i.e., contrasts of linear model coefficients and contrasts of cell means).

For each hypothesis test entertained in this portion of the investigation, the ratio of the SRS based test statistic to the asymptotically correct sample design based Wald statistic chi-square was calculated. These ratios are another measure of the effect of the sample design and are referred to in the remaining tables as *hypothesis test design effects*. Two issues will be addressed by way of these test DEFFs. First, an indication of the ordinal relationship between the two test statistics will be sought. That is, does the SRS statistic tend to be generally smaller or larger than the design based chi-square? Second, are the test DEFFs fairly constant, at least within an item or mean score? This second point is important if a simple multiplicative adjustment to the SRS test statistics is to be successful. Tables VI, VII, and VIII present a summary of the test DEFFs for each mean or item score for the indicated cross-classification. The minimum, median, maximum and mean test design effects are shown separately for linear model coefficient contrasts (test numbers 1 through 8 in Tables I and II) and cell mean contrasts (test numbers 9 through 17 in Tables I and II).

The most striking feature of these three tables is the extreme instability of the test DEFFs for linear model coefficients. In virtually every case the mean is far greater than the median, indicating a skewed distribution with a long right hand tail. It appears that adjusting the SRS test statistic for the linear model coefficient contrasts will not prove fruitful because of the extreme range they cover relative to the design based statistic. This may result from using the SRS covariance matrix to estimate the linear model parameters for the SRS test statistic. Thus, two different sets of estimated coefficients with two different covariance matrices are being contrasted rather than a common set of coefficient estimates with two different covariance matrices. In this situation, the design effect adjustment theory does not strictly apply. These results are included to illustrate the problems that arise when SRS is assumed. Conversely, Tables VI, VII, and VIII indicate that the cell mean contrast hypothesis test design effects tend to be more symmetrically distributed over a narrower range than their linear model counterparts. However, they still exhibit enough variation on both sides of unity to make a simple multiplicative adjustment questionable.

As indicated earlier, theoretical considerations suggest that the mean design effects presented in Tables III, IV, and V may provide serviceable adjustments to the SRS test statistics. This conclusion is drawn into question by comparing the mean DEFFs in these three tables with the average test DEFFs for cell mean contrasts in Tables VI, VII, and VIII. Almost without exception the mean test DEFFs are less than their corresponding p-value DEFF average. In addition, the mean hypothesis test DEFFs are generally near unity or less while the standard mean DEFFs are generally much greater than unity. This implies that dividing the SRS test statistic by the mean design effect will produce a test that is generally much too conservative for NAEP data. In fact, the adjustment suggested by Rao and Scott (1981) or Fellegi (1980) is in the wrong direction for the NAEP examples presented here.

TABLE VI. Hypothesis Test Design Effects by NAEP Item for the Race*Sex*PARED Cross-Classification

NAEP Item	Contrast of Linear Model Coefficients				Contrast of Cell Means			
	Minimum	Median	Maximum	Mean	Minimum	Median	Maximum	Mean
N0222A	.04	.82	5.42	1.41	.19	.74	1.81	.88
N0227A	.00	.57	900.26	112.96	.23	1.02	1.60	.88
N0305C	.09	.57	18.69	3.88	.62	1.33	2.40	1.38
N0323A	.00	.48	1.08	.57	.51	1.08	2.01	1.12
T0105A	.32	.99	15.73	4.02	.44	1.16	1.98	1.27
T0110A	.16	.63	1.72	.81	.56	1.18	2.18	1.19
T0203A	.10	.86	2.29	1.03	.53	1.51	2.21	1.50
T0223A	.49	5.10	284.87	45.21	.72	1.11	1.63	1.10
T0224A	.80	1.68	34.09	9.05	.65	1.10	2.41	1.27
S0108A	.03	.71	47.13	6.47	.55	.84	1.50	.93
S0117A	.19	.59	3.62	.97	.53	.75	1.75	1.00
S0121A	.00	.47	26.19	3.91	.60	.95	2.23	1.19
S0206A	.59	1.51	2.67	1.58	.59	1.10	2.09	1.12
S0225A	.34	.65	2.33	.87	.43	.92	1.09	.84
Average	.23	1.12	96.15	13.77	.51	1.06	1.92	1.12

TABLE VII. Hypothesis Test Design Effects by NAEP for the Sex*TOC*PARED Cross-Classification

NAEP Item	Contrast of Linear Model Coefficients				Contrast of Cell Means			
	Minimum	Median	Maximum	Mean	Minimum	Median	Maximum	Mean
N0222A	.48	4.28	55.14	11.51	.11	.48	2.82	.75
N0305C	.10	1.08	190.09	29.98	.19	.97	1.81	.89
T0105A	.04	.60	6.97	1.70	.13	.39	3.23	.98
T0110A	.37	.76	1.57	.80	.19	.55	3.41	.84
T0203A	.14	.44	3.93	.91	.27	1.08	1.84	.93
T0223A	.22	1.23	10.30	2.40	.45	.86	1.13	.77
S0108A	.02	.14	.64	.22	.10	.36	2.62	.73
S0117A	.46	.97	2.80	1.22	.03	.36	2.46	.70
S0206A	.11	.47	1.27	.54	.10	.64	1.27	.59
S0225A	.05	.75	2.98	.98	.23	.45	1.43	.60
Average	.20	1.07	27.57	5.03	.18	.61	2.20	.78

TABLE VIII. *Hypothesis Test Design Effects for Mean Scores*

Model/Age	Contrast of Linear Model Coefficients				Contrast of Cell Means			
	Minimum	Median	Maximum	Mean	Minimum	Median	Maximum	Mean
Race*Sex*PARED								
9-year-olds	.11	.22	3.74	.85	.29	.91	1.67	1.00
13-year-olds	.09	1.86	7064.23	885.11	.59	1.19	2.23	1.26
17-year-olds	.00	.43	1.16	.56	.40	1.08	1.32	.89
Average	.07	.84	2356.38	295.51	.43	1.06	1.74	1.05
Sex*TOC*PARED								
9-year-olds	.23	.39	1.39	.55	.19	.62	2.53	.91
13-year-olds	.05	.50	1.96	.74	.17	.72	2.87	1.09
17-year-olds	.02	.65	223.55	28.54	.03	.50	1.27	.53
Average	.10	.51	75.63	9.94	.13	.61	2.22	.84

C. *National Medical Care Utilization and Expenditure Survey*

The analysis of the National Medical Care Utilization and
Expenditure Survey (NMCUES) data offers another example of analyzing complex sample survey data. NMCUES was a large-scale
longitudinal survey conducted by RTI in 1980. Data were collected on households selected from a multi-stage cluster sample with
unequal probabilities of selection. Five such samples were independently drawn, a national household sample (HHS) and four state
Medicaid household samples (SMHS). The target population of the
analysis of the HHS data is the U.S. population during 1980,
while the target population of the SMHS analyses includes Medicaid enrollees in California, Michigan, New York, and Texas only.

An important part of the SMHS data analyses is the comparison of health care utilization rates among the four states. Because the Medicaid enrollees in each state differed considerably
with respect to various extraneous factors believed to affect
health care utilization, it was necessary to control for possible
confounding due to these factors before making these comparisons.
It was also of interest to assess the significance of the effects
of extraneous factors on utilization as well as the significance
of any effect due to programmatic differences between states.
Extensive regression analyses were carried out to accomplish
these objectives.

Regression models were fitted to the SMHS data for ten utilization measures in each of four Medicaid categories of aid.
For ease of interpretation and to avoid problems of small sample
sizes, each model included only main effects of the confounding
variables, an effect for state differences, and all two-way interactions involving the state effect. A survey regression software package, SURREGR (Holt, 1977), developed at RTI was used to
generate estimates of model parameters and the corresponding
variance-covariance matrices. With this package the variances
are estimated via a Taylor series approximation assuming independent selection of PSU's within the primary strata.

The regression equations were used to compute standardized
mean utilization rates for a comparison of the states programs.
The combined four-state population was decided upon as the standard population. Evaluating the regression equation at the four-
state average values of the confounding variables produced the
desired adjustments for each state. Because the vector of regression estimates and the corresponding variance-covariance
matrix are output from SURREGR, it was possible to compute the
adjusted means as a linear combination of the estimates and, assuming the standardizing proportions are fixed, the standard

errors of the adjusted means. Wald statistics were generated by the methods described earlier to test for significant differences among the four states.

The SMHS analyses also included estimation of various disparity ratios of utilization. For example, it was desired to calculate the ratio of mean hospital discharges for blacks to mean hospital discharges for whites in each state, adjusted to the four-state average. By applying a logarithmic transformation it was possible to express each disparity ratio as a linear contrast of the regression estimates and thereby produce the standard error of the ratio. Wald statistics were then generated to test that the disparity ratios were identical to one.

For comparison, the regression models were also fit using a standard linear models package, SAS GLM (Goodnight, et al., 1979). Weighted estimates produced by this package are identical to those produced by SURREGR but the inferential statistics are computed under inappropriate classical assumptions. The probability level for testing each effect equal to zero (after adjusting for all other effects) were compared for the two procedures. As an example, Table IX gives the results for the average number of M.D. visits per person.

Notice that all except three of the 18 SURREGR tests were more significant (i.e., smaller p-value) than the SAS GLM tests. Three other such tables were also constructed. In total, only 11 out of 72 times was the GLM p-value smaller than the SURREGR p-value. This implies that for these data the classical analysis method, assuming simple random sampling, was more conservative than the sample design based method.

This somewhat surprising result may possibly be explained by considering the state Medicaid household survey (SMHS) sample designs. In general, the Medicaid households were sampled from files of Medicaid eligible cases obtained from the states. These samples were clustered by postal ZIP codes with an average cluster size of approximately 3.25 cases within each Medicaid aid category. These samples were deeply stratified and designed to be equal weighting within each state by aid category. In addition, since the samples were drawn from the Medicaid eligibility files, they were direct samples from a homogenous, well-defined population.

The comparisons between SURREGR and SAS GLM were done within Medicaid aid category. Thus, any effects of unequal weighting were minimal. In addition, since the population within Medicaid aid category is homogenous with a small cluster size, the effects of clustering should also be small.

TABLE IX. *Probability Levels for Tests of Null Model Parameters; Mean M. D. Visits, Medicaid Aid Category: SSI Blind or Disabled*

Effect	Probability Levels	
	Method 1 (SURREGR)	Method 2 (SAS GLM)
State	0.2106	0.3825
Age	0.3663	0.5084
Sex	0.0000	0.0090
Race	0.7586	0.9151
Ethnicity	0.2941	0.7281
Family Income	0.0000	0.0021
Education of Head of Household	0.0607	0.1965
SMSA	0.9459	0.9586
Perceived Health Status	0.0000	0.0000
Age*State	0.4753	0.2667
Sex*State	0.3167	0.7322
Race*State	0.5784	0.7831
Ethnicity*State	0.0532	0.5721
Income*State	0.4210	0.4192
Education*State	0.0038	0.0873
SMSA*State	0.9593	0.9492
Perceived Health Status *State	0.1111	0.4572
Overall Goodness of Fit of Model	0	0

It appears that the SMHS design is very efficient relative to a simple random sample, and by taking advantage of the design in the analysis, more sensitive tests were obtained. Other analyses tend to support this conclusion. For example, the design effects for simple descriptive estimates within state and aid category tend to be substantially less than one.

ACKNOWLEDGMENTS

Part of the work upon which this publication is based was performed persuant to Grant NIE-G-80-0003 of the National Institute of Education. It does not, however, necessarily reflect the view of that agency.

REFERENCES

Deming, W. E. (1975). "On Probability as a Basis for Action,"
The American Statistician, 29, No. 4, 146-152.

Fellegi, I. P. (1980). "Approximate Tests of Independence and
Goodness of Fit Based on Stratified Multi-stage Samples,"
*Journal of the American Statistical Association, 75, No.
370*, 261-268.

Folsom, R. E. and Williams, R. L. (1981). *Design Effects and
the Analysis of Survey Data*, Research Triangle
Institute,Research Triangle Park, North Carolina.

Freeman, D. H., Freeman, J. L. and Brock, D. B. (1977).
"Modularization for the Analysis of Complex Sample Survey
Data," *Bulletin of the International Statistical Institute,
47, Part 3*.

Grizzle, J. E., Starmer, C. F. and Koch, G. G. (1969).
"Analysis of Categorical Data by Linear Models," *Biometrics,
25*, 444.

Holt, M. M. (1977). *SURREGR: Standard Errors of Regression
Coefficients from Sample Survey Data*, Research Triangle
Institute, Research Triangle Park, North Carolina.

Koch, G. G., Freeman, D. H. and Freeman, J. L. (1975).
"Strategies in the Multivariate Analysis of Data from
Complex Surveys," *International Statistical Review, 43, No.
1*, 59-78.

Koch, G. G., Gillings, D. B. and Stokes, M. E. (1980).
"Biostatistical Implications of Design, Sampling and
Measurement to Health Science Data Analysis," *Annual Review
of Public Health*.

Rao, J. N. K. and Scott, A. J. (1981). "The Analysis of
Categorical Data from Complex Sample Surveys: Chi-Squared
Test for Goodness of Fit and Independence in Two-Way
Tables," *Journal of the American Statistical Association,
76, No. 374*, 221-230.

Shah, B. V., Holt, M. M. and Folsom, R. E. (1977). "Inference
about Regression Models from Sample Survey Data," *Bulletin
of the International Statistical Institute, 47, Part 3*,
43-57.

AN APPROACH TO AN EVALUATION OF THE
QUALITY OF MOTOR GASOLINE PRICES

Arthur R. Silverberg

Rockville, Maryland

I. INTRODUCTION

This paper describes an approach that was used in assessing the quality of the Energy Information Administration's
(EIA) principal motor gasoline price estimates. These estimates are used by policy makers, planners, market analysts,
economic modelers, and other energy analysts who need to know
what is being measured as well as its relative accuracy.

The approach taken to evaluate the quality of motor gasoline prices combines two general techniques: an *internal
assessment* and *external comparisons*.

We define an *internal assessment* of a data series to be
an evaluation of the design, collection, processing and publishing of a data collection system. An internal assessment
attempts to describe and quantify (when reasonable) the various components of error in the data system under investigation. The internal assessment tends to be exploratory in the
manner in which it is carried out. The final summary of an
internal assessment is a listing of known error problems. In
energy statistics, it is usually not reasonable to "add-up"
the individual components of error to arrive at a total survey
error. The use of an error profile in other subject areas
include the work of Beller (1979) at the U.S. Department of
Agriculture and Brooks and Bailar (1978) at the U.S. Department of Commerce.

An *external comparison* examines the subject data series
in reference to other comparable estimates of the same
quantity. Comparisons between two or more independently
derived estimates are useful in that a difference between

estimates of the same quantity may be due to an error in one
of the data sources. The comparison itself does not tell us
which series is in error. It is also possible that what we
believe are comparable estimates are not comparable. When
differences are found between two data series we need to study
the underlying phenomenon as well as the data series, in
greater depth. Comparative analysis tends to be confirmatory
in nature. Biases in data series may be detected if only one
data series has the bias.

II. BACKGROUND

     The principal EIA data collection form for motor gasoline
prices during the time period in question (January 1977 to
June 1981) was the "Petroleum Industry Monthly Report for
Product Prices", Form EIA-460. According to form EIA-460
itself, "... Form EIA-460 is designed to provide the data necessary for the Department of Energy (DOE) to execute its role
in monitoring petroleum product prices ... (and) is also designed to facilitate the timely analysis of price and volumes
of sales at the refined product level upon which DOE will rely
in determining conformity with the established petroleum policies." EIA-460 data were collected excluding taxes. EIA published estimates of national volume weighted average price by
grade and type of sale excluding taxes in the *Monthly Petroleum Product Price Report*, and estimates of retail prices including taxes in *Petroleum Market Shares, Report on Sales of
Retail Gasoline.*

     The supply of motor gasoline comes from imports and mar-
keted production from refineries, petro-chemical plants, and
gas plants, as shown in Figure 1. Petro-chemical plants produce motor gasoline by chemically reprocessing oils that have
been produced by either gas plants or refineries. Refineries,
gas plants, petro-chemical plants and importers are the suppliers of motor gas. Once an oil has been produced (not necessarily motor gasoline), the oil may be transported by pipe-
line, barge, ship, truck, or other means of conveyance. This
oil may be reprocessed into motor gasoline at a refinery or
petro-chemical plant. Oils may also be stored at a bulk terminal. Oils can also be mechanically blended into motor gasoline at a blending station. Blending stations differ from
petro-chemical plants in that no chemical reprocessing is
performed at a blending station.

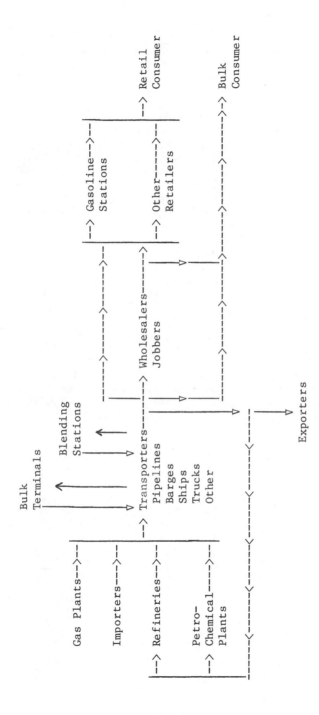

FIGURE 1. Flow Diagram of the Movement of Motor Gasoline From Supply to the Domestic Consumer

Gasoline may be exported. Exports account for only a very small amount of the total amount of motor gasoline produced or imported into the United States. During 1980, exports accounted for only .02 percent[a] of the amount supplied for domestic use (imports + production - refinery use - exports).

Motor gasoline may be sold to wholesalers and jobbers. Wholesalers and jobbers in turn sell the motor gasoline to other wholesale dealers as well as retailers. Wholesalers and jobbers are not the only types of enterprises that may sell to retailers. Any of the suppliers of motor gasoline may sell directly to retailers. Retailers include gasoline stations, and such enterprises as convenience stores and department stores.

Motor gasoline is consumed by retail consumers who buy their motor gasoline at retail gasoline stations and by bulk customers who buy from wholesalers or jobbers, or any of the suppliers of motor gasoline. Examples of bulk consumers include a farmer with a large tank on his farm, or a fleet owner such as a rent-a-car dealer.

When considering retail sales of gasoline, it makes sense to consider the retail price including taxes since this is the price that the consumer faces. On the other hand when considering wholesale or dealer-tank-wagon prices, the price excluding tax is considered, since all taxes have not yet been paid on motor gasoline at this level of distribution.

The federal government imposes a "manufacturer's excise tax" on motor gasoline. During the time period covered in this analysis, the rate was 4 cents per gallon. This tax is imposed on the "manufacturer" of the motor gasoline; commonly the refiner, gas plant, or petro-chemical plant operator is considered the manufacturer. The manufacturer will then sell the motor gasoline for a price including federal excise tax. The consumer ultimately pays the tax, reimbursing the retailer, who has reimbursed the wholesaler, who has reimbursed the refiner/manufacturer.

[a]Energy Information Administration, U.S. Department of Energy, *Crude Petroleum, Petroleum Products and Natural Gas Liquids: 1980 (Final Summary)*, Washington, D. C. December 4, 1981.

All fifty states, the District of Columbia, and Puerto Rico have their own state excise tax on motor gasoline. Licensed distributors pay the excise tax to the states. The licensed distributors are then reimbursed ultimately by the consumer in the same manner as the federal excise Tax.

State and local sales taxes may also be imposed. Several, but not all states have a sales tax. This tax may apply to the entire state, or just several counties, as the BART tax in the San Francisco area.

Form EIA-460 collected each respondent's volume sold during the reporting month as well as the respondent's weighted average selling price by grade of motor gasoline (premium, regular, and unleaded) and type of sale (wholesale, dealer-tank-wagon, and retail). Wholesale sales differ from dealer-tank-wagon sales in that wholesale sales are sales to suppliers whereas dealer-tank-wagon sales are sales to retail dealers. Therefore, nine grade-by-type categories were collected on the EIA-460. All data were collected excluding taxes; therefore, in many cases, adjustments for taxes were required before external comparisons could be made. The EIA-460 attempted to be a census of all refiners and all resellers having more than $50,000,000 in annual sales or revenues. Therefore there was no sampling error.

III. INTERNAL ASSESSMENT

The first question that should be asked is, "What needs to be estimated?" The purpose of Form EIA-460 was to collect price estimates at the refined product level so that the EIA may monitor prices, and perform timely policy and economic analyses. To this end the EIA published a national monthly volume weighted average price. No measure of price spread was given.

Figures 2 and 3 show the spread by company of reported volume weighted prices for wholesale regular and wholesale unleaded motor gasoline respectively, as a percentage of the national reported volume weighted price on a monthly basis. The top and bottom lines show respectively the maximum and minimum reported average prices. The cross-hatched areas correspond to the inter-decile range. Remember, each firm reported only one volume-weighted average price. These figures show the price spread for company average selling prices. The true price spread would be wider. Of these two

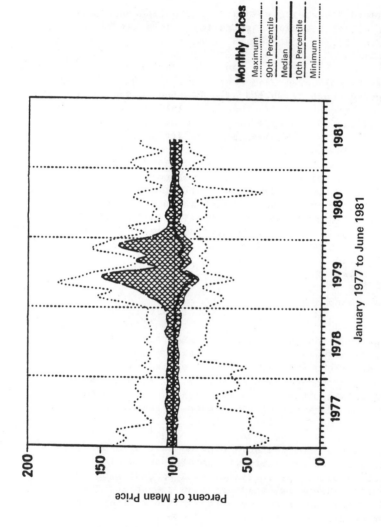

FIGURE 2. *Time Series Plot of the Variation by Company around the Regular Motor Gasoline Average Monthly Wholesale Prices Computed from an Archived File of EIA-460 Reports, January 1977–June 1981.*

Note: Vertical lines are drawn through January data values.

Source: Archived EIA computer data set "CN6329.PRJ.SOD82.EIA460.FEB1082.SAS," archived February 10, 1982.

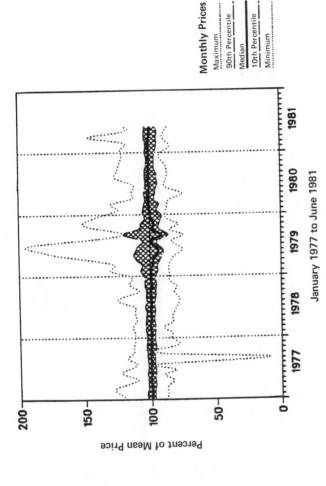

FIGURE 3. *Time Series Plot of the Variation by Company around the Unleaded Motor Gasoline Average Monthly Wholesale Prices Computed from an Archived File of EIA-460 Reports, January 1977–June 1981.*

Note: Vertical lines are drawn through January data values. We suspect that the minimum value is incorrect by a factor of 10 in September 1977. The volume associated with the highest price in September 1979 may be too large by a factor of 1000.

Source: Archived EIA computer data set "CN6329.PRJ.SOD82.EIA460.FEB1082.SAS."

grades of wholesale motor gasoline, only regular motor gasoline shows an extremely large price spread during the 1979
Iranian oil crisis when the price of motor gasoline was increasing rapidly.

Specification error is the difference between the quantity intended to be estimated, and the quantity that the respondents are asked to report. Specification error can be
caused by forms and instructions not reflecting the realities
of the phenomena being estimated or the form and instructions
not asking the correct question.

Specification error was found in the EIA-460 data collection system because the grades of motor gasoline used on the
form were not consistent with the grades being sold at that
time. The common grades of motor gasoline are premium unleaded, premium leaded, regular unleaded, and regular leaded.
The EIA-460 used the grades premium, regular, and unleaded.
It was not clear from the directions to the form as to where
premium unleaded should be reported. Based on EIA's Residential Consumption Survey, approximately 41 percent of all motor
gasoline sold to households is unleaded regular, 4 percent
unleaded premium, 50 percent leaded regular, and 4 percent
leaded premium, in 1980. (Percentages do not sum to 100 percent because of independent rounding.) No way was found to measure the impact of this specification error on the published
estimates, although obvious large bounds could be constructed.
EIA's new form EIA-782A eliminates this specification error.

When estimating refiner-marketer retail prices, the only
specification error was that discussed above. There was another specification error if we wish to estimate retail prices
without regard to the type of marketer (seller) since
independent-marketers were not covered in the EIA-460 frame,
and they did not have the same average selling price as
refiner-marketers. In 1980, the annual average retail motor
gasoline price charged by refiner-marketers was 117.3 cents
per gallon[b], whereas for independent-marketers the average
retail price charged was 120.1 cents per gallon[b] as shown in
Figure 4. During 1980, the average price for all retail gasoline sold in the U.S. exceeded the price sold by just refiner-
marketers by 1.1 cents per gallon.[b]

[b]Energy Information Administration, U.S. Department of
Energy, *Petroleum Market Shares, Report on Sales of
Retail Gasoline*, Washington, D. C.: July 7, 1981.

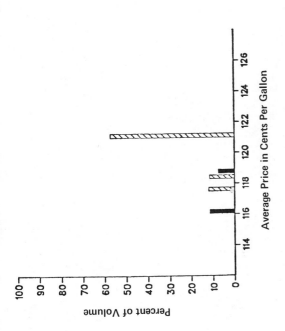

FIGURE 4. Annual Average Prices and Percent of Retail Motor Gasoline Sales in 1980 for Respondent Groups.

Source: Energy Information Administration, U.S. Department of Energy, *Petroleum Market Shares, Report on Retail Sales of Gasoline,* Washington, D.C.: July 7, 1981. Original source for independent marketer estimates (striped bars) were Bureau of Census Forms SG-1, SG-2, and SG-4. Original source for refiner marketer estimates (solid bars) were Energy Information Administration Form EIA-460.

Major refiner marketers. . . . . 118.9 cents per gallon

Other refiner marketers. . . . . 116.3 cents per gallon

Major independent marketers. . . . . 121.0 cents per gallon

Other refiner brands independent marketers . . 118.3 cents per gallon

Non-branded independent marketers. . . . . . . 117.5 cents per gallon

Selection error is caused by collecting data from frames having duplicates or from incomplete frames. The intended universe for the EIA-460 motor gasoline prices were refiners and large resellers having over $50,000,000 or more in annual sales or revenues. As part of a validation study of the EIA-460 data collection system, Transportation and Economic Research Associates, Inc. (TERA) performed an extensive analysis of frame undercoverage.[c] TERA uncovered 30 missing refiners. These 30 refiners accounted for approximately 1.5 percent of total U. S. refining capacity. No reliable estimates of the percentage of undercoverage for large resellers were available.

In order to bound the selection error, TERA performed three scenarios. The selling price for the firms that were not in the EIA-460 frame were assumed to be selling at either the highest or lowest or average selling price of the reporting firms in the missing firms stratum (refiner or reseller). Computations were performed only for December 1980 prices of dealer-tank-wagon regular, wholesale unleaded, and retail unleaded motor gasoline. By means of these scenarios, the selection error was bounded at 0.56 percent in the case of wholesale unleaded, 0.18 percent for dealer-tank-wagon regular, and 0.00 percent for retail unleaded motor gasoline.

As part of this validation of the EIA-460, the accounting firm of Alexander Grant & Company audited the records of a sample of 49 EIA-460 respondents. Of all the audited firms, 26.5 percent (not volume weighted) did not report accurate volume-weighted prices. In addition, the auditors were unable to trace the price of 12.3 percent (not volume weighted) of the audited enterprises.

Wholesale unleaded, dealer-tank-wagon regular, and retail unleaded motor gasoline data were audited for only December 1980. Since the reported volume-weighted prices were close to the traced prices (even though the firms calculated the reported prices on incorrect volumes), the national volume-weighted price was found to be quite accurate. *Respondent errors* were classified as to either computation errors, transcription errors, timing errors, misinterpretation of instructions, or different accounting conventions. The only error

[c]Transportation and Economic Research Associates, Inc., *Validation of Selected Petroleum Product Energy Information Systems*, Falls Church, Virginia, September 30, 1981.

classification that affected the overall national volume-
weighted price of the respective product by more than
0.005 percent was misinterpretation of instructions for unleaded retail gasoline where the error of this type was estimated to be 0.03 percent (with estimated relative standard
error of 0.02 percent). These errors are relatively small
despite the fact that about 80 percent of the audited enterprises included out-of-period adjustments in their sales
transaction data.

Unit non-response is the failure to obtain information,
for any reason, from entities in a sample survey. If no estimates for the non-respondents are made, implicitly, a zero is
assumed for the non-respondent's value, and an estimate of the
population total would be low biased. If an estimation procedure is used to account for the non-response, this may introduce bias. Estimates of averages of the non-respondents based
on the respondents may also be biased since respondents and
non-respondents as a group may have differing characteristics.
When a respondent omits one or more items on a survey this is
item non-response. Item non-response may cause a bias in the
data just as unit non-response.

We have found that estimation of the extent of nonresponse was quite difficult on the EIA-460. Enterprises
changing their names, enterprises merging, and enterprises
going out of business made an estimate of this type of error
difficult. The EIA did not archive a list of those enterprises receiving the EIA-460 questionnaire each month, the
current list was revised in place. When price controls were
in effect, files were kept on each enterprise listing the
months when the enterprise did not file; no files were kept by
month. The TERA validation study attempted to evaluate nonresponse for April 1981. The TERA study found that the EIA-
460 name/address list did not contain 11 refiners and 5 resellers that did actually respond during 1980. Three enterprises listed on the April 1981 name/address list did not
respond during 1980. TERA estimated the *target population*
for the EIA-460 contained 186 refiners and 77 large resellers.

The project manager for the EIA-460 did not believe that
non-response was a major problem for that data collection
system. He believed that 95 percent of all enterprises reported before the revised values were published. This
95 percent of all enterprises accounted for what he believed
to be about 99 percent of the total volume. All 15 major
refiners must report before the final average price could be

published. Implicitly a zero volume was imputed for non-respondents.

In order to obtain a feeling of how non-response might affect the estimate of volume-weighted price, we have plotted volume versus price for each grade of motor gasoline for all three types of sales (retail, dealer-tank-wagon, and whole-sale), for January 1977 through June 1981. Only two of those plots have been reproduced here. Figures 5 and 6 are scatter plots for regular wholesale motor gasoline for June 1977 and June 1979 respectively. All respondents having over 4 percent of the total reported volume are placed at the 5 percent line to protect confidentiality. No respondent reported more than 6 percent of the total reported volume. Non-response should have little effect in situations like that of 1977 where the prices tend to cluster around the average price. If the large respondents report, the lack of a response from an enterprise having relatively small volumes should make little difference in the national volume-weighted average price. A non-respondent can make a large difference in situations like that of 1979 where the distribution of prices is bi-modal. Large respondents reported at two quite different price ranges, one price range about 90 percent of the average price and the other range about 150 percent of the average price. Since the 15 largest refiners had to report before the average price could be published, we feel that non-response error was small for volume-weighted average price--less than 1 percent.

Inadvertent processing error refers to errors introduced by EIA into the estimates by losing submissions, incorrectly transcribing or coding the data, or making arithmetic errors. This type of non-sampling error is usually small as compared to other types of non-sampling errors.

To check for incorrect transcription errors, the TERA validation compared 49 hardcopy December 1980 enterprise sub-missions with the EIA computer file as of May 1981. A total of 343 data elements were compared. Three differences were found, corresponding to either a revision or a late submission by the enterprise.

TERA also performed two deterministic edit checks on all of the submitted January-December 1980 data. First the volume reported for total motor gasoline was compared to the sum of the volumes reported for the various categories of motor gaso-line. Only 0.02 percent of the January-December 1980 data failed this simple test. Second, the reported volume weighted price for "total motor gasoline" was compared to the volume

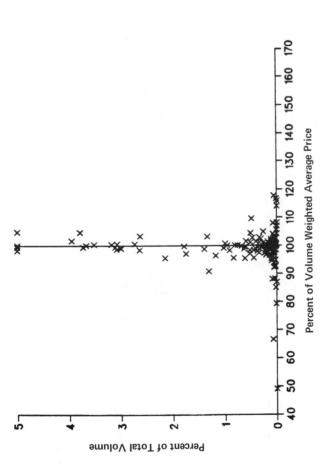

FIGURE 5. Scatter Plot of the Regular Motor Gasoline Wholesale Prices Versus Volumes by Respondent Computed from an Archived File of EIA-460 Reports for June 1977.

Note: All respondents having 4 percent or more of the total reported sales are plotted at a volume of 5 percent to protect confidentiality. No respondent has a volume over 6 percent of the total reported volume.

Source: Archived EIA computer data set "CN6329.PRJ.SOD82.EIA460.FEB1082.SAS."

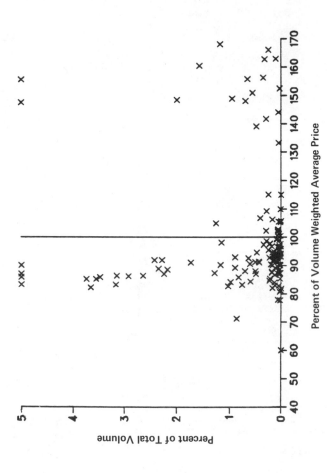

FIGURE 6. Scatter Plot of the Regular Motor Gasoline Wholesale Prices Versus Volumes by Respondent Computed from an Archived File of EIA-460 Reports for June 1979.

Note: All respondents having 4 percent or more of the total reported sales are plotted at a volume of 5 percent to protect confidentiality. No respondent has a volume over 6 percent of the total reported volume.

Source: Archived EIA computer data set "CN6329.PRJ.SOD82.EIA460.FEB1082.SAS."

weighted price computed from each of the categories of motor
gasoline. TERA found that 0.55 percent of all submissions
failed this edit check.

Additionally, we have performed the same edit tests on a
dataset archived on February 10, 1982, and have found similar
results. In addition, it was found that one enterprise reported a volume but no price. This enterprise claimed that it
did not know the volume-weighted selling price of its motor
gasoline. The only out-of-range product codes found on the
EIA-460 computer database have zero volume and no price.

As we can see from Figure 3, the September 1977 wholesale
unleaded minimum price is too low to be believed. In fact it
is too low by a factor of ten, most likely a slipped decimal
point. Correcting this value increases the volume-weighted
average price by only 0.08 percent. The June and July 1979
wholesale unleaded maximum company average prices are suspect. For wholesale regular as shown in Figure 2, we see
quite a few very low values in 1977, and one in September
1980. The high values for 1979 may be correct since the 90th
percentile is much greater than the volume weighted average
price. For all grades and types of sales of motor gasoline
there is a consistency between monthly values reported by a
particular enterprise. The lowest few prices are shared among
only a few enterprises. The highest few prices are shared
among another group of enterprises. For some of the EIA-460
product prices, we have noticed that the highest reported
prices were from enterprises that have been cited for price
overcharges.

To verify the computation that produces the published
volume-weighted average price, we wrote our own computer
program and ran it against the EIA-460 database as of
February 10, 1982. The EIA-460 database was continuously updated when late submissions or corrections arrived. Usually,
our computed price when rounded to the nearest one-tenth of a
cent agrees with the published price as illustrated for regular wholesale motor gasoline in Figure 7. For wholesale regular motor gasoline, there is only one large difference between
the two estimates. In September 1979 the price computed from
the archived database exceeds the published price by four
cents per gallon. Upon looking at the data file, it was discovered that the enterprise having the highest price has a
volume associated with it that was too large by a factor of
1,000. After correcting the error, we found that the recomputed price differed from the published price by only 0.4
cents per gallon. The only other large discrepancy between

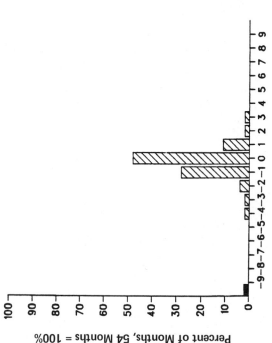

Tenth of a Cent per Gallon

FIGURE 7. *Frequency Distribution of Differences between Regular Motor Gasoline Wholesale Monthly Average Prices, Published EIA-460 Reports Minus Average Prices Computed from an Archived File of EIA-460 Reports, for the period January 1977–June 1981.*

Note: The actual value of the solid shaded bar is -4 cents per gallon.
Source: Archived data from EIA computer data set "CN6329.PRJ.SOD82.EIA460.FEB1082.SAS" Published data from EIA publication *Monthly Petroleum Product Price Report;* December 1978 issue for 1977 data, December 1979 issue for 1978 data, December 1980 issue for 1979 data, December 1981 issue for 1980 data, and October 1981 issue for 1981 data.

the prices computed from our archived database and the published prices was for the sale of wholesale unleaded motor gasoline in September 1979. Here, the same respondent, as in the case of wholesale regular, again reported a volume too large by a factor of 1,000.

No *judgmental adjustments* are made on the EIA-460 data to produce the EIA publication, *Monthly Petroleum Product Price Report*. The EIA-460 data were collected excluding taxes and the national price estimates were published excluding taxes. The EIA-460 retail gasoline prices are published with taxes in the publication, *Petroleum Market Shares, Report on Sales of Retail Gasoline*. Since the data were collected excluding taxes, EIA had to make an estimate for the tax rate. The computer program that calculated the estimates for this latter publication adds a constant value of 13.8 cents per gallon to the reported volume-weighted average price. This computer program was written in December 1978 and there is no documentation that indicates that any revisions have been performed on the program. Using data that were not available to the program office at the time the price estimates were published[d], we have computed an estimate of the tax rate for 1979 through 1981. We computed a total tax rate (federal, state, plus local) of 13.28 cents per gallon for 1979, 13.99 cents per gallon for 1980, and 14.33 cents per gallon for 1981. Therefore we estimate that the adjustment for taxes was too large by approxiately 0.5 cents per gallon in 1979, too small by approximately 0.2 cents per gallon in 1980, and too small by approximately 0.5 cents per gallon in 1981.

Auditor errors are those errors made by the auditors while checking the accuracy of the enterprise responses. *Validator errors* are those errors made by someone such as this author while attempting to understand the system under question. These errors do not affect the accuracy of the original estimates, but do affect the perceived accuracy of the original estimates.

IV. EXTERNAL COMPARISONS

Many different estimates of retail gasoline prices

[d]Federal Highway Administration, U.S. Department of Transportation, *Highway Statistics 1979, Highway Statistics 1980*, Washington, D. C., (undated).

exist. Lundberg[e] publishes estimated prices for 44 cities but
no national price since no volumes accompany the prices. The
EIA-79 estimates (last month collected, May 1980) were based
on a survey of service stations. Comparisons to the EIA-460 by
grade are not possible because of the specification error,
therefore all comparisons involving the EIA-460 must be
performed on total motor gasoline by type of sale. Two household surveys, Auto-Facts and the EIA-141, were compared to
each other by grade and were found to be very consistent. The
Bureau of Labor Statistics (BLS) estimates exceed those
published by EIA in *Petroleum Market Shares*. All national
estimates are usually within 5 percent of the EIA *Petroleum
Market Shares* estimate of retail motor gasoline prices as
illustrated in Figure 8. The EIA-460 portion of this
published estimate is lower than the overall motor gasoline
retail price.

According to estimates from EIA's Residential Consumption
Survey, urban retail motor gasoline prices are higher than
rural prices. Retail prices from the Consumer Price Index
published by the BLS, show a trend with larger cities having
higher prices. Similar trends are seen in estimates in the
Oil and Gas Journal, although in both the BLS prices and the
Oil and Gas Journal prices the trend accounts for a very small
portion of the total variation between the cities. We have no
proof that there was an urban effect, but the data we have
looked at are consistent with this hypothesis. If this
hypothesis is true, the hypothesis would explain why the city
average retail prices reported by BLS and Lundberg, Inc., tend
to be higher than the other retail price data series.

To confirm the wide spread in prices we have looked at
other data sou :es. The average retail price of motor gasoline varies widely among cities in the BLS Consumer Price
Series. Bulk terminal prices have a large price spread as
confirmed by *Platt's Oil Price Handbook and Oilmanac*.

When comparing EIA-460 estimates of wholesale and dealer-
tank-wagon volume-weighted prices with the prices based upon a
price index of the BLS, we find sizable differences for
wholesale unleaded and regular. We recomputed the EIA-460
estimated prices as a price index based upon 1977 annual sales
as BLS did. The directions of the differences between the
EIA volume-weighted price minus a price-index-based price
also calculated with EIA data, are the same as the

[e]Lundberg Letter, "Weekly Vital Statistics and Analysis in
Oil Marketing."

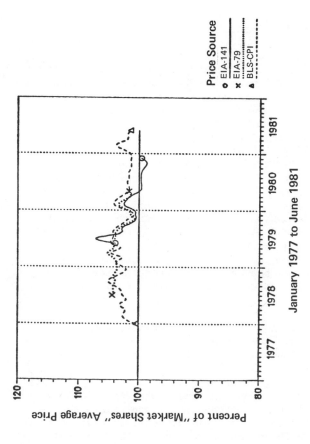

January 1977 to June 1981

FIGURE 8. Comparative Estimates of U. S. Average Retail Motor Gasoline Prices as a Percent of the "Petroleum Market Shares" Estimate, for All Grades, January 1977 to June 1981.

Note: Vertical lines are drawn through January data values.

Source: For "Petroleum Market Shares," *Petroleum Market Shares, Report on Sales of Retail Gasoline.* For EIA-141, *Consumption Patterns of Household Vehicles, June 1979 to December 1980.* For EIA-79, *Monthly Energy Review.* For BLS-CPI, *Consumer Prices: Energy and Food* (title varies by month).

EIA volume-weighted prices minus the BLS price index type
prices. It is possible that the differences that we see between the EIA published estimates of price and the BLS estimates of price may be caused by EIA using a volume weighted
price and BLS a price based upon a price index.

V. SUMMARY OF FINDINGS

a. When the price of motor gasoline increased rapidly during
    1979 a large price spread existed for some but not all
    grades of motor gasoline. The distribution of prices was
    bi-modal. Under such circumstances a national average
    price does not fully describe the phenomenon.

b. Specification error was found in that the EIA-460 collec-
    tion system used grades of motor gasoline that were not
    consistent with the grades of motor gasoline being used at
    that time. No way was found to measure the impact of this
    error, although large bounds could have been constructed.

c. The average retail price of motor gasoline exceeded the
    price of the respondents to the EIA-460 (refiner marke-
    ters) by 1.1 cents per gallon during 1980.

d. Selection error was bounded by 0.56 percent for the three
    grade/type of sale transactions considered for December
    1980.

e. During the time period considered, non-response was low
    for the EIA-460. Since the 15 largest refiners must have
    reported before the average price was published, non-
    response error was small.

f. Out of the 486 comparisons (3 grades by 3 types of sales
    by 54 months) performed between published prices and
    prices computed from an archived dataset, 2 large
    differences were found. Both were due to an enterprise
    having a reported volume too large by a factor of 1,000 in
    the archived dataset.

g. We estimate the adjustment for taxes as published in
    *Petroleum Market Shares, Report on Sales of Retail Gaso-
    line* was too large by approximately 0.5 cents per gallon
    in 1979, too small by 0.2 cents per gallon in 1980, and
    too small by 0.5 cents per gallon in 1981.

h. Comparative estimates are usually within 5 percent of the
    EIA *Petroleum Market Shares* estimate of retail gasoline
    prices. These EIA estimates tend to be lower than those
    of Lundberg and BLS. It is hypothesized that this is due
    to urban places having higher prices than rural places.

i. Other data series show the wide spread of prices found in
    the EIA-460.

j. Sizable differences were found between wholesale volume-
    weighted prices and a price index of the BLS for unleaded
    and regular gasoline. We believe these differences were
    due to EIA using a volume-weighted price and BLS a price
    index and not an error in the data collection systems.

An assessment of EIA's petroleum products and natural gas,
price and volume data series, will soon be published by the
EIA[f].

VI. GENERAL CONCLUSIONS RELATIVE TO THE QUALITY OF DATA COLLECTION SYSTEMS

    Evaluations of a data collection system provide reasons
why those individuals who are running the system need to
archive the data base used as a basis for a publication, the
mailing list of the survey, as well as any computer programs
used to compute estimates. In an evaluation, the historic
data base should be compared to the current most accurate data
base. The evaluators may want to try various estimation and
imputation schemes on the historic database. The potential
respondents are not known to the evaluator unless the mailing
list is archived. We found it nearly impossible to obtain
reasonable estimates of non-response rates or non-response
error because we did not have access to the mailing lists.
Any changes to the computer programs used to compute estimates
need to be documented. When studying the EIA-460 we were able
to know how taxes were estimated by reading the archived
computer program.

[f]Energy Information Administration, U.S. Department of
Energy, *An Assessment of the Quality of Principal Data
Series of the Energy Information Administration,* Washington,
D.C., April 1983.

For energy price data series, estimating or reducing processing error is not important; processing error is already
minute. Effort should be put into reducing other errors such
as specification error. A data base that does not satisfy deterministic edit checks is not aesthetically pleasing. If the
lack of agreement is not too bad, this may just be an aes-
thetic problem and not a real problem.

We need to look at a time series as a time series and not
just evaluate the accuracy at a few points in time. We would
not have noticed the widening of the price spread for wholesale regular motor gasoline in 1979 if we had not looked at
the time series as a whole. In addition, the plot of the
inter-decile ranges helped us to distinguish outliers from
real phenomena. A plot of the difference between the published price minus our computed price showed us two data elements where the volume found in the data base was too large by
a factor of 1,000. We found the plot of volume versus price
by enterprise valuable for understanding how price increases.

For the data collection system considered, we found that
*it is not possible to simply add errors between error types or
within error types.* A large percentage of inaccurate responses does not imply low accuracy of estimates. Eighty
percent of the audited firms on the EIA-460 included out-of-
period adjustments yet respondent error was estimated to be
less than 0.03 percent for the national volume-weighted
price. Bounding error is sometimes possible but the bounds
are sometimes so large that the reader questions the writer's
methods, not realizing the bound is an estimated bound and not
an estimated error.

We found that internal assessments seem to be much more
informative than external comparisons. It is usually not possible to make the necessary adjustments that will make two independently derived estimates comparable. It is not possible
to identify which data series has the error, or if the error
is in the comparison itself. It is even difficult to make
comparisons that give reasonably sharp bounds.

External comparisons can be used for confirmatory analysis. We have some evidence (although not strong evidence)
through external comparisons that urban prices exceed rural
prices. We also have evidence that the price spreads that
were seen in the EIA-460 data base do actually exist. In some
cases, external comparisons may be used to estimate overall
error or bias. An example would be where many *credible*
"comparable" series are all above (or below) the data series
in question.

ACKNOWLEDGMENTS

   I would like to thank T. White who performed much of this
research and C. Hebron who executed the computer graphics.
The suggestions of L. Gordon and T. Wright helped to improve
the presentation.

DISCLAIMER

   *The original research upon which this paper is based was
performed while the author was employed by the Energy Information Administration, U. S. Department of Energy.   The opinions expressed in this paper are those of the author alone
and not those of the U. S. Department of Energy.*

REFERENCES

Beller, N. D. (1979) *Error Profile for Multiple-Frame Surveys*
     (ESCS 63), U.S. Department of Agriculture, Economics, Sta-
     tistics, and Cooperatives Service, Washington, D. C.
Brooks, C. A. and Bailar, B. A. (1978) *An Error Profile:
     Employment As Measured By The Current Population Survey*
     (Statistical Working Paper 3), U.S. Department of
     Commerce, Office of Federal Statistical Policy and
     Standards, Washington, D. C.
Energy Information Administration, U.S. Department of Energy,
     Monthly Petroleum Product Price Report, Washington, D. C.
Energy Information Administration, U.S. Department of Energy,
     *Petroleum Market Shares, Report on Sales of Retail Gaso-
     line*, Washington, D. C.

HEALTH AND MORTALITY STUDY
ERROR DETECTION, REPORTING, AND RESOLUTION SYSTEM

Katherine C. Gissel
Martha L. Wray

Medical and Health Sciences Division
Oak Ridge Associated Universities
Oak Ridge, Tennessee

Martha S. Hansard

Nuclear Data Power, Inc.
Smyrna, Georgia

I. OVERVIEW

The Department of Energy (DOE) Health and Mortality Study
(HMS) is an occupational epidemiologic study of workers employed by the DOE and its predecessors since 1943. Approximately 260,000 present and former workers at more than 100
facilities nationwide currently are being studied by the
Center for Epidemiologic Research (CER) in the Medical
and Health Sciences Division of Oak Ridge Associated
Universities. Managing the large amount of data collected for
this study is, of necessity, a multi-step procedure. Figure I
shows some of the phases of the study process as it is applied
to the individual studies that comprise the overall DOE HMS.
Each phase, or step, that closely inspects and manipulates
data has the chance of detecting inconsistencies in the data.
When CER began receiving these data in 1979, several fronts
had to be attacked simultaneously: security, documentation,
record linkage, updating, query, editing and correction, and,
ultimately, production of data sets for analyses. To reduce
redundancy, a master roster was compiled of all workers under
study. Data in this master roster became denoted as the
Integrated Data Base. A commercial data base management
system (System 1022, 1983) is used on a DEC PDP-10 System.

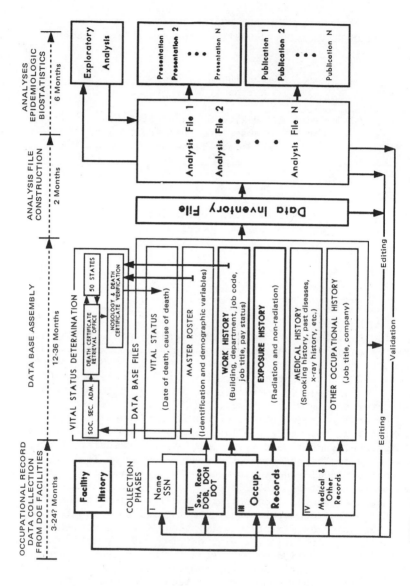

FIGURE 1. Department of Energy Health and Mortality Studies Study Process.

Since the entire HMS processing system is dynamic with many of the processes overlapping and being performed simultaneously, detection of inconsistencies occurs continually. The Error Detection, Reporting, and Resolution (EDRR) System has been developed so that each process detecting an inconsistency attempts some action that will allow the process to continue. For example, when building a file for a mortality analysis, an individual whose birth date is missing may be deleted from that study. The analysis file continues to be built including only those individuals whose birth dates are in the data base, and the inconsistencies thus detected are processed through the EDRR system.

Whereas multiple processes detect and report possible data errors, generally one individual actually attempts to resolve errors. Therefore, the EDRR system acts as a concentrator of error reports. This system organizes and summarizes these reports into a form that allows for efficiency in error resolution; it provides a systematic methodology for reporting and resolving inconsistencies and documenting any changes to the data base.

II.   TYPES OF ERRORS REPORTED

Thus far, in practice, there are five classes of data processing steps that detect and report possible data errors. These classes are described below:

A. *Loading Data into the Integrated Data Base*--At this point field checks are made for acceptable values, and consistency (including logical) checks are made with information already in the data base.

B. *Vital Status Search and Verification*--These may not be errors but inquiries for additional information. An example of a report here derives from the "impossible" social security number status made by Social Security Administration whenever a submitted social security number is one that has never been issued. Also, during the vital status search and verification, much of the data are closely inspected by researchers who recognize possible errors.

C. *Analysis File Construction* (Frome and Hudson, 1981)-- When data are merged to prepare for analysis, many different types of errors may be detected. These may be classified as
      1. Completeness (of roster and specific data items)

2. Consistency (agreement across data files)
3. Value limits
4. Logical consistency

D. *Special Purpose Editing Procedures*--These vary depending upon objectives. If some error is suspected, a special purpose program may be written to detect and report the occurrences of specific types of errors.

E. *Analysis*--During analysis, data are subjected to inspection of a type that differs from any previously encountered in processing. Univariate and multivariate distributions are checked for possible outliers or improbable outcomes. Data verification at this stage may generate additional editing procedures.

The types of errors detected to date under the various error classes just described are listed in Table 1. Error reports are standardized to avoid confusion and duplication. The error code associated with each error detected usually begins with the first letter of the attribute pertaining to the error, followed by a sequential number. For example, B1, B2, etc. are errors involving birth dates and E1, E2, etc. are employment date problems. This list of standards is expanded whenever needed. For example, if a new type of error were detected for the race attribute, then a new error code R3 would be created with the appropriate error description. In Table 1, a detection class (as given above) is specified for each error to associate it with the stage in processing which is most likely to report the error. Table 2 is a file description of the error reporting file. This file stores the error report along with the initials of the individual making the report or who is interested in getting the error resolved.

III. SYSTEM DESCRIPTION

Figure 2 shows the total data flow in the reporting and resolution portion of the EDRR system. Both researchers and computer programs can enter errors into the error file. Errors are pulled from this file, and Work History (WH) listings are created for individuals whose errors are to be resolved. Note that some external force sets the priorities for focusing on certain errors. Priorities may be based on resolving error reports in a certain study population or resolving problems that are impeding vital status searches.

TABLE 1. *Types of Errors Detected by the Error Detection, Reporting, and Resolution System*

Detection Class	Error Code	Error Description
B	A1	SSA STATUS I - SSN NEVER ISSUED
B	A2	SSA STATUS U - UNKNOWN
B	A3	SSA STATUS N - NONMATCH (SSN, SNAME DISAGREE W/SSA)
C	B1	NO BIRTH DATE GIVEN
A	B2	NEW DOB MM/DD/YY DISAGREES WITH EXISTING DOB IN MR
C	B3	DOB MM/DD/YY WHILE DOB IN MR BLANK
C	B4	INVALID DOB IN FILE XXXXXX
C	B5	POSSIBLE ERROR IN DOB - INVESTIGATION NEEDED
A	C1	TOO MANY FACS FOUND FOR PERSON (CANNOT STORE INFO)
A	C2	MULTIPLE ENTRIES IN KEY FILE FOR ONE ID
C	D1	DEPTCD DATE NOT WITHIN EMP PERIOD FOR DEPT XXXXXX
D	D2	INCOMLETE DATE FOUND IN DEPTCD FILE
C	E1	FILM BADGE READING FOUND IN UNEMPLOYED QUARTER
C	E2	URINALYSIS READING FOUND IN UNEMPLOYED YEAR
C	E3	WBC READING FOUND IN UNEMPLOYED YEAR
C	E4	NO EMPLOYMENT DATES FOR THIS PERSON

TABLE 1 (continued)

Detection Class	Error Code	Error Description
C	E5	POSSIBLE ERROR IN EMP DATES – INVESTIGATION NEEDED
C	G1	DATE FOR BADGE XXXX NOT DURING EMPLOYMENT PERIOD
D	G2	INCOMPLETE GDATE FOUND IN BADGE NO FILE
A	H1	HIRE ON MM/DD/YY GIVES AGE LESS THAN 15
A	H2	HIRE DATE MM/DD/YY WITHOUT PREVIOUS TERM
E	H3	INVALID HIRE DATE
E	H4	INCOMPLETE WORK HISTORY FOR DATE OF HIRE
A	I1	ID NOT ON MASTER ROSTER FOR THIS FACILITY
D	I2	ID NOT ON MASTER ROSTER BUT IN ONE OF KEY FILES
C	J1	NO JOB INFORMATION
C	J2	NO JOB CODE INFORMATION FOR JOB TITLE
A	N1	PERSON WITH NEW LNAME=AAAAA (PERSON NOT FEMALE)
A	N2	LNAME SAME XXX YYY NEW
B	N3	NO NAME IN NAME FILE
B	N4	CONFLICTING INFO IN NAME FILE (MULT PEOPLE ON ID)
B	N5	VERIFICATION OF NAME NEEDED
B	N6	NO LNAME. FNAME = XXX MNAME = XXX
D	P1	INVALID PAYCD X FOR GDATE MM/DD/YY

TABLE 1 (continued)

Detection Class	Error Code	Error Description
C	R1	NO RACE GIVEN
A	R2	NEW ENTRY RACE = X DISAGREES WITH OLD RACE
A	R3	INVALID RACE CODE = X FOUND
A	S1	DUPLICATE SSN IN KEY. USE WHICH ID FOR LOAD?
A	S2	NEW SSN = XXXXXXXXX DISAGREES WITH EXISTING SSN
A	S3	NO ENTRY IN KEY FILE FOR SSN = XXXXXXXXX
C	S4	SSN IN FB BUT NOT IN MASTER ROSTER FOR THIS FAC
A	S5	INVALID SSN XXXXXXXXX
C	S6	NO SSN GIVEN
A	T1	TERMINATION ON MM/DD/YY GIVES AGE GT 70
A	T2	OLD TERM ENTRY MM/DD/YY NEW ENTRY MM/DD/YY
A	T3	TERM DATE MM/DD/YY BUT NO HIRE DATE
B	T4	NO TERMINATION DATE AND EMPLOYEE DECEASED
C	T5	INVALID TERMINATION DATE
D	T6	NO TERM DATE - EMPLOYEE ON TERMINATED ROSTER
C	X1	NO SEX GIVEN
A	X2	NEW SEX = X DISAGREES WITH EXISTING SEX
A	X3	INVALID SEX CODE = X FOUND

Katherine C. Gissel *et al.*

TABLE 2.   Error File Description

VARIABLE NAME	FIELD LENGTH	POSITION IN FILE		TYPE	COMMENTS
		FROM	TO		
ID	7	1	7	INTEGER	IDENTIFICATION NUMBER
SSN	9	8	16	TEXT	SOCIAL SECURITY NUMBER
FAC	3	17	19	INTEGER	FACILITY PERTAINING TO ERROR
FILENAME	6	20	25	TEXT	FILE WHERE ERROR WAS FOUND
NAME	12	26	29	TEXT	NAME OF PROGRAM OR PERSON DETECTING ERROR
DATE DETECTED	8	30	37	DATE	DATE ERROR DETECTED
ERCODE	2	38	39	TEXT	ERROR CODE
COMMENT	80	40	89	TEXT	DESCRIPTION OF ERROR

WH listings are sent to an archivist who accesses employment history documents of the individuals in whose data errors
have been detected. Any discrepancies encountered and/or any
new information found are written on the WH listings by the
archivist and then returned to the error corrector who makes
the appropriate changes in the HMS data base. When errors are
resolved while making these changes, the error corrector takes
the error records out of the error file and stores them in the
fixed error file (Table 3).

When all corrections have been made, a new WH listing is
printed for those individuals whose data required a change.
The original WH lists (with handwritten information from the
archivist) and the updated WH lists are then checked by a

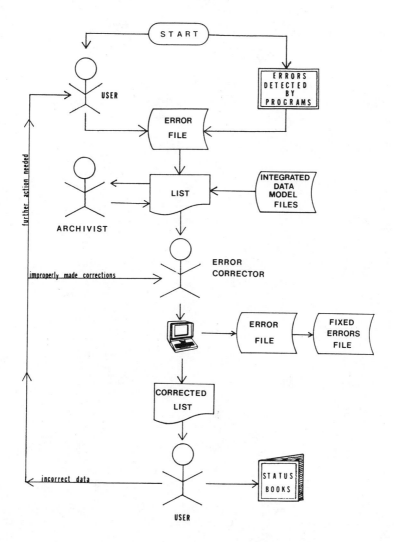

FIGURE 2. The Error Detection, Reporting, and Resolution System.

TABLE 3. *Fixed Error File Description*

VARIABLE NAME	FIELD LENGTH	POSITION IN FILE FROM	TO	TYPE	COMMENTS
ID	7	1	7	INTEGER	IDENTIFICATION NUMBER
SSN	9	8	16	TEXT	SOCIAL SECURITY NUMBER
FAC	3	17	19	INTEGER	FACILITY PERTAINING TO ERROR
FILENAME	6	20	25	TEXT	FILE WHERE ERROR WAS FOUND
NAME	12	26	29	TEXT	NAME OF PROGRAM OR PERSON DETECTING ERROR
DATE DETECTED	8	30	37	DATE	DATE ERROR DETECTED
ERCODE	2	38	39	TEXT	ERROR CODE
DATE FIXED	8	40	47	DATE	DATE ERROR FIXED
COMMENT	80	48	127	TEXT	DESCRIPTION OF ERROR

researcher with knowledge of the background and purpose of the data change. If all is in order, both WH lists are filed in the status books, which contain hard copy history of all data changes per individual. If additional work is needed, the researcher may re-enter the resolution process at any stage necessary to resolve the problem.

The entire resolution process can be monitored by reports produced from the error file and the fixed error file. Monitoring typically involves summarizing the number of errors reported but not resolved for a specific study population.

IV.   SUMMARY

The EDRR system implemented for the HMS has four main advantages. First it reduces redundancy of effort required to
resolve possible errors. The archivist receives a complete
list of all errors reported for an individual under study and
is notified if this individual's data have been previously inspected for error resolution. By consulting the status books,
the researcher can avoid repeating a lengthy data search for a
possible error which, it has already been decided, either was
previously determined unresolvable or actually not an error.
An example of this type of error is a birth date missing in
the data base and also missing in every available document.

The second advantage, documentation of data changes,
overlaps the first since the documentation provided in the
system permits the elimination of redundant resolution
effort. Documentation also allows researchers to retrace
steps whenever a question arises about how a data change was
made.

The system also tends to increase correction efficiency
by allowing errors to be grouped and resolved in a manner
which is most efficient for the archivists. Often this is
based on the physical organization of source documents.

Finally, the fourth advantage is gained from the ability
to monitor the whole detection, reporting, and resolution process. The status of any population or group can be identified
easily by running an existing report program. This enables
researchers to judge the quality of data before they conduct
an analysis. They can calculate the proportion of errors
reported and the percentage corrected at any given time.

Despite the many advantages of the EDRR System, one major
disadvantage does exist. The enormous assortment of data
encountered for the approximately 260,000 individuals in the
study requires several manual steps and varied decision
making. Therefore, it will be impossible to ever fully auto-
mate the system, and it will always remain a relatively slow
process.

REFERENCES

Frome, E. L. and Hudson, D. R. (1981). "A General Data
    Structure for Epidemiologic Studies of DOE Workers," In:
    Proceedings of the DOE Statistical Symposium, 206-218.
System 1022, Version 115A. (1983). Software House, Cambridge,
    Massachusetts.

ON USING EXPLORATORY DATA ANALYSIS AS AN AID
IN MODELING AND STATISTICAL FORECASTING

Thomas A. Curran III

Wissenschaftszentrum Berlin
West Germany

Robert D. Small

The Wharton School
University of Pennsylvania
Philadelphia, Pennsylvania

I. INTRODUCTION

In this paper we discuss and demonstrate some ways in
which Exploratory Data Analysis (EDA) can be used to improve
the quality of statistical analyses carried out on large data
sets which are, for example, often used in econometric models.
While EDA can be used as an *aid* to modeling, we believe that
it should be used as a *prerequisite* to model building. Since
that is not always the case, it is only put forth here that
EDA can and should be an important tool in model building.
The objective of this presentation is to demonstrate how to
include EDA techniques in the normal and routine functions of
modeling. Our feeling is that EDA is not used enough, especially in modeling, and a goal of this paper is to prompt modelers and users of statistical methodologies to integrate EDA,
and, in general, an assessment of the quality of the data, into their work. We also demonstrate here the use of an interactive computer package developed for EDA. This is important,
we feel, since computer software for EDA is not in abundance,
and this package is a particularly good one. Examples for
this work are taken from two existing large modeling efforts,
the STIFS model developed at the U.S. Department of Energy,
and the GLOBUS model being built at the Science Center Berlin,
Germany.

Many data analytic issues confront the analyst when working with the very large data sets needed in the common econo-

metric and simulation models used today. Among these are

- the possibility that gross errors may exist in the data and must be identified;

- the assessment of the quality of data as collected independently of transcription errors and other errors related purely to computerization;

- the appropriateness of the data for their use in the present modeling effort;

- the fit of the model to the data; and

- the stochastic properties of the data, i.e., distribution type, stationarity, etc.

In spite of the tremendous amount of research in the statistical literature on each of these subjects, the analyst is usually not concerned with carrying out every optimum test each time these issues arise in his analysis. Furthermore, he is not interested in carrying out every possible analysis, a project unfortunately possible with today's computing power. Normally, the analyst wants to know where things can go terribly wrong and affect his results, and if and where he can get more information out of these data to strengthen his conclusion.

These issues are amenable to EDA, but most applications of EDA are on small data sets that can be graphed by hand. However, here we are concerned with data sets which are usually very large. Using an interactive statistical package developed by the Wharton Analysis Center (Stine, 1980), we present examples of the application of EDA techniques on large data sets which are usually used in sizeable modeling efforts. The intention here is to show how the analyst can quickly spot errors and anomalies, evaluate the quality and appropriateness of the data at hand, check the fit of models to data, and determine certain properties of the data. In short, we pose the question, "How can one learn more about the collected data through data analysis, and especially EDA?", and clarify the answer with examples and descriptions of situations where applying EDA gave a high utility to the user. We illustrate how feedback from this kind of analysis can be used to modify a model or to modify a data storage or collection method. In addition, we discuss how EDA techniques can be integrated as an ordinary phase in the data collection and model building processes.

To accomplish these goals we draw upon examples from two
different modeling efforts: The Short-Term Integrated Forecasting System (STIFS), an energy simulation and econometric
forecasting model built by the U.S. Department of Energy
(DOE), and the GLOBUS political-social-economic simulation model being developed by the Science Center Berlin, Federal
Republic of Germany. Both of these projects involve huge
quantities of data which require detailed analysis, and these
data are critical to the models' behavior.

The STIFS model was developed by the Department of
Energy's Energy Information Administration (EIA), mainly as a
response to the severe disruption of energy flows to the U.S.
in the early 1970s. The EIA required predictions about the
state of the short-term energy economy, and the STIFS model
was destined to deliver these. As part of the project to val-
idate and improve the quality of data collected, as well as
the overall quality of forecasting at EIA, the Analysis Center
of the Wharton School undertook a study of the model. We present a short description of the model's elements and underpinnings. From this study, we then proceed to present examples
of situations where EDA was meaningfully and constructively
used.

The GLOBUS model is being developed with the objective of
anticipating "some stresses and strains which governments are
likely to confront over the next quarter-century and evaluate
strategies for coping with them" (Bremer, 1982). As a part
of the project a large amount of social and economic data was
collected by scientists, who are now confronted with the enormous task of analyzing the data and estimating the model.
Here arise various situations where EDA can be fruitfully applied to the problems which are faced. We discuss how the
techniques of EDA can be used, and we offer a proposal of how
a study-plan may be developed for undertaking such analyses.
For this, we draw upon lessons learned from the STIFS model
validation project.

We begin the paper with a general overview of some topics
which are related to our overall focus on data analysis, including a brief description of EDA, its applications, and its
lack of applications. The overview serves primarily as background information to several types of environmental problems
or situations which often confront the data analyst. In this
respect, however, it is neither comprehensive nor exhaustive;
to dwell on these problems in a more detailed manner would require much more discussion than we can fairly give here.
Rather, we attempt to present a scenario within which much
research and data analysis is conducted.

We conclude this work with a summary and some remarks on how EDA can easily be integrated into the modeling process. Furthermore, we discuss some ways in which EDA can be improved and expanded to interface with some modern technologies.

II. OVERVIEW

A comprehensive EDA assessment of the properties of the data used in quantitative models is seldom carried out. EDA can and should be considered as an initial step in the modeling process. Neglecting to explore the data before fitting a model to them often leads to serious problems.

What is EDA? As Tukey (1977) insightfully says, "Exploratory data analysis is detective work." It is concerned with the study of what is the most basic element of science -- data. EDA is a set of tools which helps one understand the nuts and bolts of data. A large batch of numbers cannot be summarized at first glance. Helpful aids, such as graphs, charts, and other diagrams, are needed. These are tools of EDA. Horwig and Dearing (1979) call EDA "a state of mind." The practice of EDA undoubtedly requires a certain state of mind or philosophical orientation. However, EDA is better thought of as a creative art of discovery and presentation.[a]

The information gained from EDA can be vital to the scientist in formulating a parametric model, and in developing a deeper understanding of the phenomena at hand. However, in the vast amount of literature describing a variety of different models, there seems to be a lack of sufficient data analysis. EDA is a time-consuming, cumbersome and strenuous task. However, it is an important one. The difficulties presented by the exploratory analysis of large collections of data can be great, but the benefits are often very noticeable. For example, EDA was crucial to the famous German astronomer and physical scientist Johannes Kepler in formulating what are known today as the Kepler Laws. The analytic work of Kepler was then later followed up by Isaac Newton who, using Kepler's findings and a model of his own, put forth the law of gravitation (Hartley, 1980). This stands clearly as an

---

[a]*For the full and basic presentation and summary of EDA, see Tukey (1977).*

example of how EDA was used in conjunction with parametric
modeling to arrive at productive results. The Kepler-Newton
experience was not only a triumph for physics but also for
EDA.

Another reason that EDA is not used when constructing
data-oriented models is that as a great number of academic
disciplines become increasingly quantitative in their basic
research orientation (take almost any branch of the social
sciences as an example), users of the sophisticated modeling
and analytical tools tend to under emphasize data analysis and
focus more directly on modeling and significance testing.
This most likely stems from the fact that the majority of in-
troductory statistics courses for social scientists do not
adequately cover the topic of data analysis (Tufte, 1970).
EDA and topics of robustness are often completely left out of
the basic statistical curriculum while classical statistical
theory and confirmatory tools and tests based on rigid assumptions, such as the normal distribution, are taught extensively
(Siegel, 1980).

When most texts on statistics introduce basic linear models, a considerable amount of effort and space is devoted to
the explanation of how one interprets "model fit" by examining
various coefficients and statistical tests, but properties of
residuals and topics concerning robustness and variable transformations (re-expressions) are seldom included in these discussions.[b] Also, perhaps because of lack of interest or
mathematical sophistication, the key assumptions of linear
models are often only lightly touched upon.

The evolution of the modern computer along with the par-
allel implementations of programmed computer packages, has undoubtedly been a key factor in the increased application of
quantitative methods to research problems in many disciplines.
The power of the computer for numerical calculations and data
storage has also spurred the tremendous increase in the amount
of information and data collected and computerized.

Although the ease of use and ease to access of computer
systems and program packages enable one to carry out many
types of statistical analyses, most programs do not require
the user to examine closely the data in order to locate
abnormalities and atypical measurements which usually exist.

[b] *A notable exception is Mosteller and Tukey (1977).*

In other words, computers and programmed packages, because they simplify the work of the user to some extent, and
perform many calculations -- the results of which are seldom either seen or understood -- have been instrumental in de-emphasi-
zing the use and practice of EDA. Many statistical package
users, having only limited experience in statistics, resort
only to what the package offers in its menu of techniques.
One tragedy of this is that a menu often excludes EDA techniques, whose computer requirements are ironically quite small.
In fact, one need only have a pencil, paper, and some knowledge
of basic arithmetic.

This raises an important quality of EDA -- that is, EDA's
strong point is its simplicity. Basically, the application of
EDA requires adventurism, creativity, the ability to make subjective decisions, and the lust for exploration of the data.
A whole analysis may result in many charts and figures, in one
stem-and-leaf diagram, or nothing. But if one explores a body
of data and finds nothing, he is still better off being able
to say that he at least looked.

III. THE WHARTON ASSESSMENT OF STIFS

A. *Description of the Project*

In response to various recent energy disruptions and
emergencies, the U.S. Department of Energy (DOE) has developed
several statistical models for the national energy economy in
order to provide information for public policy decision making. One model used by the EIA is the STIFS. The model is
actually a combination of several independent energy-sector
models and data collections which formerly existed at DOE.
Hence, the term "integrated" refers to a simulation run in
which the various models have been brought together to produce
a unified forecast. The idea of having one such model stems
from the desire for a single concise report which shows the
interactions of the main energy sectors. STIFS is formally
described as a "comprehensive automated software system and
data base that simulates the network of national energy sup-
plies, inventories, imports, conversion processes, and demands.
Its purpose is to produce automated monthly, quarterly, and
annual forecasts of integrated energy supply-demand balances,
including stock changes over the short term (e.g., 12 to 36
months)." (Dept. of Energy, 1980).

At the request of the Office of Energy Information Validation of the EIA, the Wharton Analysis Center of the University of Pennsylvania undertook a two-year-long review and assessment of the STIFS (hereafter, the Wharton evaluation). Because the review was almost entirely statistical in nature, there were no comments on or evaluation of such things as the underlying economic theory, the adequacy of the documentation, or the methods of data processing used in formulating and implementing the model -- except for those that arose in context with our main purpose. The foci of the project were primarily on the statistical performance of the model, and submodels, and the quality and apropriateness of the data used. In carrying out this research we relied heavily on EDA and other modern diagnostic techniques and their various implementations on large computers. (See especially Tukey, 1977; Mosteller and Tukey, 1977; McNeil, 1977; Velleman and Hoaglin, 1981; Stine, 1980; and Velleman, 1980.)

The Wharton evaluation consists of seventeen reports. Most of these were statistical evaluations of econometric models for forecasting procedures, two were descriptions of the integrating network, and one was an evaluation of the forecasts given in the model[c]. With few exceptions the models under study were regression models. For most of these, the fit to historical data and the quality of the forecasts were evaluated, but in a few models only the forecasts of a nonstatistical procedure could be evaluated. Compatibility, quality, and various other data characteristics were assessed in all the models.

Much of the analysis carried out was exploratory in nature, for example, plotting research, searching for systematic lack of fit, and evaluating biases in forecasts. Graphical

---

[c]*The seventeen reports are listed in the reference section. By author(s) they are: Benjamini and Curran, 1981; Bollinger, 1981; Cheng, 1982; Cheng, Newingham and Bollinger, 1981; Curran and Zimmerman, 1981; Gibbons, 1981a and 1981b; Gibbons and Tittmann, 1982; Gibbons and DeLorenzo, 1982; Mariano, 1981; Mariano and McManus, 1981; McDonald, 1982; Newingham, 1981a and 1981b; Small, 1981; Sweeney and Peacock, 1981; Sweeney and Sims, 1981. The draft paper by Green, Barnes, and Hadder (1982) also gives an independent overview to the Wharton evaluations.*

and visual displays were frequently used in the presentation
of findings. The uniqueness of this evaluation was that it
included many interacting sub-models and data series (approximately 250 data series are used in the STIFS). The type of
analysis required was conducted with the aid of interactive
computer technology and up-to-date techniques for assessing
large batches of data.

B. *Accomplishments of the Evaluations*

The STIFS is an evolving system. Some changes are made
every quarter in response to more recent demands and also to
longer range development needs. Thus, it is no surprise that
many piecemeal changes have been made in the system since the
completion of the Wharton evaluation. Virtually every recom-
mendation for change has been accommodated. In this respect,
the Wharton project was overwhelmingly successful.

The weaknesses that the Wharton evaluation discovered
fall generally into three categories: (i) data incompatibility, (ii) poor model fit, and (iii) poor forecasting ability.
These are common failings in econometric models. However, to
discover which models and data sets witnessed severe weaknesses among so many possibilities required the systematic application of powerful data analytical tools. The recommendations
can best be understood in the context of the evaluation's organization. Each model evaluation consisted of two parts, one
assessing the model and the other assessing the data. Both
parts were divided into an internal and external evaluation.

C. *The Wharton Evaluation Scheme*

The *internal evaluation of the model* consisted of an assessment of how well the model was defined, an assessment of
the model's fit and forecasting ability, a review of the advantages and disadvantages of the estimation method utilized,
and any other factors needed to define the model.

The *external evaluation of the model* compared the internal evaluation to similar, less rigorous and extensive evaluations of other models that had appeared in the literature.

The *internal evaluation of the data* assessed whether or
not the data measured the quantities defined in the models and
whether the different data series were compatible with the model
with respect to various characteristics such as coverage,

synchrony, timelines, etc. It also included a review of the
definition and documentation of the data. Various types of
incompatibility were discovered. Some were, of course,
straightforward and easily found. For example, using graphical depiction, it was found that heating degree days had a
seasonal period similar to that of price. This fact resulted
in collinearity problems when both entities were entered into
a model. Other incompatibilities were more subtle and complex. The discovery of the source of small biases in certain
derived quantities took a good deal of exploratory data analysis, as well as considerable detective work regarding the definitions and collection methods of the primary quantities. An
extensive, in-depth summary of the data's quality and properties was deemed indispensable.

The *external evaluation of the data* involved comparing
the data which were collected to those which were available in
general. Sometimes recommendations regarding the use of a
particular data series could be made. Other times, it was
concluded that there were insufficient data available to model
the process as manifested in the model definition.

D. *The Applications of EDA in the Wharton Evaluation*

An integral part of the practical and systematic application of EDA in the Wharton evaluation of STIFS was the employment of an EDA computer package developed by the Analysis
Center at the Wharton School (Stine, 1980; Stine and Cooney,
1980). Building mainly on the work of McNeil (1977), a fully
interactive computer package was developed in the APL computer
language (Iverson, 1962)[d]. The APL language is strongly
suited for data analysis. Embodied in the interactive language are very powerful commands for algebraic operations on
data structures such as arrays, vectors, and scalars. "APL is
a versatile programming language providing a direct means for
problem solving by students, engineers, scientists, educators
and businessmen." (Polivka and Patkin, 1975). It is used
widely for programming instruction, software development, and
decision support systems (see Alter, 1980; Canning, 1976; and
Keen, 1976).

[d]*For texts on APL, see Gilman and Rose (1976), and Polivka
and Patkin (1975).*

The EDA computer package was very helpful for analyzing the data used in the STIFS. In the Wharton evaluation the main types of applications of the package were in the areas of

a) *Displays* – A typical form of display of data in EDA is the stem-and-leaf diagram. The stem-and-leaf can be imagined as a histogram viewed sideways and is useful for seeing how the data are related. It is a fast way to spot suspicious measurements, erroneous data, and other anomalies.

b) *Plotting, pictures, and summaries* – Simple plotting of data was useful in locating many data anomalies. Plots can and should be done in several ways so that one gets a "feel" for the data. For instance, the data can be plotted using a letter of the alphabet for each month making it easier to see monthly trends and seasonal patterns. Box-and-whisker pictures are also plots of a batch of data. A box-and-whisker plot is shaped like a box or rectangle. The box is bounded by the upper and lower quartile values (roughly) of the batch. Somewhere in the box is a line representing the median. Lines or whiskers are drawn out from the quartile bounds to extreme points. Box-and-whisker plots are useful for plotting a 5-number summary which consists of two extremes, two quartiles or hinges, and the median. The 5-numbers are usually shown in a box resembling an upside-down U. At the side of the box there is usually a list of numbers showing the depth of the value with respect to the ordered data. It is a quick and easy way to summarize batches.

c) *Data smoothing* – A data series can usually be thought of as having two components: smooth and rough. This can be expressed by: data = smooth + rough. The smooth of a data series can be thought of as the underlying structural pattern or curve of the data. The rough is the residual, anything which is not in the smooth. Data smoothing is the process of finding the smooth of the data, through various numerical techniques, and separating it from the rough. This "smooth curve" often gives the analyst a better idea of how the data really look (see Velleman, 1980).

d) *Residual analysis* – In modeling the model, fit is regarded as important. However, especially in an exploratory approach, what is left out of the model is normally as interesting as what is included. Residual

analysis can often lead to a better model fit since
patterns found in the residuals can be included in the
model specification. Data smoothing is used widely in
residual analysis since it helps one spot patterns
more quickly (see Bollinger, 1981).

e) *Fitting lines* - Many times classical linear models do
not offer enough flexibility for use in situations
where gross data problems are witnessed. A statistical model is more robust when it is less sensitive to
extreme points. An exploratory approach normally employs a resistant and robust model, such as Tukey-line
fitting (Hartwig and Dearing, 1979), robust regression, biweight and weighted least squares (Mosteller
and Tukey, 1977). These methodologies focus more directly on the smooth of the data. It is also worth
noting here that re-expression such as quick logs,
quick roots, and reciprocals can also be very useful
in getting the data in a form more convenient for
analysis. Some examples of these applications appear in
Figures 1, 2, and 3.

E. *Summary of the Wharton Evaluation*

EDA, as mentioned above, was a keystone in the Wharton
evaluation. This was primarily due to the fact that the analytical orientation of the reports, and the study as a whole,
was one which specifically included a broad spectrum of exploratory exercises with the models and data. It was put
forth at the project's inception that EDA was to play a vital
role in the statistical review of the STIFS. The approach to
evaluation which was taken by Wharton was one that dictated a
complete summary report on the data's quality and properties
in almost every aspect. EDA was deemed indispensable as both
an instrument in studying the models and data and as an aid in
providing the modelers with a much better idea of how to
model.

One benefit of using EDA so extensively in data and model
assessment was that the recommendations were, for the most part,
easy to see and understand. In EDA, presentation of results
is often with graphs, charts, and diagrams. For instance, when
showing how to improve a simple regression model, the residuals and smoothed residuals were often shown graphically along
with the recommended changes. In these aspects, EDA was found
to be of tremendous aid to the modelers in improving their
forecasts.

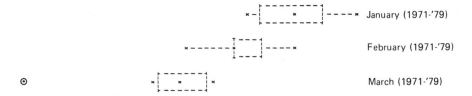

FIGURE 1. *Comparison of boxplots for January, February, and March heating degree day data over the nine year period 1971-1979.* (A question that arose in many of the models in STIFS was whether heating degree days could be modeled by a sine and a cosine term for the purpose of forecasting weather as an exogenous variable. The extreme value in March turned out to be a miscoded decimal point which had not been previously noted.)

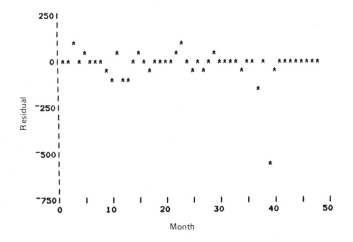

FIGURE 2. *Residuals after median polish smoothing of heating degree day data for forty-eight months.* (Median polish smoothing is a method of robust smoothing that uses both nearby values and corresponding months in other years to calculate a smoothed value. Here the technique has identified the outlier in figure 1 as the 39th month observation with the largest negative residual.)

```
-18|
-16|52
-14|9
-12|94
-10|95296
-08|71
-06|8776338877421
-04|65321973
-02|986419877222
-00|965077321
 00|17823358
 02|1246000355566778
 04|23979
 06|23482222334457
 08|7
 10|38
 12|
 14|
 16|48
 18|84
 20|1
 22|
 24|5
 26|7
 28|
 30|
 32|
 34|
 36|7
```

FIGURE 3. *Stem and leaf display of residuals for monthly heating degree day data over the nine year period 1971- 1979.* (These are the residuals from a robust fit of sine and cosine to the heating degree day data after correction of the miscoded March value noted in Figures 1 and 2. The three probable outliers at 245, 267, and 367 are from the record-setting cold winters 1976-1977 and 1977-1978. These extreme values would have biased forecasts in subsequent normal years if made from a least squares fit.)

IV. THE GLOBUS PROJECT

A. *Description of the Project*

A global simulation model is under construction at the
International Institute for Comparative Social Research in
Berlin, Federal Republic of Germany. GLOBUS, which stands for
Generating Long-term Options Using Simulations, is destined to
mature into a fully computerized simulation model useful for
the study of national and international events in the social-
political-economic spheres among twenty-five nations and a
"rest of the world" counterpart. The purpose of the GLOBUS
model is to explore and anticipate, "some stresses and strains
which governments are likely to confront over the next
quarter-century and evaluate strategies for coping with them."
(Bremer, 1982).

The scientists building the GLOBUS model intend that it
will address a host of political-economic questions concerning
current and projected world problems. Some specific focal
points include   East-West tensions, conditions in a country
most likely to lead to internal political unrest, problems
arising from the depletion of world resources (including fos-
sil fuels), and the growing schism between developed and
less-developed countries. No matter how global, a model cannot and should not address every "important" question; GLOBUS
conforms to this precept. Its purpose is to deal with a limited and particular subset of questions which are of interest
to policy analysts and decision makers. (For a more in-depth
review of the GLOBUS project, please see the following works:
Bremer, 1981 and 1982; Cusack, 1982; Pollins, 1982;
Kirkpatrick, 1982; and Widmaier, 1982.)

B. *Data Collection and Requirements*

Concomitant with the construction of global models are
a number of functional constraints which are posed to the
builder. Among the myriad of issues confronting the modeling
group are the collection and analysis of large amounts of data, and the construction of a database system to store and
retrieve data and act as an interface between the simulation
model, the statistical analysis and estimation programs, and
the data. Collecting the data for the twenty-five GLOBUS
nations has "... proved to be a rather formidable task "
(Bremer, 1981). The scope of these problems is immense and
will not be treated extensively here. However, certain points

directly related to data quality and data analysis should be brought to light.

The types of data required by the GLOBUS model are quite diverse and include a variety of political-economic indicators. These data include   economic and demographic measurements, indices of social satisfaction and political events, national income accounting figures, measurements of bilateral trade flows, international conflict and cooperation data, and military estimates.

Clearly, these data are not to be found in any one source. Many are taken from very specialized and extraordinary references, and others are measured and developed by individual scientists working on the model. For instance Taylor (1981), in a recent work on political and social indicators, cites a rather wide and remarkable variety of sources for his data collection. For the most part, however, many data are taken from more well-known and standard data sources such as *Yearbook of National Accounts Statistics,* The World Bank's World Tables, *International Financial Statistics,* and the *National Accounts of OECD Countries.* In most cases the data series from these sources must extend about twenty years into the past. (For a more comprehensive treatment of the data collection and sources see Flemming, 1982, and Bremer and Cusack, 1981).

C. Problems with the Data

The plethora of data sources and the huge quantity of data required by GLOBUS can lead one to speculate that there may exist an abundance of irregularities and errors in the data. Errors can arise from ordinary human mistakes such as misplaced decimal points or incorrect quantity conversions (for instance, converting from one currency or unitization to another). Gross errors are common and likely when the data are transcribed onto the computer. There is no formal database support for the GLOBUS Model. Therefore it is difficult to access the data and keep track of changes made to them. Updating data series and manipulating computer data files will almost always propagate errors. Furthermore, the data from some countries are simply plagued with irregularities and mysterious values. Often these are the result of an inadequate infrastructure supporting data collection, and supression or alteration of politically-sensitive data series. For instance, the data from developing countries are often affected by these circumstances.

Given the relative importance of these data to the GLOBUS project it is desirable to have a quality control mechanism. Much time and effort were spent collecting the data, and an assessment of the data quality and description of their properties is now in order. One may, for instance, want to conduct preliminary studies of patterns in the data since this type of information will be needed later in the model estimation phase. It is also crucial to the model to have the data organized in a manner which is more convenient for data analysis. This combination of problems provides for an ideal application for the techniques of EDA. In proposing how to incorporate EDA into the plan of statistical and data analysis in the GLOBUS model, we draw upon some lessons and experiences discussed in the Wharton evaluation section.

D. Using EDA in the GLOBUS Model

As Siegel (1980) aptly says, "Using robust methods is analogous to taking out an insurance policy for protection against the presence of bad data: the insurance premium is paid as an increase in sampling variation or efficiency of the estimate." (Siegel, 1980). When dealing with large amounts of data which are suspected, a priori, to be plagued with erroneous and atypical values, it makes sense to use robust techniques. Incorporating the practice of EDA into the normal functions of data collection, management, and assessment guarantees protection against atypical data.

The success of using EDA in the Wharton evaluation of STIFS was discussed earlier. However, the Wharton assessment did not alter the methods of model building used in the STIFS since the evaluation project was begun after the STIFS was already in existence. The recommendations, however, indicate that the modelers would have benefited significantly by employing EDA throughout the model-development process. In short, one may safely draw the conclusion that the systematic application of EDA techniques in the Wharton evaluation helped to reveal many pitfalls of the data and model which would otherwise have gone unnoticed. The GLOBUS project will probably witness similar difficulties unless an application of tools such as EDA is mindfully integrated in the modeling exercises.

An assortment of data files which are composed of different data structures and layouts can inhibit the data's accessibility for analysis. Difficulty to access can decrease the

user's desire to study the data in depth. An organization
scheme for the data, such as a database management system,
which could easily interface with an EDA computer package and
with the data would be excellent for the types of problems
which can be expected to arise in the modeling environment of
GLOBUS.[e]

V. CONCLUDING REMARKS

The purpose of models is to "facilitate understanding and
enhance prediction." (Rubenstein, 1975). In this paper the
aim is to point out how EDA can be useful in providing to modelers better information about data quality and model fit.
This information, in turn, can be used to improve the overall
quality of modeling and forecasting. Here, we discussed the
utility of both EDA and a computer package for EDA in the
Wharton Analysis Center's assessment of the STIFS. It was
further pointed out how the techniques of EDA can be integrated into the model-development process in a project such as
GLOBUS.

One thing which must be noted about EDA is that it is
not, unfortunately, widely used or taught. EDA offers many
subjective approaches to data analysis -- there is no set of
tests which must always be carried out. EDA is also mathema-
tically uncomplex in many of its applications. Simplicity and
clarity are emphasized more than mathematical sophistication.
These factors sometimes cast a shadow of doubt on EDA results.
EDA is unconventional and often subject to scorn because of
these factors, but more applications of it which are successful will lead to a wider acceptance.

[e]*A major weakness found in the STIFS was that a reliable
database management system was not interfaced with the
model. This made it difficult for the modelers to have an
"audit trail" of changes that were made. It was also the
case that the data were not easily accessible through such a
system. This further inhibited data analysis.*

REFERENCES

Alter, S. (1980). *Decision Support Systems: Current Practice and Continuing Challenges*, Addison-Wesley, Reading, Massachusetts.

Benjamini, Y. and Curran, T. A. (1981). "The Integration Routine of the Short-Term Integrated Forecasting System: An Evaluation," Analysis Center Technical Report. University of Pennsylvania, The Wharton School, Analysis Center for Energy Studies.

Bollinger, M. J. (1981). "An Assessment of a Model of Motor Gasoline Demand," Analysis Center Technical Report. University of Pennsylvania, The Wharton School, Analysis Center for Energy Studies.

Bremer, S. A. (1981). "The GLOBUS Project: Overview and Update," Wissenschaftszentrum Berlin, Discussion Paper, IIVI/dp 81-109.

Bremer, S. A. (1982). "The GLOBUS Model: A Guide to Its Theoretical Structure," Wissenschaftszentrum Berlin, Discussion Paper, IIVG/dp 82-105.

Bremer, S. A., and Cusack, T. R. (1981). "The National Macro-Economic Framework of the GLOBUS Model," Wissenschaftszentrum Berlin, Discussion Paper, IIVG/dp 81-106.

Canning, R. (1976). "APL and Decision Support Systems," *EDP Analyzer, 14, #5,* 1-12.

Cheng, S. T. (1982). "Stocks of Refinery Products: An Assessment of Short-Term Forecasting Models," Analysis Center Technical Report. University of Pennsylvania, The Wharton School, Analysis Center for Energy Studies.

Cheng, S. T., Newingham, L. K., and Bollinger, M. J. (1981). "The Short-Term Monthly Product Mix in the Refining Industry: An Assessment of a Model," Analysis Center Technical Report. University of Pennsylvania, The Wharton School, Analysis Center for Energy Studies.

Curran, T. A., and Zimmerman, L. (1981). "Modeling the Aggregate Level of Crude Oil Stocks: An Assessment of the Short-Term Model of the Energy Information Administration," Analysis Center Technical Report. University of Pennsylvania, The Wharton School, Analysis Center for Energy Studies.

Cusack, T. (1982). "Government Resource Allocation in GLOBUS: Budget Structure and Processes," Wissenschaftszentrum Berlin, Discussion Paper, IIVG/dp 82-106.

Flemming, G. (1982). "Towards a Comparable System of National Accounts: The GLOBUS Results to Date," Wissenschaftszentrum Berlin, Discussion Paper, IIVG/dp 82-112.

Gibbons, D. C. (1981a). "An Assessment of Procedures for
     Forecasting the Output of Natural Gas Processing Plants,"
     Analysis Center Technical Report. University of
     Pennsylvania, The Wharton School, Analysis Center for
     Energy Studies.
Gibbons, D. C. (1981b). "Short-Term Marketed Production of
     Natural Gas: An Assessment of a Model," Analysis Center
     Technical Report. University of Pennsylvania, The
     Wharton School, Analysis Center for Energy Studies.
Gibbons, D. C., and Tittmann, P. C. (1982). "An Assessment of
     the Forecast Integration Process of the Short-Term
     Integrated Forecasting System," Analysis Center
     Technical Report. University of Pennsylvania, The
     Wharton School, Analysis Center for Energy Studies.
Gibbons, D. C., and DeLorenzo, D. M. (1982). "An Assessment
     of a Model of Short-Term, Non-Utility Consumption of
     Natural Gas," Analysis Center Technical Report,
     University of Pennsylvania, The Wharton School, Analysis
     Center for Energy Studies.
Gilman, L. and Rose, A. J. (1976). *APL: An
     Interactive Approach, 2nd ed.,* John Wiley and Sons, New
     York.
Green, D. L., Barnes, R., and Hadder, G. (1982). "An Overview
     of the Wharton School Assessment of the Short-Term
     Ingetrated Forecasting System," *Draft Version.*
     Tennessee: Energy Division, Oak Ridge National
     Laboratory, Oak Ridge.
Hartley, H. O. (1980). "Statistics as a Science and as a
     Profession," *Journal of the American Statistical
     Association, 75, #369,* 1-7.
Harwig, F. and Dearing, B. E. (1979). *Exploratory
     Data Analysis,* Sage Publications, Beverly Hills,
     California.
Iverson, K. E. (1962). *A Programming Language,* John Wiley and
     Sons, New York.
Keen, P. G. (1976). "Interactive Computer Systems for
     Managers: A Modest Proposal," *Sloan Management Review,
     18, #1,* 1-17.
Kirkpatrick, G. (1982). "The GLOBUS Multi-Country Economic
     Model," Wissenschaftszentrum Berlin, Discussion Paper,
     IIVG/dp 82-107.
McDonald, W. J. (1982). "The Relationship of Short-Term
     Projections to Available Data: A Qualitative
     Assessment," Analysis Center Technical Report.
     University of Pennsylvania, The Wharton School, Analysis
     Center for Energy Studies.

McNeil, D. R. (1977). *Interactive Data Analysis,* John Wiley and Sons, New York.

Mariano, R. S. (1981). "An Evaluation of the Coal Model in the Short-Term Integrated Forecasting System of the U.S. Department of Energy," Analysis Center Technical Report. University of Pennsylvania, The Wharton School, Analysis Center for Energy Studies.

Mariano, R. S., and McManus, D. (1981). "An Evaluation of the Energy Information Administration Models for Short-Term Forecasting of Gasoline and No. 2 Heating Oil Prices," Analysis Center Technical Report. University of Pennsylvania, The Wharton School, Analysis Center for Energy Studies.

Mosteller, F. and Tukey, J. W. (1977). *Data Analysis and Regression: A Second Course in Statistics,* Addison-Wesley, Reading, Massachusetts.

Newingham, L. K. (1981a). "An Assessment of a Model for the Short-Term, Domestic, Non-Utility Demand for Residual Fuel Oil," Analysis Center Technical Report. University of Pennsylvania, The Wharton School, Analysis Center for Energy Studies.

Newingham, L. K. (1981b). "An Assessment of a Model for the Short-Term, Non-Utility Demand for Distillate Fuel Oil," Analysis Center Technical Report. University of Pennsylvania, The Wharton School, Analysis Center for Energy Studies.

Polivka, R. P., and Patkin, S. (1975). *APL: The Language and Its Usage,* Prentice-Hall, Englewood Cliffs, New Jersey.

Pollins, B. (1982). "The Political and Economic Determinants of International Trade Flows in GLOBUS," Wissenschaftszentrum Berlin, Discussion Paper, IIVG/dp 82-110.

Rubenstein, M. F. (1975). *Patterns of Problem Solving,* Prentice-Hall, Englewood Cliffs, New Jersey.

Siegel, A. F. (1980). "Teaching Robust Methods for Exploratory Data Analysis," Technical Report No. 173, Series 2. Princeton University, Department of Statistics.

Small, R. D. (1981). "Short-Term Electricity Demand Modeling: A Statistical Evaluation," Analysis Center Technical Report. University of Pennsylvania, The Wharton School, Analysis Center for Energy Studies.

Stine, R. A. (1980). "An Exploratory Data Analysis Package," *The American Statistician, 34, 3,* 187-188.

Stine, R. A. and Cooney, T. (1980). "User's Manual: Exploratory Data Analysis Package," Documentation Report. The University of Pennsylvania, The Wharton School, Analysis Center for Energy Studies.

Sweeney, K. J., and Peacock, R. L. (1981). "An Assessment of the Energy Information Administration Short-Term Forecasts of Domestic Production of Crude Oil," Analysis Center Technical Report. University of Pennsylvania, The Wharton School, Analysis Center for Energy Studies.

Sweeney, K. J., and Sims, S. W. (1981). "Monthly Nuclear Electricity Generation in the Short-Term: An Assessment of a Forecasting Procedure," Analysis Center Technical Report. University of Pennsylvania, The Wharton School, Analysis Center for Energy Studies.

Taylor, C. L. (1981). "The Third World Handbook of Political and Social Indicators," Wissenschaftszentrum Berlin, Preprint, IIVG/pre 80-127.

Tukey, J. W. (1977). *Exploratory Data Analysis*, Addison-Wesley, Reading, Massachusetts.

Tufte, E. R. (ed) (1970). *The Quantitative Analysis of Social Problems*, Addison-Wesley, Reading, Massachusetts.

U.S. Department of Energy. Energy Information Administration (1980). *Annual Report of Congress, 1979,* Vol. 3, p. 253, Washington: U.S. Department of Energy, Energy Information Administration. DOE/EIA-0173(79)/3.

Velleman, P. (1980). "Definition and Comparison of Robust Nonlinear Data Smoothing Algorithms," *Journal of the American Statistical Association, 75, #371,* 609-615.

Velleman, P. and Hoaglin, D. (1981). *Applications, Basics, and Computing of E.D.A.,* Duxbury Press, North Scituate, Massachusetts.

Widmaier, U. (1982). "Political Performance, Political Support and Political Stability: The GLOBUS Framework," Wissenschaftszentrum Berlin, Discussion Paper, IIVG/dp 82-108.

Index